The Place of the Stage

The Place of the Stage

LICENSE, PLAY, AND POWER IN
RENAISSANCE ENGLAND

STEVEN MULLANEY

Ann Arbor

THE UNIVERSITY OF MICHIGAN PRESS

First printed by the University of Chicago Press, 1988
© 1988 by the University of Chicago
Copyright reassigned to Steven Mullaney 1995
All rights reserved
Published in the United States of America by
The University of Michigan Press
Printed and bound by CPI Group (UK) Ltd, Croydon, CR0 4YY

2003   2002   2001   2000   6   5   4   3

A CIP catalogue record for this book is available from the British Library

LIBRARY OF CONGRESS CATALOGING-IN-PUBLICATION DATA
Mullaney, Steven.
    The place of the stage.
    Includes bibliographical references and index.
    1. Theater—England—History—16th century.
2. English Drama—Early modern and Elizabethan, 1500–
1600—History and criticism.   3. Shakespeare, William,
1564–1616. Pericles.   4. London (England)—Intellectual
life—16th century.   I. Title
PN2589.M78 1988   792'.0942   87-17327
ISBN-13 978-0-472-08346-6

Contents

Contents

Preface

This is a study of popular drama in Elizabethan and Jacobean society, and of the cultural conditions that made possible, for a relatively brief period of time, a theater of ambivalent status but considerable ideological range and license.

The drama of Shakespeare and his contemporaries has long been accorded a special and privileged position in literary history; all too often, however, such an aesthetic perspective has been insufficiently grounded in the particularities of time and place that defined the conditions of possibility for such drama. In order to provide such a grounding, we need first to recognize that the drama we regard as one of the supreme literary achievements of the English language was viewed quite differently by the period in question—as a troublesome and potentially subversive social phenomenon that threatened religious and civic hierarchies and yet, despite considerable antagonism, could neither be outlawed nor put down. Popular drama in Renaissance England was born of the contradiction between a Court that in limited but significant ways licensed and maintained it and a city that sought its prohibition; it emerged as a cultural institution only by materially embodying that contradiction, dislocating itself from the confines of the existing social order and taking up a place on the margins of society. Erected outside the walls of early modern London in the "licentious Liberties" of the city, the popular playhouses of Elizabethan England occupied a domain that had traditionally been reserved for cultural phenomena that could not be contained within the strict or proper bounds of the community.

The cultural and ideological significance of such marginality is the focus of my opening chapters, which survey the symbolic topography of Elizabethan London and provide a compressed history of the ideology of space in the early modern city. I approach the city as a cultural artifact, a social text composed by varied rites of initiation, celebration, and exclusion—by a diverse body of ritual practices, that is to say, through which a ceremonial social order could maintain and manifest itself, in time and in space. In a premodern or ceremonial city, civic pageantry and annual repetitive customs provided the vehicles with which a community could chart, in its actual topography, the limits and contradictions of its authority; such ritual passages of power served to inscribe the common places of London with cultural value and significance, making the city a legible emblem or icon of community. Within the walls of the medieval and Renaissance city, the ideals and aspirations of community were staged in an extensive repertory of rituals, ceremonies, and cultural performances. The inscription of ideological values on civic space, the ritual creation of the social topology, did not halt at the boundary of the city walls, however. The margins of the city were themselves a crucial part of its symbolic economy, but they served as a more ambivalent staging ground, as a place where the contradictions of the community—its incontinent hopes, fears, and desires—were prominently and dramatically set on stage.

Readers familiar with the work of Michel Foucault will note a significant indebtedness throughout this book, particularly in my own analysis of the politics of space and the topology of contestatory powers in Renaissance London. Although the debt is as undeniable as it is (at least in my estimation) productive, it is also a general rather than a specific one as far as the rhetoric of civic space is concerned. In particular, my own analysis of the rise of leprosariums in the High Middle Ages differs markedly from Foucault's in *Madness and Civilization*.[1] There, Foucault argued that the exalted seclusion of leprosy on the margins of society, a product of a medieval shift in the cultural significance attached to the disease, created an institutionalized structure of confinement that outlived its original purpose and was thus available when new and otherwise unrelated figures of cultural ambivalence emerged on the social horizon. Where the leper was once housed, according to Foucault, the madman was later incarcerated. Of debatable historical validity in France, such a genealogy of confinement is even less readily apparent in the history of hospitals, madhouses, and prisons in England. Moreover, in isolating the leprosarium from other forms of marginal spectacle and ritual, Foucault to a large degree obscured the civic structure of which the leprosarium was but one manifestation. Analyzing the leprosarium in the context of other marginal phenomena, I argue that the ideological and topological structure of the walled medieval and Renaissance city was a tertiary rather than a binary one; long before the emergence of popular drama, the Liberties of London had served as a transitional zone between the city and the country, various powers and their limits, this life and the next—as a culturally maintained domain of ideological ambivalence and contradiction, where established authority reached and manifested, in spectacular form, the limits of its power to control or contain what exceeded it. Viewed from a religious perspective, the Liberties unfold as a place of sacred pollution, reserved for figures like the leper, who was made at once holy and hopelessly contaminated by his affliction. From a political perspective, the Liberties were the forum for ambivalent displays of power exercised on the body of the exile or the traitor—figures who were subjected to the extreme effects of early modern power but who also served to mark, in their place of banishment or death, the threshold and vanishing point of such power. More generally, the margins of the city were places where forms of moral incontinence and pollution were granted license to exist beyond the bounds of a community they had, by their incontinence, already exceeded. Social and civic margins, the Liberties also served as margins in a textual sense: as a place reserved for heterogeneous and overdetermined cultural phenomena and for divergent points of view—for commentary upon and even contradiction of the main body of their text, in this instance the body politic itself.

In tracing the symbolic topology of London and its Liberties, I undoubtedly neglect certain aspects of the socioeconomic and political functioning of the city and its negotiations with the world beyond—with the country that began not at the city walls but at the extreme verge of the Liberties themselves. Any perspective is bound to emphasize some issues at the expense of others, and my own has both its necessary limits and what I hope are its insightful blindnesses. The civic and social structure I analyze was neither unchanging nor uncontested, but it was a remarkably stable one, maintained for centuries by the combined powers of city, state, and church because it could make room for what more rigid civic and moral hierarchies could not contain, and could include all that exceeded the strict bounds of binary or antithetical definition. It was a structure that could cope, however, only with a limited range of social and demographic pressures; the social, political, and religious upheavals of the sixteenth century exceeded its capacity to accommodate new forms of cultural incontinence, but it did not as a consequence vanish overnight. When popular drama moved out into the Liberties, it appropriated this civic structure and converted the moral license and ambivalence of the Liberties to its own ends, translating its own cultural situation into a liberty that was at once moral, ideological, and topological—a freedom to experiment with

a wide range of available ideological perspectives and to realize, in
dramatic form, the cultural contradictions of its age.

The remainder of the book turns to particular plays that exemplify the ideological license of the popular stage and, in so doing,
help to decipher the shifting bases of power, license, and theatricality in Elizabethan and Jacobean England. With the exception of
passing references to plays by Marlowe and Jonson, my focus is on
Shakespeare, one of the few playwrights whose career encompassed
both the height and the decline of popular theater in Elizabethan
and Jacobean England. While I have not attempted to trace the
fortunes of the popular stage in any comprehensive sense, the plays
discussed are purposefully drawn from the primary genres popularized by that stage—history, comedy, tragedy, romance—and
from different phases of Shakespeare's career, thus providing a
foreshortened if largely implicit overview of the shifting grounds
of popular drama in the period. To a significant degree, however,
the comprehensiveness of more traditional literary history and
interpretation is not a goal of the present work. Employing a kind
of "thick description" in Clifford Geertz' sense of the phrase,[2] I
examine diverse sources and events, cultural as well as literary, in
an effort to situate the popular stage within the larger symbolic
economy of Elizabethan and Jacobean England. Rather than provide extensive readings of an entire corpus, I have sought to devise
what might be described as an open-ended sociohistorical herme-
neutics, to view the popular stage not merely or primarily as a
literary phenomenon but as one of a diverse body of cultural
practices whose relation to the larger social formation was at once
culture-specific and provisional. In *The Place of the Stage*, literary
analysis is conceived not as an end in itself but as a vehicle, a means
of gaining access to tensions and contradictions less clearly articulated in other cultural forums but all the more powerful for their
partial occlusion. Literature itself is conceived neither as a separate
and separable aesthetic realm nor as a mere product of culture,
but as one realm among many for the negotiation and production
of social meaning, of historical subjects, and of the systems of power
that at once enable and constrain those subjects.

Such concerns and assumptions are obviously not mine alone
but are to a significant degree shared by recent developments in
Renaissance literary studies on both sides of the Atlantic. I refer
to what has come to be known in this country as the New Historicism
and to a related trend in England, characterized by its practitioners
as a form of cultural materialism.[3] The latter phrase, adopted from
the theoretical writings of Raymond Williams, is in many ways

preferable as a description of recent developments in this country as well; unlike the term "New Historicism," it does not suggest a unified theoretical movement—no one has been moved to speak of *the* cultural materialism—nor does it encourage the false dichotomies (old vs. new, history vs. literature) that have colored recent discussions of New Historicism. More significantly, both New Historicism and cultural materialism share certain assumptions about the nature and functioning of hegemonic culture which, if not derived from Williams, are most ably articulated by him. Hegemonic culture, in Williams' development of Antonio Gramsci's concept, is neither singular nor static, nor is hegemony synonymous with cultural domination; on the contrary, the culture of any given historical period is conceived as a heterogeneous and irreducibly plural social formation, and as a dynamic process of representation and interpretation rather than as a fixed ensemble of meanings and beliefs. In such a view, culture is an ongoing production, negotiation, and delimitation of social meanings and social selves, composed through both discursive and nondiscursive means and in various and competing forums. Moreover, as Williams reminds us, the dominant culture of any given period is never either total or exclusive, never an accomplished fact but rather a process that "has continually to be renewed, recreated, defended, and modified" because it is being "continually resisted, limited, altered, challenged by pressures not at all its own"—by marginal, residual, and alternative cultures that, together with the dominant, comprise the hegemonic.[4]

However we designate them or articulate their differences and similarities, recent developments on both sides of the Atlantic have begun to problematize and break down the boundaries that literary study of the past has tended to enshrine—by which I mean not only the traditionally enabling but suspect distinction between "history" and "literature," "text" and "context," but also the disciplinary boundaries delimiting the terrain of the so-called human sciences. This salutary blurring of disciplinary genres has not, of course, been limited to Renaissance or even to literary studies in recent years; it is part of a larger movement that, at its best, represents a significant reconfiguration of social thought and social theory. There will always be studies that merely borrow reigning concepts or data from sociology or anthropology or history, import them into literary studies and apply them, more or less reductively, to produce a study of kinship, courtship, or the family in Spenser, Shakespeare, or Donne. But the sociohistorical work emerging today represents a more thorough and significant incorporation of theoretical and

methodological perspectives from other fields—an incorporation
necessary if we are to produce not merely historically informed
readings of literary texts but a broader semiotics or poetics of cultural production.[5] Such a cultural poetics must situate literary texts
in relation to the larger social text that is itself an unstable, heterogeneous, continually rehearsed and renegotiated production:
an agonistic and dramaturgical network of "cultural performances,"
by which I mean the various discursive and nondiscursive, licensed
and illicit ways in which "this people or that, this period or that,
makes sense of itself, to itself."[6] Crucial to such a project if it is to
be more than a reinscription of dominant ideologies—and hence
a repression of what Frank Lentricchia has described as those "histories within history . . . [which] thicken and make heterogeneous
historical textures that tradition and system would homogenize"[7]—
is the recognition that the ways in which a culture makes sense of
itself, to itself, are never restricted to its intentional or ideologically
determined efforts along this line: that the cultural performances
of any given society are produced not only by its reigning hierarchies or institutions but also by the contestatory, marginal, and
residual forces which the dominant culture must endlessly react to
and upon in order to maintain its dominance.

If the early modern period seems of particular moment to such
historical analysis, it is at least in part because of the complex ways
in which the sixteenth and seventeenth centuries bear upon the
historical present. *The Place of the Stage* explores a historical terrain
that is at once intimate and foreign to us, strange but with a resonance of the uncanny to its strangeness; in negotiating this terrain,
I have sought to keep both historical difference and similarity in
mind, in the hope of providing a poetics of Elizabethan and Jacobean culture that allows an occasional glimpse of a larger and
more significant project—of something that could rightly be called,
in Michel Foucault's sense of the phrase, a genealogy of the present.

Acknowledgments

Portions of this book have been presented to the English Department at Berkeley, at the First Annual Bronowski Conference on the Renaissance, and at meetings of the MLA, the Renaissance Society of America, and the Shakespeare Association of America; my thanks are extended to both the sponsors and the audiences on these occasions. Chapter 3 originally appeared in *Representations*, no. 3, 1983, pp. 40–67 (copyright © 1983 by the Regents of the University of California; reprinted by permission of the Regents); an earlier version of Chapter 5 appeared in *ELH*, and is reprinted by permission of The Johns Hopkins University Press.

The Giles A. Whiting Foundation provided time and support when the book was first being conceived, and I am grateful both to the Foundation and to Stanford University for this. An Old Dominion Fellowship, awarded by the Massachusetts Institute of Technology, aided the completion of the book by freeing me from other duties at a critical time. Less tangible debts are more difficult to acknowledge adequately, given all that I owe to a generous community of scholars and readers. I want to thank the members of the Literature Faculty of MIT for their support and encouragement, especially Peter Donaldson, David Halperin, and David Thorburn. A number of colleagues read the manuscript in whole or in part at various stages of its development, and for their contributions I am grateful to Terry Comito, Jonathan Goldberg, Stephen Greenblatt, Leah Marcus, Louis Montrose, Stephen Orgel, David Riggs, and Peter Stallybrass. John Bender oversaw the initial stages of the project with patience and extraordinary insight, and deserves special mention for the role he played in its development. Others who have benefited from her friendship and intelligence will understand why I dedicate this book to Linda Gregerson.

1

Toward a Rhetoric of Space in Elizabethan London

I

Anthony van den Wyngaerde composed his Panorama of London around 1543. In its broad expanse, the spires of Westminster stand out to the west against a backdrop of open fields punctuated with shrubs and trees (see fig. 1). Charing Cross—the original monument erected by Edward I to honor the memory of Eleanor, his queen, rather than the Victorian facsimile built in 1863 by Thomas Earp—rises prominently from a Scotland yard that is yet a yard, open and undeveloped, that has not yet given up its name or its place to the Metropolitan Police. To the north is open countryside, a few randomly scattered churches, and the anachronistic memorial of the Jews' Cemetery, unused, one must imagine, since Edward's expulsion of the Jews from England. To the east, the Tower of London is dwarfed by the White Tower; hand-operated cranes can be seen unloading barges at the docks around Traitor's Gate, and the scaffold on Great Tower Hill can be readily discerned, even down to the planks of its raised platform. The houses, churchyards, hospitals, and stews of the Bankside are rendered in photographic detail, from their chimney stacks and shingled or thatched roofs to the trees that partially obscure the latticework of their windows. The city itself, dominated by St. Paul's, is a forest of roofs watched over by church steeples and towers, but even here, with so much to portray in so small a space, the Panorama reveals a great deal of the varied architecture of Tudor London, and reveals it in fine detail, from the cruciform windows of Leadenhall to the gabled front of the Cross at Cheapside.

F I G U R E 1. On the following pages, an 1849 engraving by N. Whittock based on Anthony van den Wyngaerde's *Panorama of London* (1543). By permission of the British Museum.

The Panorama is an urban landscape, a view or representation of the city, rather than a map of it. So it appears to our eyes, at any rate, accustomed as they are to a cartography that is distinctly willing to forego the particularities of local detail and architectural spectacle for the sake of a less cluttered world view, a more abstract and schematic apprehension of distances and orientations in space. A map in the modern sense of the term is a guide to the present: a graphic index to the location of things in space, a traveler's aid which makes the passage from here to there less difficult, the mastery of a given topography available to newcomer and native alike. The routes of access presented by a panorama like Wyngaerde's are cultural and temporal as well as spatial; the city, represented in spectacular detail, is its own map, to be reproduced rather than abstracted because its edifices stand as monumental signposts to a community, a culture, a history defined and embodied by the traces it has left behind in the urban landscape. Whether we view the Panorama as a map of a city or as a portrait of a culture, however, the general configuration of London remains the same. The city before us is one that is still relatively well-contained by the ancient Roman wall that hedges it against the Thames. Although there are signs of growth to the east and west, the outlying suburbs known as the Liberties of the city lie for the most part open and unoccupied, and some free space—customary sites reserved for trade and recreation—even remains visible within the walls themselves. To a considerable extent, the city is still aloof and continent, as well defined in its territory as it was in the less immediately visible yet manifest domain of its rights, privileges, obligations, and powers.[1]

At the time of Wyngaerde's Panorama, Elizabeth was a child scarcely ten years of age; it would be more than thirty years before the first of the popular playhouses of Elizabethan London would appear on the scene, to translate the Liberties outside Wyngaerde's city into an arena for Elizabethan and Jacobean drama. This is an inquiry into that drama—or more precisely, into the situation of the stage in relation to the society that, in one sense or another, produced it. Before turning to the playhouses or individual plays, however, I want to consider the mise-en-scène of Elizabethan drama, to set it in context as the rather massive and unprecedented historical event that it was, and to gain some overview of the social drama out of which popular theater in Elizabethan England arose. To do so will mean beginning with the city itself and pursuing terms such as "situation" and "place" with as much literal-mindedness as can be mustered—more than might seem appropriate to readers trained, as I was, to regard plays as poems, and drama as primarily (if not entirely) a literary phenomenon. But then drama, unlike poetry, is a territorial art. It is an art of space as well as words, and it requires a place of its own, in or around a community, in which to mount its telling fictions and its eloquent spectacles.

Of all the arts, drama is the most social, indeed the most metropolitan: it is political in the finer sense of the word, intimately related to the life of the polis it at once depends upon and recreates, in one form or another. "It is the poetry of the city," writes Muriel Bradbrook, who goes on to note the incontrovertible kinship that has historically prevailed between theater and cities. "The theatre reached its greatest heights in fifth-century Athens, in Elizabethan England, and in the Paris of Louis XIV."[2] Such an observation is something of a critical commonplace, customarily pursued no further even though it links, for purposes of comparison, forms of theater and of cities that have little in common beyond their exemplary status as high points, dramatic and civic, in the course of Western culture. The analogy between Athens and Elizabethan London should in particular give us pause.[3] Each belonged to a hierarchically constituted and ritually oriented culture, in which the situation of drama was partly defined by its coherence with or divergence from the annual repetitive customs of the city. In fifth-century Athens, however, drama essentially cohered with the ritual life of the community; in Elizabethan London it diverged, in fundamental and even radical ways.

Of Athens, it is not overstating the case to say, along with Victor Ehrenberg, that the theater *was* the polis.[4] Drama in Athens was fully incorporated into the civic and religious life of the city. Serving as the climax to the spring festival of Dionysus, the annual dramatic competition sponsored by the city stood as a central event in the civic calendar, one that lay at the heart of the community's concern. And in Athens, the centrality of drama's cultural situation, its "place" in the sense of its status, was reflected in its topographical situation. In the premodern city, at any rate, topography tends to recapitulate ideology. The theater of Dionysus nestled at the heart of fifth-century Athens; situated thus, it provides us with what Richard Schechner has called an accurate map of Athenian culture and social structure. At the center of the theater stood the altar of Dionysus, open to the heavens; around it, encircling the sacrificial nexus of Athenian drama, danced the chorus. The *agons* of the actors were similarly bound and contained by the solid ranks of the audience, and the theater as a whole was further circumscribed, its agonistic contest contained and secured, by the city that surrounded the entire theatrical event. Beyond the open amphitheater, visible throughout performances, stretched Athens itself, providing the final "nest of solidarity" in an expanding series of agonistic conflicts, culturally contained and delimited. In both the shape of the theater and its situation in the city, we glimpse the configuration of the social system which produced Athenian drama, a system, in Schechner's terms, "which alternated *agon* with solidarity; which was open about debate and interrogation, but closed about who was or was not a member, a citizen."[5]

The cultural terrain of Elizabethan drama is fundamentally different. If we want to view the stage of Marlowe and Shakespeare as a historical event, a cultural phenomenon that took place in a particular social and ideological setting, we must not, in the process, lose sight of it as something that "took place" in a slightly altered sense of the phrase. Popular drama in England got under way by occupying or taking up a place in the cultural landscape that was not quite proper to it. However central that drama has come to be in our own understanding of Elizabethan culture and society, we need to keep well in mind the fact that, in the sixteenth century, what has come to be known as popular drama situated itself neither at the heart of the community nor even within it. Born of the contradiction between Court license and city prohibition, popular drama in England emerged as a cultural institution only by materially embodying that contradiction, dislocating itself from the strict confines of the existing social order and taking up a place on the margins of society, in the Liberties located outside the city walls and, to the south, across the natural barrier of the Thames. As it does in fifth-century Athens, the place of the stage in Elizabethan London reflects the cultural and ideological situation of drama, but the map of Elizabethan culture thus provided reveals the configurations of a distinctly different social system: not a geographically and ideologically closed system, but one that was in the process of opening up, of becoming unbound and less tightly coherent.

Popular drama was one of the things that would, as the sixteenth century progressed, obscure the clear outlines of Wyngaerde's London. From the standpoint of the reigning hierarchies of the city, the popular stage was an eccentric phenomenon, an extravagant and incontinent form of recreation. London regarded plays with (at best) suspicion, players as "doble-dealing ambodexters,"[6] and their audience as an imminent and unruly threat to the health of the body politic.[7] Yet the city was unable to control or suppress the stage, and not only because of Court resistance to the antitheatrical endeavors of the city. Although outside of the city proper, the Liberties were an integral part of a complex civic structure common to medieval and Renaissance cities, a geopolitical domain that was crucial to the symbolic and material economy of the city and that had traditionally been reserved for cultural phenomena that could not be contained within the strict or proper bounds of the community. The purpose of this study is to delineate the traditions of moral and cultural license that had for centuries been maintained in the Liberties, and to examine the ways in which popular drama appropriated such license to achieve, for a relatively brief period of time, an ideological liberty of its own. The place of the stage was a marginal one, and in the world of early modern culture such marginality was in itself significant. It was a world where place, in all senses of the term, mattered; where to ascertain what something was or meant, one first located it in the order of things.

To locate popular drama both culturally and topologically; to define the significance, at once literary and ideological, of the marginal situation of the Elizabethan stage; to explore some of the ways in which the plays produced on that stage not only reflected their marginality but also put it to use, deriving from their removed, exterior vantage point a critical perspective on the cultural conditions that made such plays and such a stage possible—these will be my concerns in the pages that follow. The course before us is not a simple one, however. Approaching another culture is of necessity an oblique and tentative maneuver, especially when the culture in question is, like Elizabethan England, well on its way toward becoming our own, on the verge of our world but not yet a part of it. Whether it is a city or a poem we intend to read, we need to exercise certain basic cautions as we set about defining, interpreting, reconstructing, or deconstructing the utterances and symbolic configurations of the past. The language we encounter is at once intimate and foreign to us, familiar yet often deceptive in the lines of its familiarity. Where language is concerned, we have long been accustomed to the need to gloss words and supply historical contexts—a philological and hermeneutical enterprise which, when properly undertaken, serves not only to bring what is distant closer to us, but also (and perhaps more importantly) to qualify and even question many of our unfounded assumptions of proximity to another time or culture, making it possible, by thus identifying our false cognates with the past or the sheerly Other, to approach what is different as difference, what is far from our world as precisely that. When it is not a poem but a city we intend to read, as I intend to do here, the interpretive enterprise is compounded by the need to gloss not only words and tropes and figures of speech, but figures of space as well.

II

Any city could be described, regardless of its time and place, as a projection of cultural values and beliefs: as a casting of ideals and ideologies into concrete form, an inscription of cultural practices and concerns in the very landscape of community. But as the work of Sydney Anglo, Natalie Davis, and others has begun to detail,[8] our talk of cities and cultural inscription means something altogether different when it refers not to the constructs of the modern age but to those of a traditional, more public, and more ritually oriented society. As a human artifact and a socially created image, Wyngaerde's city belongs to the latter category; we might call it, for the sake of convenience, a *ceremonial* city. It was shaped not by the dictates of urban planning and population control—prime movers in the shaping of the modern city—but by the varied rites of initiation, celebration, and exclusion through which a ceremonial social order defined, maintained, and manifested itself, in time and in space.

The late medieval and Renaissance city was the fullest expression of a world in which, to adopt Johan Huizinga's apt phrase, the outlines of things were more clearly *marked* than they are in the world we occupy.[9] Huizinga's reference was not to the unmediated simplicity of premodern existence. Things were not clearer in and of themselves, as if possessed of some radiant phenomenological purity, but were instead more clearly outlined, delimited, set apart, or underscored by the "proud or cruel publicity" of a social order governed and to a considerable extent constituted by customary ritual and ceremony. In the late medieval and Renaissance city, civic pageantry served as a spectacular advertisement of social structure; ceremony and annual repetitive customs provided vehicles with which a community could chart, in its actual topography, the limits and coherence of its authority. The outlines of things, of the community itself, were marked by means of ritual process. The city was a dramatic and symbolic work in its own right, a social production of space, an *oeuvre* (as Henri Lefebvre has rightly characterized it)[10] composed and rehearsed over the years by artisanal classes and sovereign powers, for whom meaning was always a public event, culture an "acted document,"[11] and power a manifest thing, to be conspicuously bodied forth and located in the urban landscape.

The most conspicuous embodiments of social hierarchy and power were those occasioned by the dramatic movement of royalty. On the day before her coronation in 1559, Elizabeth Tudor passed in procession through London, on a course that began at the Tower and concluded at Westminster; in so doing, she provided the populace with an engaging example of the dexterity with which she would rule, and us with one of our more impressive instances of the city in symbolic action, as a cultural performance.

"If a man should say well," as Richard Mulcaster commented in *The Quene's Majestie's Passage*,[12] "he could not better tearme the citie of London that time, than a stage wherein was shewed the wonderfull spectacle, of a noble hearted princesse toward her most loving people" (16). Mulcaster's theatrical figure, of the city as a stage upon which the royal spectacle was performed, exceeds the bounds of metaphor as we follow his account of the procession. London provided the dramatic setting of Elizabeth's passage, as Mulcaster suggests, but the city was also converted, for the sake of that passage, into a series of quite literal stages and scaffolds, erected at significant junctures along the way: at Fenchurch Street, Gracechurch Street, Cornhill, Sopers Lane, Cheapside, St. Paul's, Fleet Street, and finally St. Dunstan's. The series was a dynamic one. Elizabeth's presence as she made her progress became the moving and vital force that brought the pageants to life and gave voice to the figures they contained. And the scenes that unfolded before Elizabeth were dynamic in import as well as in form. They did not merely pay tribute to their royal audience; they also subjected her, as it were, to didactic and even prescriptive allegories on the arts of government. While they invited Elizabeth's response, making her both audience to and central actor in the ongoing dramaturgy of state, they also shaped and qualified that response, eliciting vows of a peaceful, harmonious, and above all Protestant rule from the incipient queen. "The symbolism of the progress," as Clifford Geertz, one of the more recent of its many commentators, has observed, "was . . . admonitory and covenantal: the subjects warned, and the Queen promised."[13]

At Gracechurch, the stage extended from one side of the street to the other; as Elizabeth approached, this central platform revealed "iii. several stages in degrees" (18), each of which was occupied by appropriately robed figures of royalty. On the lowest sat Henry VII and his wife Elizabeth; on the next, Henry VIII accompanied by Anne Boleyn—chosen from among numerous possibilities, of course, because she was the mother of Elizabeth herself. On the third and highest stage, a solitary figure was enthroned: a proleptic figure in this instance, drawn not out of England's past but from its imminent future, seated before Elizabeth's eyes but located in time at a point just beyond the present moment, and "representynge the Queen's most excellent majestie Elizabeth nowe our most dradde soveraygne Ladie, crowned and apparelled as the other prynces were" (19). It was a genealogy of the houses of Lancaster and York, a *tableau vivant* not only representing and legitimizing Elizabeth's ascension but also specifying the terms of that legitimacy. The theme of the spectacle was unity and peaceful rule, and Elizabeth acted out her part in the scene, receiving its admonitory message and then, in an address to the crowd, publicly interpreting the significance of the setting while assessing and addressing its tone. "After that her grace had understood the meaning thereof," writes Mulcaster, "she thanked the citie, praised the fairnes of the work, and promised, that she would doe her whole endeavor for the continuall preservacion of concorde, as the pageante did emporte" (20).

The platforms and scaffolds erected in the public thoroughfares did not merely act as the passive setting for the drama of state that was played out upon them, but actually entered into the covenantal dialogue thus established with Elizabeth. The very gaps and interstices of the scaffold at Gracechurch addressed themselves to their royal audience, for "all the empty places thereof were furnished with sentences concerning unitie." At Fleet Street, too, the city was inscribed with an occasional significance. "The void places of the pageant were filled with pretie sentences" (33) concerning good council, the topic of that locale. On such an occasion, the city and its common places unfolded before the eyes of the knowing spectator to become an extensive emblem or commonplace book— "a great Book-faire printed," as Donald Lupton would remark of London in 1632, *"cum privilegio Regis."*[14]

The dramatic movements of early modern power are of great interest to our age, and such interest has been nurtured by the extensive written accounts of royal processions and triumphal entries which began to be composed and preserved during the course of the sixteenth century. Processions like Elizabeth's have consequently received an extraordinary degree of attention. Other forms of public ritual and ceremony did not go unrecorded, however. Less frequently translated into documentary form, they may be largely inaccessible to us, yet they left a record nonetheless—one effaced with the passage of time but crucial to the functions of civic ritual. Focusing primarily on those ceremonies preserved in the archives of the document, we tend to view them as initiatory rites of passage, vehicles by which figures of power or authority were conveyed to their proper place in the social hierarchy, their passage into prominence realized and celebrated by ritual means. Such a perspective is not false, but it is misleading. It removes civic ritual from its urban context, obscuring the degree to which that context—the landscape of community itself—was the record being simultaneously composed and interpreted by such ritual processes.

Public ritual and ceremony did not merely take place in the city. They provided what Charles Phythian-Adams has described as a "living mirror" of the community,[15] and the glass thus created was one fashioned of stone and mortar and cobbled streets. Ceremony was the vehicle by which the urban landscape was articulated and defined, the civic terrain shaped and translated into significant space. In the varied ceremonies and festivities conducted throughout the year in sixteenth-century London, the city's image of itself was at once dramatized and, through repetitive performance and mnemonic association, made inseparable from the physical body of the community. When a lord mayor's pageant achieved its plotted course through the city the ceremony itself was at an end, but the concerns of community thus celebrated and conveyed were not exhausted by their ritual progress. Rather, such concerns were set in context, transcribed into a language of monuments and common places. When ceremony ceased, the city remained: a trace, a record, a living memory of the cultural performances it both witnessed and served to embody.[16]

The ceremonial city was a "great Book-faire" printed, in the case of royal processions, *cum privilegio Regis;* it was a text to be inscribed and interpreted, not by historians but by the interaction of ritual process and community, the action of ritual process *on* community. When we regard a royal procession or a panorama of the city like Wyngaerde's, part of what fails to register with us is the degree to which the city at large, in its unadorned streets and conduits, its everyday markets and common places, was a monumental record of the various ceremonies and rituals which had annually shaped and articulated it. The city was a symbolic artifact, a cultural emblem or device conceived in ceremony, ritual, and not always harmonious community, impressed with significance but difficult to read, as any emblem or device must be. "The device," as D. J. Gordon reminds us, "does not exist by itself; it has to be read; moreover, it has to be difficult to read. To read it is a kind of play, and its function is to define the group that *can* play—to establish the group's sense of coherence, identity, and security."[17] The group that could read the emblematic or ceremonial city—that was defined

and maintained by a ritual play of interpretation which took all the
city for its stage—was, of course, the urban community itself.

Literally tracing the outlines and avenues of community, rituals
of state and city in the Renaissance did not so much celebrate power
as negotiate it; by a ritual process or play of signification, they served
to define, articulate, and interpret both the social hierarchy and
the communal landscape in which it was reflected. Such rituals acted
first as a means of embodying cultural values in the urban topography, and second, as a vehicle for rehearsing or performing those
values. The ritual life of the city was organized, in other words,
around a process of cultural inscription and interpretation that was
at heart dramaturgical, and the city itself—the body politic in its
most concrete manifestation—was both the product and the exegetical object of that dramaturgy.

Prior to the sixteenth century, the inscriptive and interpretive
process of civic ritual was sufficient to its object. Written accounts
of public ceremonies begin to proliferate only in the middle and
later years of the sixteenth century, at a time when traditional forms
of public ritual were on the wane; the landscape of community,
traditionally informed by a ritual play of signification, was becoming
increasingly obscured, in need of the supplementary gloss provided
by documentary transcription. In order to read a ceremonial city
like early modern London and to understand, at least to some
extent, a sense of space alien to the modern world yet substantially
embodied in such a city, we stand in need of a guide; fortunately
for our purposes, the later sixteenth century shared our inadequacy
to an increasing degree and produced, as a consequence, a quite
exemplary guide in the person of John Stow—antiquarian, scholar,
and surveyor of Elizabethan London.

Fifty years before its appearance in 1598, Stow's *Survay of London*[18]
would have been superfluous. The city was an emblem of cultural
identity and security, a symbolic text that was both inscribed by
the passage of power and communal spectacle, and interpreted or
made accessible through such ritual processes. Reading the city,
as Stow does in his *Survay,* was something every citizen could be
expected to do. Not without difficulty, of course; it was precisely
the play of interpretive difficulty (to adopt Gordon's phrase once
again) that distinguished citizen from noncitizen. In order to define a community or coherent group, symbolic devices had to be
difficult to interpret. Informed by what we might call a strategic
obscurity, they invited and even demanded explication. Emblems
of the period were always accompanied by their explanatory poems,
devices by their mottoes, and cities by their public ceremonies and

ritual processions: all were forms of commentary, examples of what Stephen Orgel has called the Renaissance pressure toward explanation.[19] As we move away from the clear outlines of Wyngaerde's London and into the more ambiguous cultural terrain of the Elizabethan city, however, the period's pressure toward explanation also shifts ground, becoming more anxious and problematic, requiring new and unprecedented forms of commentary. Stow's *Survay* is one of the results: a timely work, prompted by the economic, social, and cultural changes that were transforming the face of London, making the city unrecognizable to its own citizens and obscuring the emblems and devices of community.

III

In his preface to the reader, presumed to a be a citizen of the city, Stow describes his *Survay* as a "Discovery" of London, and it is precisely that: an archaeology of the city, systematically uncovering its lines and sites of significance.

In the *Survay,* Stow sifts patiently through the chaos of present detail—the effects of London's unprecedented growth in the sixteenth century[20]—to locate, by means of a quite substantial memory as well as by archives, chronicles, and oral accounts, the traces of a past whose outlines were daily growing more tenuous. The social order he records in passing is a ceremonial one, and the city that unfolds before us is as much a dramaturgical creation as a juridical or political one, a cultural text both composed and performed by ritual processions and ceremonies. For Stow, London is a palimpsest of the many who have lived and died within its confines, of the people and events that were shaped by the city and that shaped it in turn, leaving the signs of their passage on its streets and conduits, its customs and rituals. In an entirely literal sense, the *Survay* is a reading of London and those various signs of passage. With Stow, we move from place to place in a careful and ruminative perambulation, inquiring at each site after the significance of the place: the images it holds, the events it has witnessed, the changes it has felt and had impressed upon it.

The *Survay* is organized not as an analysis of the city but as a walk through it: as a peripatetic representation of London, in which the city serves as its own map, an open book for those (like Stow) who know how to read it. "I will beginne at the East," writes Stow, "and so proceede through the high and most principall streete of the cittie to the west . . . then by the said Stockes (a market place both of fish and flesh standing in the midst of the Cittie) through the Poultrie (a street so called) to the great conduite in West Cheape,

and so through Cheape to the Standard . . . then by the Standard
to the great crosse . . . and then to the little conduite by Paules
Gate" (1:117–18). Stow's course is largely the one followed by Elizabeth in her precoronal procession, and his progress is properly
viewed as a documentary supplement to more spectacular passages
like the queen's. Where Elizabeth's passage inscribed the common
places of the city with meaning, Stow's retrieves and recreates not
only the meaning of such events but also the eventfulness of such
manifest forms of significance. The *Survay* views urban topography
as a cultural artifact or creation, providing us with one of our
clearest portraits of the ways in which communal territory intersects
and is shaped by cultural concerns and ideologies in the premodern
city. The streets of London determine the shape of Stow's interrogation, and his questions and comments conform to the irregular
configurations of London's customary topography—the emblematic embodiment of meaning, power, and memory.

Indeed, Stow's London serves its surveyor as a vast memory
system, an extensive memory theater. His passage through it amounts
to an attentive transcription of the memory-traces impressed upon
the city by time and ceremonial circumstance. But if Stow's London
is a memory theater, where images of the past adhere to particular
places and can be retrieved or recreated by the sort of topical and
ambulatory inquiry that structures the *Survay,* it is also a city: a
symbolic and even a rhetorical device, but an inhabited one. As
such it stands significantly apart from the intricate, hermetic, and
highly artificial memory theaters designed by the likes of Giullio
Camillo and Giordano Bruno, and admirably described, in all their
intricacy, by Frances Yates in *The Art of Memory.* Artificial memory
theaters were the products not of widespread cultural practices but
of individual practitioners of the arts of memory. They were too
elaborate ever to be realized in mortar and stone, and it is doubtful
that their designers even fostered such concrete intentions. Stow's
London, however, is very much in the world, and it is rooted in a
more concrete and substantial sense of place. Its common places
were actual sites, visited and frequented by the citizens of London,
and at the same time they served as commonplaces in the rhetorical
sense of the word: as topoi or *loci communes,* sites of potential meaning, open and available to various figures and uses, even capable—
as rhetorical topoi often are—of antithetical or ambivalent
significance.[21]

The art of memory was born of the experience of actual places,
according to Quintilian; it was the places of memory systems, at
once actual and rhetorical, that provided Aristotle with his term

for the "topoi" of invention, among which a speaker moves as he develops his theme.[22] A coincidence of actual place and rhetorical commonplace characterizes the ancient and partly shared heritage of both artificial memory and rhetoric, and it is this heritage that is made visible in the city Stow records for us. A rhetoric of space informs Elizabethan London, and Stow's *Survay* is the closest thing we have to a commonplace book for such a city. The common places of London are Stow's topics; as he moves through the city, it unfolds as his theme.

Surveying London thus, Stow recreates not only a city and its history but also a vanishing sense of space, one perceived and recorded at the point of its vanishing, at least insofar as Western culture is concerned. Stow's London stands on the verge of the Cartesian world—on the verge, that is to say, of a new concept of space, one whose philosophical development has been admirably traced by Ernst Cassirer in *The Individual and the Cosmos,* and whose more mundane ramifications were what Weber had in mind when he spoke of the "disenchantment of the world" that accompanied the rise of early modern capitalism.[23] We are the offspring of that disenchantment; our world is a more abstract one, stripped of the materiality that previously governed notions of space and place. Stow's world was a more substantial one. The London he records belongs not to a quantitative cosmos but to a qualitative one, informed by a hierarchical sense of space and its significance; what something means in such a world is a function, first and foremost, of its situation in the order of things.

"All our affirmations concerning any concrete 'what,' " as Cassirer writes of the pre-Cartesian world, "are always accompanied by affirmations concerning its 'where.' "[24] In such a world view, in a world viewed thus, place and meaning are inseparably intertwined:

> Places have their nature and peculiar characteristics, the same as bodies—or, if not the same, at least in an analogous way. And there exists a very definite relationship of community or of conflict, of sympathy or of antipathy between the two natures. The body is by no means indifferent to the place in which it is located and by which it is enclosed; rather, it stands in a real and causal relation to it. Every physical element seeks "its" place, the place that belongs and corresponds to it, and it flees from any other opposed to it. Thus, with relation to specific elements, place itself seems to be endowed with powers. . . .[25]

Place is endowed with meaning, and with power. When Cicero speaks of the inherently spatial character of rhetorical topoi, his own topic is the power of rhetoric, and he suggests, in this context, that rhetorical topics function in a manner analogous to certain places in the world at large—natural places to which a particular power or efficacy is thought to adhere. "Behind the topoi," as Terry Comito aptly notes, "we may discover a more primitive sense of the sacred potency of space."[26]

Whether sacred or secular, power is a phenomenon difficult to locate in the memory theaters discussed by Yates, but it is, as we have seen, the informing presence that structures and inscribes the common places of Stow's London. They are natural but culturally determined sites of significance, endowed with meaning not by nature but by the inscriptive, ritual arts of a traditional society: a society organized around and by the annual customs which served to translate urban topography into culturally significant *topology*, as Robert Thornton has defined the term. In Thornton's study of non-Western traditional societies and their "pre-Cartesian" sense of space, topology refers not to the physical landscape alone but to the intersection of topography and culture; the topology of a community is a cultural recreation of physical space, fashioned and maintained through ritual process. It is something made, a civic or communal form of *poesis*. Thus the Iraqw of Tanzania speak of making or creating the land they occupy: the circulation of ritual over a given territory translates natural or physical patterns of the landscape into a cultural framework by inscribing them with value, delineating boundaries and defining territories in a way that refashions space into an image or icon of community, a symbolic representation of cultural values and hierarchies.[27]

Stow's *Survay* represents for us, then, a pre-Cartesian or Aristotelian world; a memory theater whose topoi or commonplaces are no less significant than they are substantial; a topological device on the scale of a city, to be compared to the spatial constructs of other traditional societies, Western or not, for whom place and its significance are ritually constituted phenomena. Stow does not impose or create meaning; in his terms, he merely transcribes what is already there. It is the ritual passages of power, whether civic, royal, or ecclesiastic, that have inscribed the common places of London with significance, and it is the traces of such power, at once moving and monumental, that Stow records for us as he makes his topical progress through the city—affirming *what*, by first affirming *where*.

As the publication of the *Survay* itself reminds us, however, such affirmations were becoming increasingly difficult to make. Stow's perspective on the city is like that of Walter Benjamin's angel of

history: he faces the past, but is being irresistibly propelled into
the future by the catastrophic storm we sometimes call history,
sometimes progress, usually both.[28] At the moment in history that
Stow conducted his *Survay of London,* the traditional structures of
heirarchic society in England were breaking down; Elizabethan
culture was taking a decidedly alien warp, such that even native
forms of significance began to appear in contexts far removed from,
if not subversive of, their customary usage. It was in 1589, in the
midst of unprecedented social and cultural upheavals, that John
Lyly described Elizabethan England as a kind of *genera mixta* writ
large, a highly complex emblem or device that was increasingly
resistant to interpretation or explication:

> At our exercises, Souldiers call for Trajedies, their object is bloode;
> Courtiers for Commedies, their subject is love; Countriemen for
> Pastorelles, Shepheardes are their Saints. Trafficke and travell hath
> woven the nature of all Nations into ours, and made this land like
> Arras, full of devise. . . . Time hath confounded our mindes, our
> mindes the matter; but all commeth to this passe, that what here-
> tofore hath been served in several dishes for a feaste, is now minced
> in a charger for a Gallimaufrey. If wee present a mingle-mangle,
> our fault is to be excused, because the whole world is become an
> Hodge-podge.[29]

What was true of Lyly's England—"like an Arras, full of devise"—
was most emphatically true of Elizabethan London. As the city
expanded far beyond its customary social, cultural, and geographical limits, it indeed became a "Gallimaufrey" of the nation (if not
of all nations) as a whole. Distinguishing citizen from noncitizen
became a doubtful task as the displaced and marginal population
of the country came to London in increasing numbers, to take
advantage of the anonymity the city offered and to escape from
the rigid traditional structures which the city itself had once served
to embody. In Lyly's terms, the result was confounding; in Gordon's, the play of interpretive difficulty that the city both invited
and demanded became a more serious and dramatic sort of play,
an enterprise that could as readily challenge coherence, identity,
and security, as establish them.

The dismay expressed by Shakespeare's contemporaries over
their increasingly unfamiliar and unruly city was the dismay of a
community helplessly watching the symbols of its coherence, the
devices of its integrity, being taken over and turned against it.
Informed by a strategic obscurity, of necessity difficult to read if it
is to function as a means of cultural self-definition, any cultural
symbol has an equivocal potential. In Elizabethan London, that

potential came to the fore in the latter half of the sixteenth century, and it reached its greatest pitch just outside the city walls, in the margins of Stow's London.

IV

The ultimate emblem of London's coherence and integrity, the most prominent of its figures of space, was the ancient Roman wall which, in Wyngaerde's day, still defined the city with relative clarity. It had long been useless for purposes of defense, and with the advent of gunpowder and cannon as martial tools-in-trade it ceased to act in even the most residual capacity as an effective barrier against the outside world. In the sixteenth century it functioned solely as a means of symbolic definition, a monumental demarcation of the limits of community, an emblem of civic integrity that was annually "refortified" by the ceremonial repertoire of the city.

During the secular half of the year, running roughly from Midsummer's Eve to the initiation of Christmas festivities, there was little public ceremony; the city was given over to commercial concerns. But during the six months dominated by the Church calendar, ceremony circulated throughout the confines of London. Ritual progresses ranging from a lord mayor's pageant and Corpus Christi processions to the more errant and wanton motions of Misrule crossed and recrossed the city proper, defining the terrain of community and charting, in all its particulars, the province of communal concerns. At Rogationtide the line of London's wall was itself traced, in a ritual that marked the horizon of community on the one hand and served, on the other, to locate and give access to those areas of "licentious libertie" (as Henry VIII called them)[30] traditionally preserved just beyond that horizon, at the threshold of the city.

Stow devotes over half of his *Survay* to the area outside the walls of the city. Once the wards within the walls have been traversed, he moves outside the city proper to chart, in a progress that again proceeds from east to west, the outlying suburbs and Liberties. In so doing, he reminds us that the definition provided by London's wall was more equivocal than its clear outline at first suggests. From our vantage point, it is easy to be taken in by the walls of a medieval or Renaissance city—to regard them, as even Fernand Braudel does in his inspired overview of early modern towns,[31] as sheer, antithetical boundaries defining inside against outside, what is native and integral to the community against what is foreign and alien to it, the city against its polar opposite, its counterexample, the "Countre." But the country did not begin as one passed through the city gates of sixteenth-century London. What was defined by ritual's progress through the city and over the course of the ceremonial calendar was not a binary construct, composed within a system of polar oppositions, but a tertiary one. Between city and country stood "an uncertain and somewhat irregular territory"[32] where the powers of city, state, and church came together but did not coincide. From the walls of London out to the bars located up to a mile beyond them—outposts where pilgrims and other travelers could be examined for signs of leprosy or plague, turned away or diverted to nearby lazar-houses and hospitals—stretched the marginal and ambivalent domain of London's Liberties.

The outskirts of the premodern city were places of a complex and contradictory sort of freedom, ambivalent zones of transition between one realm of authority and another. In France, they were known as *banlieux:* places of proclamation where the law was made known, its ban announced, but also, as their name suggests, places of exile or banishment. It was here that exiles were conveyed, shackled so as to be fully and visibly under the sway of authority, and it was here that exiles were released from their bonds—the visible ones of iron, the invisible ones of the community—to be cast altogether outside the magic circle described by power, authority, and community. In the margins of the premodern city, the law could be felt and witnessed in its most extreme forms and also at its furthest limits, at its extremity, its verge or vanishing point.

If anything, the Liberties of London were an even more ambiguous realm, a borderland whose legal parameters and privileges were open-ended and equivocally defined. "Strange relics of medieval customs, precincts which were at the same time within and not within the city, conflicts of jurisdiction, privileged persons, edicts which were never enforced—all these," writes Virginia Gildersleeve, "make the situation [of the Liberties] hard to grasp."[33] The Liberties were free or "at liberty" from manorial rule or obligation to the Crown, and only nominally under the jurisdiction of the lord mayor. While belonging to the city, they fell outside the purview of the sheriffs of London and so comprised virtually ungoverned areas over which the city had authority but, paradoxically, no control. Liberties existed within the city walls as well, but they too stood outside of London's effective domain; like the Liberties outside the walls, they were a part of the city yet juridically set apart from it. Entering a Liberty, whatever its location, meant crossing over into an ambiguous territory that was at once internal and external to the city, neither contained by civic authority nor fully removed from it. They were the suburbs of the urban world, forming an underworld officially recognized as lawless; they stood in a certain sense outside the law, and so could serve as privileged or exempt arenas where the anxieties and insecurities of life in a rigidly organized hierarchical society could be given relatively free reign.

It was to the Liberties, according to Stow, that citizens retired to pursue pastimes and pleasures that had no proper place in the community. Their place of retreat was a heterogeneous one: alongside gaming houses, taverns, bear-baiting arenas, marketplaces, and brothels, stood monasteries, lazar-houses, and scaffolds of execution. Whatever could not be contained within the strict bounds of the community found its place here, making the Liberties the preserve of the anomalous, the unclean, the polluted, and the sacred. Like the French *banlieux*, London's Liberties were places of exile, yet the banishment enacted in them was of a more ambivalent order. What was lodged outside the city was excluded, yet retained; denied a place within the community, yet not merely exiled. The licentious, dangerous, unclean, or polluted was cast out of the city, but was then maintained as such and even placed on public display. The horizon of community was thereby made visible, something that could be seen and apprehended, but the apprehension involved was a double-edged one. What London saw when it gazed out into the Liberties were things without a proper place in the community, things that in a certain sense had already exceeded the limits of community. Fitting emblems with which to articulate the city's threshold, to be sure, but also unsettling or discomfiting sights, potential sources of anxiety or dread—of apprehension in a different sense of the word. If within the city walls the ideals and aspirations of community were staged in an extensive repertory of civic rituals and cultural performances, then the margins of the city served as a more ambivalent staging ground: as a place where the contradictions of the community, its incontinent hopes and fears, were prominently and dramatically set on stage.

V

During the latter half of the sixteenth century, it was in the Liberties that the alien warp of Elizabethan culture became most pronounced, and it was in such areas, of course, that Elizabethan drama established its most radical roots—in the public playhouses located outside the city walls.

As we move out into the Liberties, it will be important to keep in mind the fact that popular drama did not move into a blank or neutral field when it occupied the margins of the city. It moved into a province with its own tradition of ambivalent spectacle and cultural license: a tradition which served, in a sense, to prepare the ground for Elizabethan drama, and which the stage appropriated and adapted to its own dramatic ends. Effectively banished from the city by increasingly strict regulations, popular drama translated the terms of its exile to its advantage. Like Rosalind's withdrawal from court in *As You Like It*, the withdrawal of drama from the city was a flight "to liberty, and not to banishment" (I.i.138). It was an act of cultural translation, and we can best understand what the stage translated its situation into, by first understanding what it was translating from: the traditions of marginal ritual and spectacle that had previously defined the significance of London's Liberties.

Ritual and spectacle are not spontaneous; they are staged events, orchestrated manifestations of power, studied representations of authority and community. In early modern society, power was inseparable from such public manifestations. In a sense, it existed in any effective form only insofar as it made a moving spectacle of itself. "Traditionally," as Michel Foucault writes, "power was what was seen, what was shown and what was manifested and, paradoxically, found the principle of its force in the movements by which it deployed that force."[34] Foucault is not alone in making such an observation, nor in the focus of concerns that underlie it. With the once-sacrosanct boundaries separating the human sciences beginning to blur, a new and multidisciplinary interest in the public world of the Renaissance has begun to take shape; whatever our particular field, we find it increasingly fruitful to consider the various stages occupied by early modern power, the various rituals and spectacles that comprised its moving and self-constituting dramaturgy. Whether we call the final product of such considerations history, anthropology, sociology, or (not to exclude my own province) literary studies, the effects have been salutary. We are developing a more public sense of culture and its ideological complexities, and along with it a more public sense of "sense" itself, of meaning, its social contexts, and the interplay of dialectic that informs them both. Such a development is most clearly manifested when the object of concern is a particular court with its progresses, triumphs, and other moving dramas, but a broader interest in the dynamics of culture is also apparent in recent approaches to more diverse cultural phenomena, such as (to cite but a few examples) a pastoral poem, a carnival at Romans, the inquisition of a Friulian miller, a treatise on Virginia, or an outbreak of organized violence in seventeenth-century Westmoreland.[35] "All represent attempts," writes Clifford Geertz, himself an influential figure in this ongoing refiguration of social thought, "to formulate how this people or that, this period or that, makes sense to itself."[36]

In a hierarchical yet resolutely plural society like Elizabethan England, power, authority, and community involved a delicate and continually renegotiated balance. Neither the city nor the Court could hope to exert full control over its own cultural performances—over the ways, that is to say, that civic and royal authority (like a people, a period, or a person) made sense to itself. Lacking a professional army and even the rudiments of a paid bureaucracy, Elizabeth wielded little real coercive force. She could maintain her throne only by devoting herself to the arts of political persuasion and performance, and by turning those arts toward "the arduous and constant wooing of the body politic."[37] Royal power depended upon its "privileged visibility," in Stephen Greenblatt's excellent phrase, and as Greenblatt especially has shown, such visibility was theatrically constituted and theatrically maintained. "We princes," as Elizabeth herself announced to an audience of Lords and Commons, "are set on stages in the sight and view of all the world."[38]

In our brief overview of the ceremonial city, we have seen Elizabeth thus on stage, negotiating with the city for the power and authority she would need for effective rule, making the city through which she passed an enduring record of such a negotiation. But the spectacle of power in early modern society, whether royal, civic, or ecclesiastic, was not limited to such center-stage productions. Nor was it always organized around those mobile figures of authority, be they monarch, lord mayor, or divine, who made any place they occupied both a center and a stage. Some of the most extreme and paradoxical manifestations of power, the most equivocal acts of cultural definition and performance, were reserved for the margins of early modern society: for that culturally, socially, and politically ambiguous domain outside the city walls, where the powers of city, state, and church were most resolutely plural and most equivocally defined. Here it was not the commanding figures but, as we shall see, the limits and contradictions of society that occupied center stage.

Neither a part of nor fully apart from the city, the Liberties served as a kind of riddle inscribed in the cultural landscape. The riddle was one of community, its limits and its threshold, and up until the second half of the sixteenth century it was the citizens of London who could correctly parse its message, and so reconstitute and define themselves as a community, through a ritual process of interpretation. As the sixteenth century progressed, however, those citizens found themselves increasingly excluded from such an interpretive enterprise—defined, to their discomfort and dismay, as part of a group that could no longer play. There were new players in the field, and they were redefining or appropriating to themselves the former grounds of community. It is the riddle of London's margins that will occupy us now, as we endeavor to situate Elizabethan drama in the context of marginal spectacle and to relate its discomfiting appearance on the horizon of the city to a long-standing and ambivalent tradition of cultural displacement and display.

CHAPTER
2
The Place of the Stage

I

On July 21, 1557, two men were conveyed out of London and ferried across the Thames to a hospital located on the outskirts of Southwark. It was known as the Lock: a place of incarceration but also, as the name suggests, a *site de passage*, a place where the new inmates could live out their lives in peace if not in comfort, fed and tended by the Warden of the hospital, the Guider, whose duty it was to oversee the passage of God's afflicted as they made their way from this life to the next. The men remain nameless, but their anonymity can hardly obscure the significance that attaches to them. They were the last recorded lepers of early modern London and its environs.

Coming when it does, their brief appearance on the stage of history is a reverberating one, and for our purposes the timing— less than two years shy of Elizabethan England—is most opportune. History, like a literary text, offers innumerable points of entry. Some are more resonant than others, and a few are capable of providing an expansive opening of the kind once described by Erich Auerbach: an *Ansatzpunkt* or point of departure comprising "a firmly circumscribed, easily comprehensible set of phenomena, whose interpretation is a radiation out from them, and which orders and interprets a greater region than they themselves occupy."[1] Where the symbolic topography of London's Liberties is concerned, few points of departure could be as radiant as leprosy's final excursion from the city. The history of London's margins is a history of such excursions—a history of persons and things, of persons made into things, conveyed out of the city and lodged on its threshold. In the Liberties, the spectacle of the outcast and the marginal traditionally held sway; much that was without a proper place in the customary order of the community found a place here. Being the final procession of its kind, the ritual progress of London's last lepers points us in two directions at once. On the one hand, it orients us toward the history of London's Liberties, opening a line of inquiry that will allow a genealogy of those Liberties, a rhetoric or poetic of marginal spectacle, to be composed. On the other hand, taken as a conclusive ritual, a point of historical closure, it points us toward all that was new on the horizon of London's concern—toward what was taking the place of customary forms of spectacle and display, displacing tradition and transforming or troping the significance of London's Liberties.

Eclipsing all other forms of the new—both from the vantage point of literary history, and from the perspective of the city itself—were the public playhouses of Elizabethan London. It was in 1576, some twenty years after leprosy's last rites were performed, that James Burbage, a joiner by trade, left the city to erect a playhouse in the Liberty of Holywell, to the north of London. He christened his handiwork with a resoundingly pagan but apposite name: the Theatre. An imitable precedent was set, and others immediately followed suit. In 1577, the Shoreditch Theatre was joined by the Curtain; the Rose appeared on the Bankside in 1587, followed by the Swan in 1595 and the Globe, refashioned from timbers of the original Theatre, in 1599. By the turn of the century, when the Fortune completed the scene, the city was ringed with playhouses posted strategically just outside its jurisdiction (see fig. 2)."Houses of purpose built . . . and that without the Liberties," as John Stockwood complained in a sermon delivered at Paul's Cross in 1578, "as who woulde say, 'There, let them saye what they will say, we wil play.' "[2]

The playhouses of early modern London no longer speak to us so clearly or so outrageously; the voice that Stockwood projects upon the new theaters, at once mocking and assertive, is in need of some amplification if it is to be heard and comprehended at a historical remove such as ours. Literary historians have conducted an extensive archaeology of the Elizabethan theater over the past century and a half, but their monumental enterprise has understandably focused upon those aspects of the playhouses—galleries for the spectators, tiring houses, the shape and orientation of the scaffold itself—that would have directly affected performance.[3] For the most part, modern scholarship has sought to gloss the first

---

F I G U R E 2. On the following pages, London buildings used as theaters or intimately connected with dramatic performances between 1520 and 1642. Based on M.C. Bradbrook, *The Living Monument: Shakespeare and The Theatre of His Time* (Cambridge: Cambridge University Press, 1976), pp. xii-xiii.

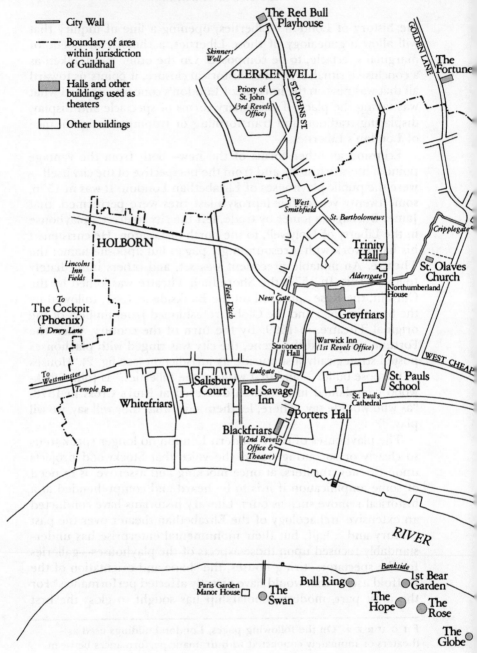

THEATERS OF LONDON

Legend:
- City Wall
- Boundary of area within jurisdiction of Guildhall
- Halls and other buildings used as theaters
- Other buildings

The Red Bull Playhouse

Skinners Well

GOLDEN LANE

The Fortune

CLERKENWELL

Priory of St. John (3rd Revels Office)

ST JOHNS ST

West Smithfield

St. Bartholomews

Cripplegate

HOLBORN

Trinity Hall

St. Olaves Church

Lincolns Inn Fields

Aldersgate

Fleet Dich

New Gate

Northumberland House

To The Cockpit (Phoenix) in Drury Lane

Greyfriars

Stationers Hall

Warwick Inn (1st Revels Office)

WEST CHEAP

To Westminster

Temple Bar

Ludgate

St. Pauls School

Salisbury Court

Whitefriars

Bel Savage Inn

St. Paul's Cathedral

Blackfriars (2nd Revels Office & Theater)

Porters Hall

RIVER

Bankside

Paris Garden Manor House

The Swan

Bull Ring

1st Bear Garden

The Hope

The Rose

The Globe

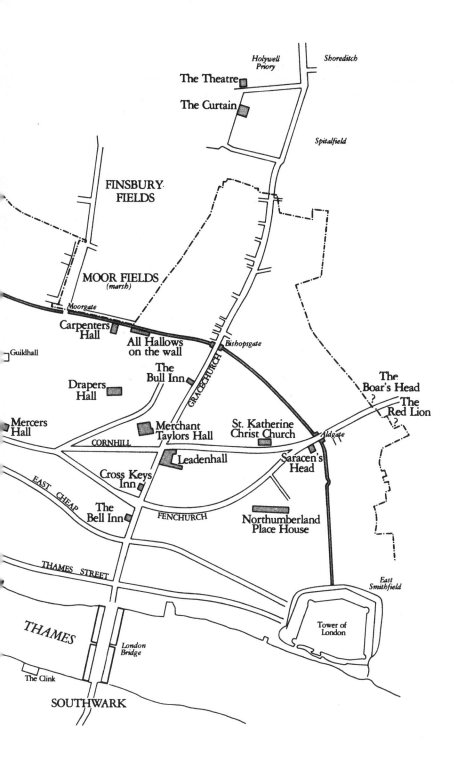

Holywell Priory
Shoreditch
The Theatre
The Curtain
Spitalfield
FINSBURY FIELDS
MOOR FIELDS
(marsh)
Moorgate
Carpenters Hall
Guildhall
All Hallows on the wall
Bishopsgate
The Bull Inn
GRACECHURCH
The Boar's Head
?
The Red Lion
?
Drapers Hall
Mercers Hall
Merchant Taylors Hall
St. Katherine Christ Church
Aldgate
CORNHILL
Leadenhall
Saracen's Head
Cross Keys Inn
EAST CHEAP
The Bell Inn
FENCHURCH
Northumberland Place House
East Smithfield
THAMES STREET
THAMES
Tower of London
London Bridge
The Clink
SOUTHWARK

clause of Stockwood's complaint against the theaters—that they were "houses of purpose built"—and the effort has met with at least some success. Working from Court, city, and parish records, the observations and sketches of foreign visitors like deWitt and Hollar, a building contract for the Fortune Theatre, and other documentary evidence, we now think we could construct a facsimile that a native would have taken for a playhouse, or a foreigner like Wenceslaus Hollar might have at least mistaken for a bullring or "Beerebayting" arena—as Hollar does mistake the Globe in his panorama of London, published in 1647. Much doubt and confusion remains over what we know and what we have yet to learn, however, largely because English sources are so chary of detail when it comes to the construction or the theatrical capabilities of the Elizabethan theater. What Shakespeare's contemporaries found noteworthy about the playhouses, however, was neither their facilities nor their design, but (as O. L. Brownstein has recently reminded us) their *location*.[4] They were houses of purpose built, as Stockwood says, but they were of purpose built "without the Liberties"; it is the second clause of his complaint that speaks to and even mimes the unsettling significance of the Elizabethan playhouse. What Stockwood finds distinctive and scandalous, even to the point of an audacious and unruly eloquence—"As who woulde say, 'There, let them saye what they will say, we wil play' "—is not the architecture but the place of the stage, its marginal yet commanding situation on the threshold of early modern London.

However difficult it is to recreate the physical architecture of the Elizabethan theaters, their moral and ideological architecture is a great deal more resistant to recreation. Yet it was the place of the stage—both its status and its locale—that most occupied Elizabethans, and will occupy us here, as I attempt to sound out both the social and the aesthetic reverberations of Elizabethan drama's marginality. In a certain sense outcast, the popular stage also possessed, by virtue of its situation, a power to shock or scandalize; while an integral part of Elizabethan culture, the stage was also set apart from that culture, displaced from it to a degree that would be crucial to the development of a new and ideologically mobile drama—a marginal but by no means superfluous form of theater. When Burbage dislocated theater from the city, he established a social and cultural distance that would prove invaluable to the stagecraft of Marlowe and Shakespeare: a critical distance, I will be arguing, that provided the stage with a culturally and ideologically removed vantage point from which it could reflect upon its own age with more freedom and license than had hitherto been possible. It was a freedom, a range of slightly eccentric or decentered perspectives, that gave the stage an uncanny ability to tease out and represent the contradictions of a culture it both belonged to and was, to a certain extent, alienated from. The place of the stage was an ambivalent one, even a para-doxical one—but so is the situation, in less concretely manifested ways, of any viable literature in relation to the culture that produces it and is in turn produced by it.

The marginality of Elizabethan drama was not, however, merely a literary affair. Ambivalence, paradox, and cultural contradiction were not new to the margins of the city, and the liberty or license popular drama gained when it moved out into the Liberties had long existed there. It was a liberty that was at once moral, ideo-logical, and topological; a license to exist outside the strict confines of community, traditionally reserved for a different kind of outcast phenomenon and for less artistic but equally dramatic displays of cultural ambivalence and contradiction. Marginal spectacle was a complex variety of cultural performance, an equivocal way that premodern European cultures had of making sense of themselves, to themselves. It was through such spectacle that the Liberties be-came inscribed as areas of anomaly and arenas of cultural ambiv-alence, open to forms of signification more contradictory, more extravagant and incontinent, than those allowed to manifest them-selves within the city gates. And it is through such spectacle that we can come to understand the ideological mobility and license which popular drama found available when it abstracted itself from the city and moved into the Liberties, to translate them, in all their complexity and ambivalence, into a new forum for theater.

II

Inside the ceremonial city, ritual and spectacle were organized around central figures of authority and power, emblems of cultural coherence and community. The figures we encounter outside the city walls are liminal ones, figures of the threshold rather than the center of society. Marginal ritual and spectacle placed such figures in the context proper to them, on the *limen* or threshold of the community. The dramaturgy of the margins was a liminal breed of cultural performance, a performance *of* the threshold, by which the horizon of community was made visible, the limits of definition, containment, and control made manifest. The vehicles for such a performance ranged from hospitals and brothels to madhouses, scaffolds of execution, prisons, and lazar-houses. Although I will be concerned with the entire field of marginal spectacle, I begin at the point where such spectacle comes into sharpest focus—at the extreme verge of London's Liberties, where we enter into the province of the city's lazar-houses. By the sixteenth century they hedged the city in all directions, and they marked, with the circle they described, the boundary at which the ambiguous and equivocal domain of the Liberties gave way, finally and fully, to the country itself.[5]

Leprosy was a prominent inhabitant of the outskirts of medieval and Renaissance cities. In London, the passing of the disease was muted and anonymous; elsewhere, in cities where its cultural profile was less obscured by the new, leprosy was accompanied by great festivity when it made its final withdrawal from a community. In Reims in 1636, for example, the citizens celebrated the event with a procession through the city, one last rite of purification that enacted, at long last, leprosy's final Triumph.[6] What passed from the community in either case was much more than a disease. Leprosy entered into the moral imagination of medieval culture at an early date, such that it altered and determined not only the lives of those afflicted but also the metaphors, customs, and institutions that shaped the lives of those otherwise untouched by the disease. It was an exemplary disease, comparable to tuberculosis in the nineteenth century or to cancer in our time. The symptoms of leprosy were taken to be manifestations of a disorder that was both particular and pervasive, signs of disease in an individual body and signs whose frame of reference extended to the culture as a whole, signaling on a figurative level a disorder to which the body politic itself was vulnerable. Leprosy was to be witnessed and interpreted: it was a form of symbolic commentary composed in living flesh, a telling memorial addressed both to those who suffered from it and to those who watched over its inevitable progress.

Long before leprosariums appeared on the horizon of European cities, leprosy was regarded as a form of monumental spectacle. In a funeral oration delivered in 379 A.D., St. Gregory of Nanzianzus turned for a moment to consider the devastated features of the deceased. The face was beyond recognition. But while the countenance could no longer recall the man who lay before him, it did remind Gregory of comparable monuments of human ruin and decay: the seven-gated city of Thebes, the fabled colossus at Rhodes, the long-fallen walls of Babylon and Egypt, the still-standing sepulchers of the pyramids and the Carian Mausoleum. In modern French, where a mouldering stone wall can still be called a *lépreuse*, we encounter a trace or cultural memory of the spectacle of decay that Gregory saw when he looked upon the face of leprosy. According to Gregory, however, none of the examples he lists are as mortifying or as radical as the harsh and pitiful spectacle ("triste et miserandum spectaculum")[7] of leprosy, where the dissolution of human constructs and architectures extended to the body itself. As his disease progressed, the leper grew increasingly inarticulate and disarticulated. Leprosy assailed the body from without and from within. It left its mark on the skin, but it also attacked the vocal chords and skeletal structure, subjecting the voice and limbs to a slow deconstruction from within. The leper became a walking ruin, the wandering wreckage of a former self who was beyond recognition and could be identified in name alone, if at all. He was the figure of a death beyond dying, the image of a mortality that did not even need death to make its message known.

Late antiquity and early Christianity took note of that message but banished its bearers; lepers were driven from the community in relatively straightforward rites of exclusion, exiled to wander the countryside, ringing a bell to announce their presence. By contrast, the High Middle Ages embraced the disease. England's Queen Maud, for example, was famous for entertaining large companies of lepers at Westminster, where she bathed and even kissed the lesions of the afflicted, treating their wounds as if they were errant or ubiquitous stigmata. It was Maud who, in 1118, founded London's first lazar-house at St. Giles-in-the-Fields.[8] During the eleventh and twelfth centuries, leprosariums began to appear throughout Europe, always situated on the outskirts of a community or "betwixt the townis," and their sudden rise signals a fundamental shift in the cultural significance of the disease. Leprosy was no longer excluded from society in any full sense, as it once had been, but was instead stationed at the perimeters of cities and towns, set apart but maintained in ritual seclusion. Once free (or condemned) to wander, the leper was now bound fast to the horizon of community. His role as a form of marginal spectacle had commenced.

Alive yet dead to the world, described as one of the living dead, the leper was already a walking oxymoron; violating the sacrosanct boundary between life and death, he had long been a figure of anomaly and hence of pollution. With the institution of the leprosarium and the customs and rituals surrounding it, however, the leper was no longer a figure of mere dissolution or pollution. His separation from the community was not intended to banish or suppress the disorder but, as Michel Foucault writes, "to keep it at a sacred distance, to fix it in an inverse exaltation."[9] Medieval biblical commentary had brought its exegetical machine to bear on leprosy, and through a curious conflation of Old Testament figures, the leper became a lazar. Figural exegesis merged Lazarus the beggar, who lay at the rich man's gate "full of sores" (Luke 16:19–26), with Lazarus of Bethany, raised from the dead by Christ in a miracle prophetic of the final resurrection. The sickness of the one, traditionally assumed to be leprosy, was transferred to the other, and this compound Lazarus became the namesake and *figura* for the lazar of the High Middle Ages.[10] As a historical repetition and fulfillment of his scriptural prefigurations, the lazar was a figure of sacred pollution, no longer a mere *memento mori* but a constant and monumental reminder that resurrection awaited even the most ravaged and devastated of bodies. The lazar was relegated to the margins of society according to Levitical code (Lev. 13:5), yet he was also granted the full if distanced visibility reserved for things touched by the power of God.

The medieval world did view leprosy as a contagious disease, but the sudden and startling rise of leprosariums is difficult to explain if we view it, as many have tried to do, as an effort to contain the disease and keep it from spreading. Leprosy was commonly thought to be transmitted by touch, and by sight as well—a notion of spectacular contagion which, while curious to us, had some currency even in Shakespeare's day. Margaret of Anjou objects not to the theory of infection by sight but to its momentary relevance—its application to her own person—when she demands,

> Why dost thou turn away and hide thy face?
> I am no lothsome leper, look on me!
> *(2 Henry VI,* III. ii. 74)

To some of Shakespeare's contemporaries, Margaret's disclaimer was less than convincing. According to William Rankins, she was indeed a loathsome leper, along with all of her (or rather, his) fellow actors. Like lepers, players were without a place among traditional callings or social categories; figures of categorical ambivalence, they were also viewed by a wide body of Elizabethans (by no means all or even primarily Puritan) as spectacles of human deceit, incontinence, and general depravity. Rankins' topic in his aptly titled *Mirrour of Monsters* (1587) is "the manifold vices, and spotted enormities, that can be caused by infectious sight of Playes"; whatever it tells us of the consequences of viewing Elizabethan drama, Rankins' tract, an elaborate moral application of spectacular contagion to Shakespeare's medium itself, does serve to remind us of the inordinately high fears of infection once occasioned by leprosy. But the leprosarium was hardly designed to shut leprosy off from human contact or to remove it from the light of day. Far from rig-

orously isolating the disease, the institution of the lazar-house placed
it prominently on display, and even put it into fuller circulation
with the community. Lepers were let out of their asylums to beg,
and selected inmates were licensed to shop for food and other
necessities. Unaffected citizens were granted free access to the hospital. "A curious ambivalence of separation and participation," as
Peter Richards has noted, "pervades the regulations" that governed
life in a lazar-house.[11] Codes of behavior in the leprosariums were
strict, infractions severely punished. Extreme violations were met
by expulsion—a curious measure, if leprosariums were designed
to correct, as unhealthy, the earlier custom of banishment. Lepers
found in violation of the code at St. Julian's and at Sherburn Hospital were simply driven away, however, as lepers traditionally had
been. At the hospital at Ilford in Essex, after a notoriously lecherous
inmate was once again discovered *in flagrante delicto* with a prostitute
from a neighboring brothel, he was cast out to wander the countryside at will, ringing the leper's bell just as his fathers in affliction
had always done.[12] Neither the codes of the lazar-house nor its
promiscuity—by which I mean its prominence and ease of access,
as well the ease with which this particular inmate satisfied his desires—argue strongly for a view of the leprosarium as a prophylactic
institution.

Difficult to align with any shift in medieval fears of contagion, the
rise of the leprosariums does figure prominently in new developments that were reshaping the life of European cities. Leprosariums
date from a period of urban renaissance throughout Europe—in the
West, the first real flourishing of cities since the end of the Roman
Empire. Many new towns were founded at this time, many old ones
transformed along lines that would remain stable until the late Renaissance. Cities became worlds in themselves, strong and privileged
urban bodies defined and maintained by new forms of ritual and
ceremony. The walled medieval town makes its appearance at this
time: as the city became more autonomous, it developed new needs
for protection and self-definition. "It had to break away from other
human groups," as Fernand Braudel notes, "from rural societies, and
from old political connections. It even had to stand apart from its
own countryside."[13] But as I have previously suggested, the process
of defining urban powers and limitations was an equivocal one, and
it is during this same period that the margins of European cities began to develop into arenas of cultural license and anomaly. Both new
towns and old girded themselves with a wide variety of marginal rituals and spectacles, establishing a middle ground or buffer that stood
between themselves and the country, a domain where figures of ex-

treme ambivalence and contradiction—such as the leper had come to be—could be arrayed, as actors in an ongoing and spectacular dramaturgy of the margins.[14]

Leprosy's drama began within the framework of community. In a series of stages it moved outward, progressively displacing the leper or lazar from the human order of things. Upon discovery of a leper, a priest or lay person would come to speak comforting words and lead the stricken one to a church, according to the office of seclusion set out in the *Manuale ad Usum Ecclesiae Sarum.*[15] Although still living, the leper bore the marks of death and putre-faction on his body; lodged in time and space, still a creature of history, his disorder made him a figure of the end of all worldly orders and measures. In a certain sense it removed him from time and the world of the living, and he was treated accordingly. Once in church he made what would be his last confession, for the mass that followed was a mass for the dead. The leper lay supine throughout the service: he assumed "the manner of a dead man, although by the grace of God he yet lives in body and in spirit." At the conclusion of the service the leper's spouse was declared free to remarry, and in England the leper was stripped of all com-mon-law rights, including the right to inherit or bequeath an estate. Removed from the legal and ecclesiastic community, cut off from his past and future lineage to become a sign of full exteriority, the leper was then led outside the city walls. A spade of earth was cast upon his feet; the priest intoned, "Be thou dead to the world, but alive again unto God," and, with the entrance into the lazar-house, the ritual was complete.

The audience for such a ritual, being the community itself, did not disappear once leprosy entered its designated abode; the in-stitution of the lazar-house reminds us, as it once reminded lep-rosy's contemporaries, that the lazar's life as a spectacle was initiated rather than concluded by his passage out of the city. Ritual seclusion was a rite of passage, to use a phrase popularized by Victor Turner, but it was a special variety. It was not a pilgrimage, a journey beyond the bounds of society and back again, as are most of the ritual processes studied by Turner and his followers.[16] Ritual seclusion was a one-way street. What mattered was not the experience of the leper (he was not a pilgrim or "passenger" in Turner's sense) but the results of his passage, the lasting impression he made on the cultural landscape. Leprosy's ritual conveyance was an inscriptive process: it defined the leper as a figure of anomaly, and at the same time it defined the site to which he was conveyed as an anomalous territory, reserved for marginal and ambivalent figures. Rites of passage such as leprosy's are instruments or tools deployed by a culture, ritual devices with which a community defines itself and, most relevant to our purposes, delineates those areas of uncertainty or contradiction that circumscribe its powers and desires.

Like any ritual, leprosy's rite of passage was performed to make a point, and such marginal zones—*marges de transition,* as Arthur Van Gennep characterized them[17]—were among the points being made. Leprosy was an incontinent disorder. It exceeded the bounds of community and classification, and it was also accompanied, according to traditional wisdom, by an extreme sexual incontinence. One of its signs, admirably illustrated by the leper cast out of Ilford, was a carnal excess that went beyond the bounds prescribed for the body and its passions. Both physically and morally, the leper exceeded or confounded the network of classifications that normally locates persons, states of being, and values in cultural space. The proper place for such exorbitance, as Plato long ago noted, was outside the boundaries of community, at a point where cultural containment and definition cease to reign:

> It is not the fact, as it would seem, that in the case of all objects boundary is contiguous with boundary; but where there is a neutral strip, which lies between the two boundaries, impinging on each, it will be midway between both. And that is precisely the description we gave of the passionate action, as one which lies midway between. . . . (*Laws* 878b)

The ritual and ongoing spectacle of leprosy was but one of the devices that inscribed such ambiguous zones in the cultural landscape of premodern cities. Such areas existed outside of fifth-century Athens, and in his ideal state Plato preserved the tradition of publicly exposing perpetrators of violent, passionate crimes "at the frontiers of the country" (*Laws* 855c).[18] Neither here nor there, the margins were areas that fell "betwixt and between" the categories and norms prescribed by law, custom, and cultural convention. Arenas of representation and cultural performance, they were informed by a sort of rhetoric, but it was a rhetoric of the margins rather than of the agora—a system of ambivalent figures and incontinent commonplaces.

The cultural significance of giving such a prominent place to persons and things that exceed the bounds of the community—its powers to contain, define, or even control—remains to be seen. By way of introducing such questions, however, we could say that any structure of ideas, values, or beliefs, whether it takes the shape of a political philosophy, a religion, or a ceremonial city, is vulnerable at its margins. Such is the conclusion of Mary Douglas in *Purity and Danger*,[19] a work that serves in many ways as an extensive gloss on Plato's recognition, quoted above, that there are not only limits to cultural boundaries and definitions but also equivocal realms that stand beyond those limits, places of passion and anomaly, margins of ambiguity and contradiction. In traditional or pre-Copernican cultures, the margins of the social structure were embodied in literal areas like the Liberties of London. When the margins of society are thus realized on the threshold of the community, shaped into arenas of representation and given over to public ritual and spectacle, part of what is manifested in them will be the vulnerability of the social structure itself. The Liberties of the city were social and civic margins, and they also served as margins in a textual sense: as places reserved for a "variety of sences" (to borrow a phrase from the translators of the 1611 Bible, describing their own margins) and for divergent points of view—for commentary upon and even contradiction of the main body of their text, which in this instance would be the body politic itself.

III

By the end of the sixteenth century, there were ten lazar-houses stationed on the outskirts of London. They were licensed by the Crown, and up until the dissolution of the monasteries in 1540 they were jointly administered by the city and the church. What they presented to the citizens of London was leprosy's *spectacle:* both its monumental aspect, that is to say, and its significant form. Spectacle is never a matter of sheer monumentality; it carries its own weight of meaning and cultural significance. "Spectacle is the existing order's uninterrupted discourse about itself," according to Guy Debord. "It is the diplomatic representation of hierarchic society to itself, where all other expression is banned."[20]

The spectacles mounted in the Liberties were tensed by ambivalence and ambiguity; the representation of society they made was one that revealed the gaps and seams, the limits and contradictions of the social fabric. A broad expanse of ground separated the lazar-house from the city walls. It acted as both a barrier to set leprosy apart from the citizens' daily rounds, and as a foil to set it off, to throw the profile of the lazar-houses into relief. The lazar-houses framed the city: they hedged it in and placed it in context, with a result that could best be described as a form of dramatic irony. Manifesting the authority of the city, London's ancient wall defined the community and proclaimed it, in a language of mortar and stone, to be an integral and coherent whole. This proclamation of authority, however, was hedged by contradiction—by the Liberties themselves. The arc described by the lazar-houses echoed the more substantial enclosure of London's walls, but the echo was a ghostly and parodic one, a monumental reminder that to declare a province of authority was also, of necessity, to declare its limits. An organization, a community, or a culture is bound together by its acts of definition, but the bind is an inescapably double one, defining at the same time the limitations of organization, community, or culture. Anomalous and ambiguous, uncontained by either the categories or the powers that be, leprosy stood in the Liberties as a constant reminder of such limits: a marginal gloss on the ambivalence that circumscribes any will to contain.

The message was borne out by other forms of marginal commentary. In his *Survay* of London's Liberties, John Stow describes a graveyard located outside the city walls, where unknown foreigners—all who were not citizens of London, whether they hailed from the countryside or further abroad—were brought when they died, nameless and unmourned, to be buried in a communal cemetery aptly known as No Man's Land (2:81). The epithet could easily be applied to the Liberties as a whole. What escaped classification within the social structure of the city was lodged outside the physical embodiment of society. As we follow Stow around the city's perimeter, we encounter a heterogeneous collection of outcast things, things without a proper place in the customary order of things, and as such, sources of anxiety and dread, potentially unsettling or discomfiting.

In close proximity to scaffolds of execution stood hospitals, established not so much to cure the sick or prevent contagion as to provide a place set apart—a site of passage, a *marge de transition*—for those whose ailments had already, like the misdeeds of the condemned, dissociated them from the social body. The juxtaposition of gallows and hospital has its own marginal decorum. Both served as sites of transition, where those who were neither living nor dead but were embarked on an ambiguous passage between the two states could be accommodated and displayed, according to their kind. Stow provides an example of such accommodation when he pauses to comment on Wapping-in-the-Woze, more commonly known as Wapping Marsh. It was "the usuall place of execution," Stow writes, "for hanging of Pirats & Sea rovers, at the low water marke there to remaine, till three tides had overflowed them" (2:70–71). Execution under such circumstances was slow. The condemned thieves were not so much hung as staked out in a liminal realm where land and sea held equal claim, a tidal zone between the

powers of human and divine authority. As the lives of the condemned ebbed slowly with the incoming tides, so did the power of
the community over those lives. Dead or alive or at some point in
between, the condemned marked the frontier beyond which human
authority did not extend. Once dead, their bodies remained and
continued to serve as ambiguous signs of power, marking at once
the manifest efficacy of the reigning social structure and the all-
too-immediate limits of social and political control.

To view such a spectacle merely as a display of efficacious power
would be to ignore half the scene being composed. In an age of
conspicuous expenditure, when a family fortune accumulated over
centuries could be consumed in a single day of ostentatious display
(as in the funeral mounted to observe the death of Sir Henry
Sidney),[21] rituals of power and authority were paradoxical affairs.
Whenever power or prestige was at stake, Renaissance authority
achieved the full apogee of its assertion, its most extreme manifestation, at its own expense—when most conspicuously expended
or consumed. Ceremonies of power were ceremonies of loss as well,
and in the margins of the city such ceremonies amounted to ritual
demarcations of the limits of social and political authority. Marginal
spectacle conformed to an ambiguous dynamic, whether it took the
shape of public execution, the ritual seclusion and display of leprosy, or the more benign manifestations of civic incontinence represented by the brothels and gaming-houses of the Liberties. When
a man was conveyed out of the city, to be released either into exile
or into the ready hands of the executioner, it was as an outlaw
rather than a criminal; the latter is a modern concept, the former
a fitting description of the place the condemned had come to occupy
in the cultural landscape. Having removed himself from the human
community by his actions, he was taken beyond that community to
a liminal arena outside the law, where he became a figure as ambiguous and equivocal as the place he occupied. Whether alive or
in the throes of a protracted death, he served at once as a sign of
power and authority in its fullest manifestation and as a marker of
authority's limit, of the place where law, authority, and community
gave way to something else, something Other.

IV

Insofar as he manifested the contradictions and limits of power,
the condemned joined his fellow marginal citizens to become a
liminal figure, inscribed in the civic landscape, articulated upon
and serving to articulate the threshold of community. The margins
of the premodern city were not only host to a series of mortifying

spectacles. They were also places of sanctuary and incontinent pleasure, of license and extravagant liberty. In our view, unaccustomed
to its rigor or its paradoxical logic, public execution looms above
other forms of marginal spectacle as one of the most unsettling
and noteworthy. For contemporaries, however, more discomfiting
by far and more in need of justifying commentary were those
aspects of the city's margins that conspired to make them "licentious
liberties," potentially dangerous areas of sanctuary and disorder.

Although the period is not known for its urban theory, in his
treatise *Of the Causes of the Greatnes and Magnificencie of Cities* Giovanni
Botero does address the reasons why a city might find it necessary
and even desirable to obscure the clear outlines of community. "It
cannot be denied," writes Botero, "but that a moderate libertie and
a lawfull place of safetie, very greatly helpeth to draw a multitude
of people to a resting place."[22] The demographic economy of the
premodern city, like its symbolic economy, did not lend itself to
sheer or absolute demarcation. Cities are precarious creatures in
Botero's estimation, subject to desolation by plagues, tyrants, and
external foes, and often impoverished by the errant desires of their
citizens to relocate in more appealing climes. A city that wants to
survive must counterbalance the entropic forces that threaten its
existence. It must provide for such forces and in some fashion
incorporate them into its civic landscape if it is to attract a steady
flow of "strangers and forreine people" and at the same time satisfy
the curiosity and desires of its present inhabitants. For Botero, "the
opening of Sanctuary and giving of liberties and freedome to all
that would" serves what is a necessary function in the *rhetoric* of
the city, for sites of sanctuary and license are above all persuasive.
They "allure the people (who are of a nature indifferent to be
heere or there) to the choyse of one place before another," and in
the process, by providing a variety of "alluring sights," they make
continued residence in the city both desirable and pleasurable.

Among the alluring sights Botero lists are triumphs, impressive
buildings, battles on water, competitive swordplay, and "Theatres,
Porches, Circles, and Rases for running horses." His prime example
is pagan Rome, but even canonized Christian commentators recognized the need to preserve a less than sweet disorder in the
"Skirtes and Confines" of the city. What Botero views as a rhetorical
lure, necessary for the maintenance of the physical population,
Thomas Aquinas grudgingly regards as a safety valve, necessary if
the spiritual well-being of the community is to be maintained. Citing
Augustine, Aquinas compares prostitution—one of the most alluring pastimes located in London's Liberties—to the sewer in a palace.

"Take away the sewer, you fill the palace with pollution . . . remove prostitution from human affairs, and you will pollute all things with lust."[23] In an ideal world, lust and other forms of pollution—outbreaks of moral and social incontinence, things neither the physical nor the social body can entirely contain—would be sheerly proscribed, eliminated, or excluded from human affairs. But Aquinas is too much of a pragmatist for such a solution: to exclude lust, to deny it a prescribed place in the social order, would pollute all things. It would have the effect not of banishing lust but of subjecting all order to its disordering impulse; not of excluding pollution but of fully including it, overwhelming the social body with an incontinence that can never be fully excluded, contained, or controlled.

Aquinas' solution is not less paradoxical, merely more economical. His cure for pollution can only displace it, and in doing so will inevitably promote it—an inevitability that Botero, as we have seen, fixed upon as the equivocal hope of urbanity. Displaced into the margins of the city and licensed to operate there, prostitution is both a remedy for lust and a precipitator of it, both an antidote to the ills that infect the body politic and a source of further contagion. With social ills and vices that admit of no final solution, efforts to contain or displace them will be tinged with paradox, haunted by an irreducible margin of ambiguity. "For such vices," as the Athenian of Plato's *Laws* announces, "the legislator must find in each instance a specific remedy"—what Plato calls a *pharmakon* (919b).

In many respects, Plato remains our fullest commentator on the equivocation that hedges any effort to contain or control. Like Aquinas, Plato's Athenian specifies the need for a particular solution adapted to the social ill in question. In this context, *pharmakon* refers to such a cure, but the word is a curiously double-edged one. It can mean either a cure for an illness or its cause, either a remedy for pollution or a source of contagion. As Jacques Derrida has brilliantly argued in his reading of Plato,[24] *pharmakon* is a term that resolutely resists translation, such that it must be taken—like Aquinas' cure for lust—as both a remedy and a poison, at once a cure and a cause of pollution. Like *sacer* and *altus*, *pharmakon* belongs in the company of those cultural designations Freud called antithetical words: terms in which oppositions meet and do not easily resolve, which mean both one thing and a mutually exclusive other, and which accumulate (in the West, at any rate) around those objects, persons, and places that elicit extreme cultural ambivalence.[25] This is one way to describe the margins of the premodern city: as the boundary of inside and outside, the place where the holy and polluted combine in an irreducible *coincidentia oppositorum*, the breeding ground of antithetical words and figures.

In ancient Athens, the outskirts of the city were the domain of the *pharmakos*. The name, indissociably related to *pharmakon*, identified a figure akin to the scapegoat, who was first exalted and then degraded in an annual ritual that culminated on the margins of the city, where the *pharmakos* was flogged and stoned to death. In medieval and Renaissance London, the range of marginal displacement was more varied but no less a register of cultural ambivalence. Viewed from a religious perspective, the Liberties unfold as a place of sacred pollution, reserved for figures like the lazar, made at once holy and hopelessly contaminated by his affliction. From a political perspective, they are the forum for ambivalent displays of power, personified in figures like the exile or traitor—figures that mark the threshold and the vanishing point of power's efficacy. From a more general point of view that encompasses the religious and the political, the margins of the city were places where forms of moral incontinence and pollution were granted license to exist beyond the bounds of a community they had, by their incontinence, already exceeded.

When it did not exile or execute them, early modern power licensed those things it could neither contain nor control. London's stews and other marginal pleasures, the libidinal economy of the "licentious liberties" (to employ Henry VIII's phrase once again), were one of the results. Although less formally maintained than the other cultural phenomena manifested in the Liberties, "license" also bears, like leprosy or Plato's *pharmakon*, the seeds of its own contradiction. It refers at once to what is permitted and to what transgresses the bounds of permission. License shades into licentiousness without even the trace of a seam—as Aquinas and Henry fully recognized, and as even Lord Chesterfield was forced to admit, when he voiced his opposition to the Theaters Act of 1737:

> There is such a Connection between licentiousness and Liberty, that it is not easy to correct the one, without dangerously wounding the other. It is extremely hard to distinguish the true limit between them; like changeable silk, we can easily see there are two different colors, but we cannot easily discover where the one ends, and the other begins.

"The word changes color while you look at it," writes Tony Tanner, "transforming itself into its opposite."[26] The ambiguity is not merely linguistic, if ambiguity ever is. Like the word, the act of licensing is two-sided and ambidextrous. A license is a token of the agent who grants it, and so can serve its bearer as an emblem or imprimatur of authority. Once issued, however, a license leaves the control as well as the hands of the licensing agent. With a license, one can take license or liberties; issuing a license is at once an assertion of authority and a declaration of its limits.

It is one thing, however, to choose to display one's limits or to participate, as the powers of the city, church, and state traditionally did, in the staging of one's own incontinence. The margin of ambiguity that circumscribes and to an extent subverts authority is not thereby reduced, but a certain power, albeit an ambivalent one—a power grounded in its own limits and contradictions—is thus maintained and manifested. Any spectacle implies the institution or institutions that mount it; however ambivalent the spectacle, the implication of authority is of some use and profit, serving to assert an image of authority even if that image is a liminal one. It is quite another matter, however, when a community finds the spectacle of its own vulnerability and limits thrust upon it, as London did in the latter half of the sixteenth century. It was upon the unstable ground of license that Elizabethan drama established itself, of course, but it was not only the popular theater that was thus fostered by the ambiguity and ideological mobility latent in the margins.

With the dissolution of the monasteries in 1540, a great deal of land, verging on the city yet exempt from its control, was opened up to new uses by so-called New Men, with ties to neither feudal customs nor guild hierarchies.[27] In addition, the changes taking place in the countryside created a new class of displaced persons, who were ineluctably drawn to the alluring refuge and anonymity of London's Liberties. In close proximity to graveyards for the nameless dead there came to reside a growing population of the living, who escaped civic classification and control by being neither here nor there—by taking up a place that was, properly speaking, no place at all, but betwixt and between proper places and the proprieties that adhered to them. The ideological misfits and masterless men of Elizabethan society ranged from early modern entrepreneurs and victims of enclosure to outlaws, Puritans, and players. Revealing how far they did indeed exceed customary modes of classification, Elizabethan law knew the bulk of them as vagabonds. "For the sixteenth century vagabond," as Christopher Hill has noted, the privileged places of London increasingly became "what the greenwood had been for the medieval outlaw—an anonymous refuge."[28]

When they gazed out over their Liberties and suburbs in the sixteenth century, what the city fathers and religious authorities of London saw was a discomfiting and anamorphic scene. Traditional forms of marginal spectacle were being overlaid with new forms of anomaly; traditional license was being translated into new forms of licentiousness, making the community the victim of its own ritually inscribed and maintained contradictions. The civic and social structure I have been tracing here had been remarkably stable for centuries, but only because that structure had made room for what it could not contain, had included all that exceeded the strict bounds of binary or antithetical definition. The city thus conceived was in a sense a perpetual stasis machine, its stability powered by the incontinence and instability it so rigorously hedged itself with and gave way to. In the latter half of the sixteenth century, however, the Liberties were taking liberty, and London was a captive audience to the unfolding social drama. The cast of that drama was a large one, but the city reserved its most strident outrage for the newly emerged companies of professional players. It was the latter who were creating a viable and highly visible institution—and one erected, moreover, on the grounds of the city's own carefully maintained contradictions.

V

We do not know how long London's last lepers survived in their anonymous confinement. We do know that the symbols of their anomalous status, the lazar-houses themselves, continued to stand and even to operate well into the seventeenth century, gradually coming to house a less discriminate cast of the afflicted. Standing thus, they and other traditional forms of marginal spectacle created an incongruous scene, an anamorphic combination of the new and the old. No matter what our point of view, any perspective on such a scene becomes what Kenneth Burke calls a perspective by incongruity:[29] an uncanny juxtaposition of things that do and do not fit together, and that clarify, in the tension of their congruence, the lines of similarity and difference that make up their incongruous bond.

For the authorities of London, the incongruity was shocking and scandalous. It served as a constant and monumental reminder that the license being appropriated by the Liberties had always existed, albeit in different forms; that the community was to an extent responsible for its inability to control its own margins, and was even an accomplice in the subversion of its own authority. The message was an unsettling one, and it produces a curious strain of nostalgia in the city, a longing for even the most grotesque former emblems of the city's limits. In other cities, if we recall the example of Reims, the passing of leprosy was an occasion for rejoicing: a centuries-long seige was finally lifted, and the community understandably celebrated the end of its long subjection. Such festivity is significantly absent in London. When John Stow looks out on the margins of the city and is forced to consider all that has come, by 1598, to obscure and eclipse their ambivalent but relatively austere profile, he gives a sidelong glance to the passing of leprosy. Far from relief, however, his tone is one of regret verging on mourning:

> but now wee see the thing [the Liberties] in worse case than ever, by means of enclosure for Gardens, wherein are builded many fayre summer houses, and as in other places of the Suburbes, some of them like Midsommer pageantes, with Towers, Turrets, and Chimney Tops, not so much for use or profite, as for shewe and pleasure, bewraying the vanity of mens mindes, much unlike to the disposition of the ancient Cittizens, who delighted in the building of Hospitals, and Almes houses for the poore, spent their wealthes in preferment of the common commoditie of this our Citie. (2:78)

Among the hospitals he has in mind are the lazar-houses of the city. They served the "common commoditie" of the community by contributing to its symbolic economy—to that delicate balance of civic powers and city limits I have been tracing here. What unsettles Stow is a displacement of values that is all too easy to read in the open book of the Liberties. It is a shift away from marginal spectacle, properly speaking, toward new forms of apprehension and display.

Stow does not include the Elizabethan playhouses in the scenario of his discontent. Unlike a great many of his contemporaries, he does not make the new theaters either an emblem or a cause of the Liberties' increasing license—"a continuall monument," as Thomas White described them, "of London's prodigalitie and Folly."[30] In his relative reserve, however, Stow does suggest a term that will help gloss the less discriminating reactions of his fellow citizens, who did make drama the scapegoat for the ills that quite literally surrounded them. In Stow's view of things, London's outlying areas are being taken over by new forms of excess, by things shaped "like Midsommer Pageantes . . . not so much for use or profite, as for shewe and pleasure." He objects neither to ostentatious display nor to the customary pastimes of London, but to the displacement of marginal spectacle into something new, more freewheeling and uninstitutionalized, devoted not to use or profit in the city's symbolic economy but to show and pleasure. The term he does not use but verges upon, the source of his and his contemporaries' discontent, is the unruly and profligate *theatricality* of the Liberties.

"Let them saye what they will say, we wil play." We are now in a position, at long last, to turn to Burbage's excursion, and along the way to realize the full audacity of the message conveyed to men like Stockwood by the playhouses that circumscribed Elizabethan London. The playhouses were a scandal: that is to say, they made apparent a tradition of cultural license that had always reigned in the Liberties, but whose subversive potential had remained latent, to an extent mystified or obscured by the ceremonial needs and pretensions of the community. If the margins had not for centuries said what they did, Elizabethan drama would not have been able to shape the audacious message it did. Without such a tradition, theater would not have been in a position to scandalize Stockwood and his fellows; it would not have had a place from which to proclaim its occupation of the margins, its theatricality.

VI

In its remove from the city, drama gained a local habitation and a name; embodied for the first time since late antiquity in a permanent architecture designed expressly for it, the concept of theater, as Stephen Orgel writes, gained a concrete sense of place. "All at once, theater was an institution, a property, a corporation. It was real in the way that 'real estate' is real; it was a location, a building, a possession—an established and visible part of society."[31]

Playing moved from a mere pastime toward an art when it extended itself beyond the city; players, from a wandering and vagrant existence toward a status of substance if not of respectability. To men like Stockwood, however, the place of drama—both its status and its location—was an appropriated one, proper neither to players, plays, nor playhouses. To the extent that theater became a more established and visible part of society, it was all the more scandalous. If it became an institution of sorts, it was the bastard sort. Companies of players organized themselves along the lines of corporate guilds, but to the city such imitation hardly represented social respectability. It registered instead as a bold mockery of civic hierarchies. Drama earned its living by a theatrical sleight of hand, translating work into play. "Outraged by their profits," as Muriel Bradbrook aptly notes, "the City saw the players as a horrible parody of a guild."[32]

Long before Burbage's enterprise, drama had flourished within
the city in a variety of guises. Religious cycles, originally developed
out of responses to the liturgy of the mass—a dramatic extension
of the *quem queritis* trope[33]—supplemented and to some degree
merged with secular plays performed in the streets, innyards,
schools, and private houses of London. The humanist drama of
the schools was especially wide-ranging and ideologically complex.
As Joel B. Altman has recently demonstrated in *The Tudor Play of
Mind,* such drama was greatly influenced by the rhetorical exercises
of the *argumentum in utramque partem,* designed to cultivate a bud-
ding scholar's powers of persuasion, including his ability to argue
for mutually exclusive points of view. Recast in dramatic form,
exercises like the *argumentum* fostered a drama of freewheeling
inquiry, characterized by a high degree of rhetorical and ideological
mobility. Plays took the form not of exemplary solutions to moral
problems but of extended questions; they served as forums in which
a number of potentially incompatible perspectives could be entertained. It was a dialogic form of theater, devoted to what Altman
eloquently calls "the moral cultivation of ambivalence." Plays served
not as mere extensions or reflections of the world offstage, but
rather as "liberties within the actual world—neutral places in which
to arouse emotions, ask certain broad philosophical questions, and
expound a variety of attitudes."[34]

A certain ideological range and license was unquestionably
available to intramural drama. If we move, however, from Altman's figurative liberties to those that indeed existed in the actual
world—if we follow, that is to say, the movement of the stage
itself during the period—we find a drama that few, if any, of its
contemporaries would characterize as moral. It is a drama less
tidy and well-contained than even the humanist drama of Altman's study—a drama whose place in the ideological landscape
was not neutral, but highly controversial.

From innyard playing to religious cycles and academic exercises,
the drama that preceded the public playhouses was an *interstitial*
form of theater. Like the Athenian stage, the pre-Elizabethan theater was a forum for agonistic debate and inquisition, a place where
questions that could not be framed elsewhere could be raised and
explored. "Many woulde resorte to the commonhouses called Theatres," Sir Thomas Elyot writes in 1540, "and purposing some matter of philosophy, wold there dispute openly."[35] But such drama fit
comfortably into the gaps and seams of the social fabric; no matter
how agonistic or inquisitive, it was fully circumscribed by the structures of authority and community. In a stable hierarchical society,

proper rule or authority often lends itself to misrule: it gives itself over to its own disruption, producing an inverted image of itself that it entirely contains. Holiday provides both an escape from and a return to everyday routine; it would not be holiday if its festive impulse were not thus hedged by everyday. Secular drama in the city often played with the festive inversion of cultural norms, but rituals of misrule, dramatic and otherwise, are precisely what their name implies: misrule, defined against and delimited by proper rule, its reigning antithesis.[36] The public playhouses were born, however, at a time when traditional hierarchies were breaking down, and neither they nor the plays they fostered were thus contained by the customary antitheses of rule and misrule, order and disorder, everyday and holiday. With their advent we are no longer concerned with an interstitial stage, but with what we might call an *incontinent* one.

Incontinence was not new to the Liberties, but drama was, along with a great deal else that was "pestering the Citty." The other ills infesting the Liberties ranged from masterless men, "strangers and foren Artifficers," to the ever-present plague. Like drama, they also stood beyond London's powers of containment, control, and even understanding; according to the city fathers, however, drama was to blame for the increasingly unruly situation found in the Liberties. Whatever was unsettling, whatever was polluting the margins with new forms of incontinence, was relentlessly attributed to the unhealthy climate fostered by the playhouses. "Some things have doble the ill," as Sir Nicholas Woodrofe, lord mayor of London, wrote to Lord Burghley on June 17, 1580, "both naturarly in spreading the infection, and otherwise in drawing God's wrathe and plage upon us, as the erecting and frequenting of houses very famous for *incontinent rule* [my emphasis] out of our liberties and jurisdiction."[37]

Public playhouses were often accused of being forums for sexual incontinence during the period; Woodrofe's "incontinent rule," however, appears to be the earliest use of "incontinence" in its modern, broader sense, encompassing any activity or cultural phenomenon that exceeds the bounds of societal norms—that stands, like the playhouses in their incontinent rule, outside the limits of community or control. The infestation Woodrofe decries was as much moral as it was physical or biological. Conflating plagues and playhouses was one of the city's trump cards in its efforts to suppress drama in the Liberties.[38] The two were assumed to be pathologically congruent—playhouses produced plague by acting as breeding grounds for the disease—but they were bound to one another by metaphor as well. What replaces leprosy on the horizon of the city's concern and in its moral imagination is not plague alone, but this curious coupling of pestilence and drama, the odd rhyme they produce in tract after city tract. Leprosy had been a grotesquely disfiguring disease, yet curiously well-bred. It announced its coming long in advance, whether with its customary bell or with the first signs of epidermal rash—the harbingers of a death that was already present in the body, and yet would take years, even decades, to make its mortifying figure literal. Leprosy isolated individuals from the community rather than the community from itself; with its politic yet apocalyptic style, it gave a community ample time to draw itself together again in rites of exclusion and seclusion.

Plagues and players were, by contrast, difficult to identify and impossible to put down. Neither lent themselves to institutionalized ritual and spectacle; like leprosy in its time, they dominated the margins of the city, but in the way an invading army might. In *The Wonderfulle Yeare* Thomas Nashe deploys such an image to describe the outbreak of plague in 1603. He begins by comparing the epidemic to a seige laid upon the city by the much-reviled Spanish, and then corrects his simile and redirects its thrust in mid-campaign. "All this while, Death (like a Spanish leager, or rather like a stalking *Tamburlaine*) hath pitcht his tents . . . in the sinfully-polluted Suburbes."[39] Tamburlaine, of course, did stalk the sinfully-polluted suburbs—on the boards of those houses famous for incontinent rule, erected outside the jurisdiction of the city. Nashe's shift of figures, from Spanish to Marlovian, is an appropriate one. It correctly identifies the threat to the city: a threat posed not by a merely foreign presence but by one that is both utterly alien—from outside the confines of Western culture—and hauntingly homegrown. Intimate yet foreign, an external threat nurtured from within and growing without restraint: such terms are equally commensurate, in London's apprehension, with plague and with theatricality.

Like a plague or a stalking Tamburlaine, theatricality subjected the city. It was a plague in its own right, contaminating morals and manners when it did not, in its pathological alliance, contaminate the flesh itself. It infected the body politic. "The youth thearof," as another lord mayor testifies, "is greatly corrupted & their manners infected with many evil and ungodly qualities, by reason of the wanton & profane divices represented on the stages by the sayd players."[40] The devices of the stage were divisive in a way that marginal spectacle, however licentious, had never been. Theaters of-

fered a new form of "recreation"—a form that drew out the
unsettling etymological reverberations of the word:

> The refuse sort of evill disposed & ungodly people about this Cytie
> have opportunity hearby to assemble together & to make their matches
> for all their lewd & ungodly practices; [playhouses] being also the
> ordinary places for all maisterless men & vagabond persons that
> haunt the high waies, to meet together & *to recreate themselves*.[41] (My
> emphasis)

This is not, it should be noted, a Puritan response to the theatricality
of the popular stage, although many a Puritan voice in and around
the city raised the same hue and cry. Responding to the social threat
of the popular playhouse, the city fathers created an unintended
alliance with the emerging Puritan culture of Elizabethan England;
antitheatricality was a topic around which Puritans would become
an increasingly powerful force in English society, eventually eclipsing the traditional voices of civic authority. Antitheatricality was
not merely dear to the heart of Puritan ideology; for a culture
attempting to emerge out of the fluctuating currents of Elizabethan
and Jacobean society, it was also something of a strategic necessity.

Beyond mere entertainment or diversion, the re-presentation
and disguise of theatricality suggested a potential social fluidity, a
recreation of the self, that extended beyond the playing space of
the scaffold. Playhouses were viewed as Houses of Proteus, and in
the metamorphic fears of the city it was not merely players who
shifted shapes, confounded categories, and counterfeited roles.[42]
In the theater, masterless men could take on a new appearance; vagabonds, like the players included in their motley company, could
make themselves over again. Theater played with the social order,
representing a cultural and ideological instability whose consequences verged on the apocalyptic, as Stephen Gosson stressed in
his *Plays Confuted in Five Actions* (1582):

> If privat men be suffered to forsake their calling because they desire
> to walke gentlemen like in sattine & velvet, with a buckler at their
> heeles, proportion is so broken, unitie dissolved, harmony con-
> founded, that the whole body must be dismembred, and the prince
> or heade cannot chuse but sicken.[43]

The warning runs throughout the period, as E. M. W. Tillyard
most notably documented.[44] What Tillyard failed to take into
account, however, is the frequency with which such assertions of
order and degree fix upon the stage as their overarching emblem
for the shaking of degree, the untuning of the string, the displacement of order into chaos and contradiction. Tudor doctrine

was not an expression of a world view or consensus but rather, as Louis Montrose has recently suggested, "an ideological response to unprecedented changes affecting English society in the sixteenth century"—changes which the Elizabethan world picture "was wholly inadequate to represent, contain, and explain,"[45] and which Tudor ideology explicitly sought to suppress. Elizabethan popular drama arises out of the growing contradictions between English society as it was in actuality and as it was portrayed by the official organs of government. The popular stage was one of the cultural contradictions which the unchanging and analogic hierarchy of Tudor ideology sought to suppress, and that ideology was frequently invoked against the theatricality of popular drama. When Shakespeare's audience heard Gosson's words returned to them some twenty years later, in Ulysses' notorious speech on degree, they heard what Tillyard refused to hear. Not a commonplace verbal portrait of the Elizabethan world picture, but an ironically framed parody of such portraits: a commonplace charge against players, assimilated by the stage and cast back by the players themselves. Let them say what they will say, we will play.

Drama had not previously made such bold assertions, or had the room to echo Elizabethan culture in this fashion, subjecting it to its own unsettling reverberations. Both within and without the playhouse walls, the new theaters were redefining the place and powers of their audience. Drama on the public stages had a great many fathers; its mixed patrimony includes common and noble, popular and learned predecessors. One of the traditions it grew out of was a participatory form of theater, in which spectators took an active if unrehearsed part in the performance. Irony and criticism, under such conditions, were more often located in the audience than onstage. The drama of Kyd, Marlowe, and Shakespeare evolved, however, by "growing out of" this participatory tradition quite literally. The stage dissociated itself from the audience, establishing "a firm degree of distance between the spectator and the play."[46] It was a distance that allowed for a more aesthetically complex and ideologically resonant theater to take root in the new playhouses, and it was reflected or reproduced in the complementary dissociation that defines the relationship of those playhouses to the city. When Stockwood and his contemporaries looked out upon their Liberties, what they saw was a sort of stage, an arena reserved for cultural representation and performance in their most extreme forms. Traditionally, London had played a double role in the rituals and spectacles mounted in its margins, acting as both audience to and participant in them. In the latter half of the sixteenth century, the city continued to occupy the place of an audience, but merely of an audience. The sensation was a new one, as the outraged protestations of the period eloquently testify.

Private playhouses within the city were sometimes included in such protestations, but more as an afterthought than as a focus of London's concern. They did not, of course, subject the city to the spectacle of its own incontinence, nor did they redefine the place or power of their audience within the theater to the degree characteristic of the public stage. Spectators took an active part in the plays presented by the boys' companies at theaters like Blackfriars and St. Paul's, voicing their own objections, comments, quips, and quiddities as the drama unfolded, even seating themselves on stage (like the Citizen of Beaumont's *The Knight of the Burning Pestle*) to enter more fully into the play. The repertories of the private theaters lent themselves to such participation. Over 85 percent of the boys' plays were comedies, largely satires: in terms of dramatic genres, a contained form of social criticism, one that relies, as pre-Elizabethan drama had always done, on a stable and circumscribing social structure.[47] In terms of repertory, audience, and topology, the private theaters within the city located themselves in the gaps and seams of the social fabric which had traditionally provided a forum for intramural drama. Until their takeover by adult companies in the Jacobean period, the private stages of London remained an interstitial form of drama, representing a less incontinent breach of civic authority than the playhouses outside the city.

The public playhouses were not a minor irritation to London; they represented a threat to the political well-being and stability of the city. Their rise and continued existence marked a radical shift in the delicate balance traditionally maintained between the city and the Court—a balance that had been graphically enacted in the past at the point where civic and royal authorities met and in a sense combined, to display their mutual limits and limitations through the vehicle of marginal spectacle. As we have seen, many of the spectacles traditionally mounted in the Liberties were, like the lazar-houses themselves, sponsored by both the city and the Crown. The public playhouses, however, were manned by companies of players licensed by the Court despite the incessant objections of the city. A royal license neither provided a place for drama nor subsidized it; once they secured a sponsor, players were merely free to play, and thus to earn their livelihood exempt from the Vagabond Acts that otherwise would have curtailed their performances. Exempting drama from royal statutes did not release it from civic authority, but it did encourage the stage to seek out a place beyond the bounds of that authority. Merely by granting theatrical license, Elizabeth accomplished a great deal. She guaranteed an extensive dramatic repertory for her occasional entertainment, at no cost to the Crown; and she also put an increasingly powerful city, lodged on the doorstep of the Court, off-balance and continually on the defensive. Like its royal license, the removed prominence of the popular stage manifested a breach that had opened in the political landscape—a breach that the city, try as it might, could never successfully close.

A social and cultural distance was thus established when popular drama took liberties with its royal license and appropriated the Liberties of the city. In so doing, it gained a different kind of license: a liberty that was at once moral, ideological, and topological, a freedom to experiment with a wide range of available perspectives on its own times. The stage decentered itself, and its displacement provided it with something approaching an exterior vantage point upon the culture it was both a part of, yet set apart from—a vantage point from which it could occasionally glimpse the fragile conditions of its own possibility. Literary criticism has long acknowledged this mobile eccentricity of Elizabethan drama. S. L. Bethell speaks of the "multi-consciousness" of Shakespeare's stage; A. P. Rossiter, of its "two-eyedness," its power to produce, in dramatic form, an anamorphic scene that always seems to call for yet one more perspective, for what are oftentimes mutually exclusive points-of-view, if it is to be adequately comprehended.[48] To be able to bring such varied perspectives to bear on the actions and morals of its own times meant that Elizabethan drama had to be capable, according to Robert Weimann, of "a standpoint involving more freedom, more 'license' and imagination, than the particular social attitude or moral concept in question."[49]

To locate such a standpoint in the physical landscape of the city might seem a crude kind of materialism, but the Liberties had long represented such freedom and such license. The premises or gounds of cultural phenomena like marginal spectacle do not vanish overnight; oftentimes, as Maurice Godelier suggests, the domain established by a given cultural tradition will outlast that tradition, to be consequently taken over and adapted by new cultural formations, as their grounds of possibility:

> We cannot understand the forms and direction taken in changing
> from one mode of production and social life to another without fully

accounting for the premises which caused such changes to develop. Former relations of production and other social relations do not disappear suddenly from history, but they are changed; they influence the *forms* and *places* which will assume and manifest the effects of the new conditions in material life, within the former social structure.[50]

Without the dissolution of the monasteries and the social and cultural disruptions of the times—changes that opened up the Liberties to new forms of cultural excess and incontinence—Elizabethan drama could not have occupied the place it did; without the traditions of marginal spectacle that both preceded and overlapped the brief reign of the playhouses, the ground would not have been prepared for the popular stage, and it could not have enjoyed the license and liberty that it did. The opening of the Liberties created a brief interlude in history, a time when liberty—what is for us an abstract concept of modern ideology—was still concretely realized in the topology of the community, yet was open and available to new cultural developments. For the limited duration of that interlude topology continued to recapitulate ideology, in the place of the popular stage.

VII

Elizabethan drama is a relatively transient phenomenon. In the broad chronicle of literary history, the theater of Marlowe and Shakespeare is a brief and flaring thing, something of an aesthetic fluke, an oddity, an anomaly. But the odd case can be illuminating, and Elizabethan drama has from its inception been regarded as exemplary. What it is taken to exemplify, however, has shifted dramatically. For the sixteenth century, the Elizabethan playhouse and its productions were supreme manifestations of "incontinent rule," tokens for all that stood in a certain sense outside its own age, for everything—from residues of past cultures to emerging forms of the strange and the new—that lodged on or just beyond the ideological horizon. For us, viewing the same object from the standpoint of literature, Elizabethan drama has achieved the status of a supreme fiction, one of the apogees of literary art in the West.

Such perspectives are not as far removed from each other as they first appear. One of the reasons I have undertaken such an oblique approach to Elizabethan drama—this long excursus through the topologies of premodern cities—is to bring cultural and literary points of view into some proximity. When modern literary theory seeks to describe the relationship of literature to its own culture,

it finds itself in a position analogous to that of the city fathers of
Elizabethan London. It tries to account for a cultural phenomenon
which seems to reside both within and without its given context,
and which consequently, like Nashe's stalking Tamburlaine, wields
a certain power. A power, in Hayden White's estimation, "to transcend, criticize or at least self-consciously comment on the structure
of those social conditions under which literary works are produced."[51] Occurring when and where it did, Elizabethan drama
came into being only by dissociating itself from the community to
which it owed its livelihood. It continued to depend upon that
community, and to stand apart from it. In so doing, it provided
us with one of our most concrete realizations of the situation of
literature itself.

For the student of Western culture, the playhouses of Elizabethan London can precipitate an uncanny sense of cultural déjà
vu. In the place of the Elizabethan stage, we find the place prescribed for the mimetic arts by Plato when he banished drama
from the *Republic*. A figurative banishment from an ideal republic,
to be sure; but history at times reveals an acute capacity for
literalizing the metaphors of its past. In exiling drama from his
ideal polis, Plato did not intend to be taken quite so literally, by
his readers or by history. But he did intend to codify a vagrancy—
a vagabondage, in Elizabethan terms—which he regarded as con-
stitutive of drama and poetry. Homer was always a wanderer, as
Socrates says, errant and homeless as the songs he sang (*Rep.*
600d–e); poetry and drama begin in exile, and whether actually
returned to their proper place or not, are to be viewed as marginal
pastimes. Literally or figuratively, they take place outside the polis,
society, or episteme to which they ambiguously belong. They stand
not outside history, but at a slight remove from the historical
conditions that make them possible—able to transcend, criticize,
and even comment upon those conditions by virtue of a certain
marginality.

Feeling transcended, criticized, and commented upon by the
popular stage, watching its values and pretensions enacted at a
critical distance, Elizabethan London would have understood our
formulations of the ideological power of literature quite well. Compared to us, however, Elizabethans would have had a more concrete apprehension of the spatial metaphors we rely upon in our
efforts to locate the ambivalent and contradictory place of the
literary. A literary text, according to Terry Eagleton, is "a momentarily liberated zone in which the exigencies of the real seem
to evaporate, an enclave of freedom enclosed within the realm of

necessity."[52] A liberated zone, an enclave of freedom: the terms are unwittingly borrowed from an age when "liberty" was not a political or juridical concept but a geographical domain, a literal if ambiguous enclave of license and incontinent rule. Whether we take our own metaphors literally or not, what we mean to describe when we speak of literature's liberty or license, its momentary dissociation, is at best a tenuous and two-sided affair. The literary stands at a slight remove from its cultural context, and yet it continues to be a product of that context, to depend upon the entire field of language and ideology that becomes, through dissociation, literature's Other. We look to literature, according to Louis Althusser, for its ability to provide us with a paradoxically removed and critical perspective on this ideological Other. Balzac and Solzhenitsyn, writes Althusser, "give us a 'view' of the ideology to which their work alludes and with which it is constantly fed, a view which presupposes a *retreat*, an *internal distantiation*, from the very ideology from which their novels emerged. They make us 'perceive' . . . in some sense *from the inside*, by an *internal distance*, the very ideology in which they are held."[53]

No literature of any vitality ever existed fully outside of the ideology which produced it; conversely, no literature achieves vitality or ideological complexity without establishing at least a virtual distance from its reigning culture or ideology, a perspective on its own time and place that is by no means limited to or definitive of the literary, but that can, in a given cultural milieu, provide it with the ideological equivalent of an external vantage point. In describing such a virtual distance or "internal distantiation," Althusser's examples are novelistic, but the situation he depicts is essentially dramatic, like the language he employs. Drama is the literary art of space, virtual or otherwise; it is the art that most concretely employs distance—literal, aesthetic, ideological, and historical—to bring reigning ideologies and cultural climates into view. Drama is also the art that, in its Elizabethan manifestation, realized and embodied in substantial form the terms we use to characterize the power of literature, whether we speak of a certain marginality, an internal distance, a paradoxical dissociation, or (like Nicholas Woodrofe) an incontinent rule. The spatial metaphors of a later age do not always figure so prominently in the literal situations of the past, but Elizabethan drama took matters of place and space, distance and displacement, quite seriously. They were the conditions of its possibility.

At times, when the domain outside the city walls is itself brought on stage, we catch a glimpse of such conditions, of the ambivalent but recreative potential of such a place occupied by such a stage. Something like Althusser's internal distance opens before our eyes when Marlowe's Jew, presumed dead, is cast over the walls of Malta:

Firenze: For the Jew's body, throw that o'er the walls
          To be a prey for vultures and wild beasts.
          So, now away, and fortify the town.

                                                              Exeunt

Barabas: What, all alone?

                                                         (V.i.58–61)

The stage before us is neither an illusionistic one nor the stage of Bottom's rude mechanicals; it is doubtful that the wall Barabas is cast over was represented by anything but a bare, flat platform. In this theater, we credit what we are told, we are wherever the play situates us. When he rises to his feet, Barabas does not cancel the illusion we have supplied. But in rising from his apparent double death, Barabas does transform the space he occupies; he translates it back into the theatrical space it has always been, now glimpsed at its recreative and nihilistic extreme. For a moment we are outside the city walls in a double sense: still outside the walls of Malta, but reminded, as we are forced to readjust our image of that scene, as we for a moment doubt it, that we are also outside the walls of Elizabethan London. We are in a place, that is to say, where classes, occupations, states of being, even definitions of place come together to form an incongruous composition; where life and death reach an ambivalent congruence, once most starkly manifested by the lazar-houses built to house those who belonged, at once and impossibly, to both the quick and the dead. Marlowe's Jew has now become the full figure of such ambivalence. Rising from his double death, standing in a place twice-removed from the city—once in representation, again in actuality—Barabas stands before us as the master of an incontinent vitality. And standing where he does, he situates that vitality, ambivalent and recreative and theatrical as it is, in the place where it most emphatically belongs: at the heart of the Elizabethan stage.

He stands, and he speaks. Unlike the marginal spectacles of the past, the stage was not silent. Like some of its predecessors in the Liberties, the Elizabethan stage was a paying proposition, but it was also a literary phenomenon, making the plays it produced a peculiar breed of commodity: a commodity that speaks, and that speaks about the conditions of its own culture and its own production. The Liberties of the city had always been places of cultural commentary. Like the margins of the 1611 Bible, they were reserved for "a varietie of sences," for a certain excess or incontinent significance that extended, as I suggested earlier, to commentary upon and even contradiction of the main body of their text, the body politic itself. With the advent of popular drama, the margins attain a new capacity for commentary, a new license for contradiction. They become outspoken.

If the place of the stage was a marginal and ambivalent one, so were the figures that occupied that stage most prominently. Having considered the topology of early modern London and its Liberties, it is now time to turn to a select few Shakespearean plays, chosen because of the ways in which they reflect upon and put to dramatic use the marginality of the popular stage. Here our concern will be not the place of the stage but the broader ramifications of its cultural situation, and our focus will be on those figures of license, both dramatic and rhetorical, through which Shakespeare explored the conditions of his art and, in so doing, the ideological horizon of his age.

3

The Rehearsal of Cultures

I

In the autumn of 1599, Thomas Platter of Basle visited the London apartments of Walter Cope—gentleman, adventurer, and member of Elizabeth's Society of Antiquaries—to view Cope's collection of curiosities gathered from around the world. No catalogue of the objects displayed in the room could presume to be complete. Platter himself records only a selection, but he does take an evident pleasure in compiling his list—a *plaisir de conter* akin to that which Jean Céard has found at work in contemporaneous accounts of nature's oddities and marvels, such as the anonymous *Histoire prodigieuses* published in 1598.[1] It is a pleasure in the recollection, literally, of such wonders as an African charm made of teeth, a felt cloak from Arabia, and shoes from many strange lands. An Indian stone axe, "like a thunderbolt." A stringed instrument with but one string. The twisted horn of a bull seal. An embalmed child, or *Mumia*. The bauble and bells of Henry VIII's fool. A unicorn's tail. Inscribed paper made of bark, and an artful Chinese box. A flying rhinoceros (unremarked), a remora (explicated at some length), and flies of a kind that "glow at night in Virginia instead of lights, since there is often no day there for over a month." There are the queen of England's seal, a number of crowns made of claws, a Madonna made of Indian feathers, an Indian charm made of monkey teeth. A mirror, which "both reflects and multiplies objects." A sea-halcyon's nest. A sea mouse (*mus marinus*), reed pipes like those played by Pan, and a long narrow Indian canoe, with oars and sliding planks, hanging from the ceiling. They are all strange things, *frembden Sachen.*[2]

The canoe lodged on the ceiling may have been a convention of sorts, judging from its promiscuity of appearance in better-known collections of the same variety (fig. 3). Cope's room is a *Kunst* or *Wunderkammer*, a wonder-cabinet: a form of collection peculiar to the late Renaissance, characterized primarily by its encyclopedic appetite

F I G U R E 3. Frontispiece from *Museum Wormianum* (1655). By permission of the Houghton Library, Harvard University.

for the marvellous or the strange and by an exceptionally brief historical career.[3] The first *Wunderkammer* was established in Vienna in 1550; for perhaps one hundred years such collections flourished, but by the middle of the seventeenth century they were rapidly vanishing. As early as *The Advancement of Learning* (1605), where Bacon calls for the "substantial and severe collection of the Heteroclites or Irregulars of nature," wonder-cabinets were derided as "frivolous impostures for pleasure and strangeness."[4] The well-known Dresden collection proved to be a late survivor: founded in 1560, it remained intact until 1721, when it was broken up to form the separate exhibits—works of Nature, Art, Science—whose outlines can still be observed today.

The dates serve to remind us that a wonder-cabinet is not a museum, not even a vague or half-formed gesture toward one. Its relation to later forms of collection is a discontinuous one, even when the objects displayed were themselves preserved and carried over, as in the case of Dresden. The museum as an institution rises from the ruins of such collections, like country houses built from the dismantled stonework of dissolved monasteries; it organizes the wonder-cabinet by breaking it down—that is to say, by analyzing it, regrouping the random and the strange into recognizable categories that are systematic, discrete, and exemplary. The museum represents an order and a categorical will to knowledge whose absence—or suspension—is precisely what is on display in a room such as Cope's.

As Platter notes, these are strange things: a category that in fact withholds categorization, that neither specifies nor defines but rather sets the objects to which it refers aside, grants them the freedom to remain as they are. Rhetorically, Platter's designation duplicates the effect which the wonder-cabinet itself produces in the objects thus displayed: it maintains them as "extraneous" in the Latin sense of the word, lodges them, at least for the time being, beyond the bounds of cultural hierarchies or definitions. Regarded as such, anything could reside in a room like Cope's. No system determines the organization of the objects on display or separates one variety of the marvellous from another. We are surprised upon entering the room, but our surprise is occasioned not so much by the individual items we encounter, impressive though they are, as by the immediate, even immoderate familiarity they show for whatever joins them. These are things on holiday, randomly juxtaposed and displaced from any proper context; the room they inhabit acts as a liberty or sanctuary for ambiguous things, a kind of halfway-house for transitional objects, some new but not yet fully assimilated, others old and headed for cultural oblivion, but not yet forgotten or cast off. Taken together, they compose a heteroclite order without hierarchy or degree, an order in which kings mingle with clowns, or at least the props of their respective stations do; in which the outworn relics of Folly and the inconsequential charms of Alchemy (the unicorn's tail: neither its most potent nor even its most distinctive feature) hold court with icons of the Crown, and with such genuine novelties as the Indian artifacts collected by Cope himself.

In the space of such a room, under the gaze of a spectator like Platter, the New World coincides with the Old and is even woven into the very fabric of European beliefs—as in the case of Cope's feathered Madonna, the handiwork of some forever unknown Archimboldo of the Americas. How are we to interpret signs of such consubstantiality between the Old World and the New? Is this Madonna, for example, the record of a heathen brought into the Christian fold and eager to portray the image of his new faith—or is it rather a blasphemous parody of such conversions, an infernal representation in which the immaculate image finds itself appropriated by pagan craft? In the sixteenth century, there was cause for apprehension when Christian and pagan cultures mingled, even in so token a fashion as this. "There is scarce anything," as Father Joseph de Acosta noted in his *Natural and Moral History of the Indies* (1598), "instituted by Jesus Christ our Saviour in his Lawe and his Gospels, the which the Devil hath not counterfeited in some sort and carried to his Gentiles."[5] Such questions, however, do not occur to Thomas Platter, our remarkably incurious Swiss curieux. This is a room of wonder, not of inquiry. It requires and to a certain extent produces an audience that is at once passive and attentive, willing to suspend its critical faculties in order to view "strange things" as precisely that: as known but in a certain sense unaccountable, alien yet recognized as such, and so granted temporary license to remain without "authentic place" (as Ulysses says in his speech on Degree) in the cultural and ideological topography of the times.

What it means to be thus maintained, as something Other, is a question that will take us beyond the confines of the wonder-cabinet and into the field of a broader cultural dynamic, one that is dramaturgical at heart and is organized around the spectacle of strange cultures during the period defined by the wonder-cabinet. In this context, Cope's display of strange things will serve as our introduction not to Renaissance collections, but to Renaissance collection: to the process rather than the product of what we might call the collective activity of the period. The late sixteenth and early seventeenth centuries collected and exhibited not only the trappings but also the customs, languages, and even the members of other cultures on a scale that was unprecedented. In forums ranging from wonder-cabinets to court masques and popular romances, from royal entries and traveler's narratives to the popular playhouses of Elizabethan London, the pleasures of the strange are consistently invoked to solicit our attention as spectators, auditors, or readers, but the motives of what the period knew merely as its "curiosity" are far from clear. This is an essay into that curiosity, or more precisely, an inquiry into the attention which the period ostensibly devoted to the cultivation of wonder, but directed, often with paradoxical ends, toward its various cultural Others—toward the old and the new, the residual, emergent, and otherwise strange cultures that occupied an expanding horizon of concern for the dominant cultures of early modern Europe.

The wonder-cabinet and the suspension of cultural decorum and discrimination it exhibits provide us with the most literal but by no means the fullest representation of what the early modern period embraced as strange. I will be concerned, in the pages that follow, with a large and often lively cast of what the period perceived as alien, anomalous, dissimilar, barbarous, gross, or rude, and yet (if this is the proper conjunction of ambivalence) sought out for purposes of exhibition and display—what the period maintained and produced, as something Other. What comes to reside in a wonder-cabinet are, in the most reified sense of the phrase, strange things: tokens of alien cultures, reduced to the status of sheer objects, stripped of cultural and human contexts in a way that makes them eminently capable of surviving the period that thus produced them. Although many *Wunderkammern* did indeed provide the raw materials for later collections and institutions, what we encounter in them is not the proleptic beginning of a civilizing process—the confused and somewhat frivolous origins of the museum—so much as the final stage of a historical dynamic specific to the period in question. In less objective forums, where other cultures were not—or at least, not yet—so radically reduced to their representative trappings, the attention directed toward strange ways and customs reveals an ambivalent and even paradoxical rhythm; in such forums, as we shall see, the maintenance and production of the strange takes on its most dramatic form, as a process of cultural production synonymous with cultural performance.

II

Within and without the wonder-cabinet, the "spectacle of strangeness"[6] enjoyed a remarkable currency during the early modern period. Upon first encountering Caliban's indeterminate form, Trinculo observes that any strange beast could make a man: a comment which condenses in a phrase the period's investment—both mercenary and imaginative—in the sheerly Other, and the increasing instability, even interchangeability, of cultural categories such as self and other, monster and man:

> Were I in England now, as once I was, and had but this fish painted, not a holiday fool there but would give a piece of silver; there would this monster make a man; any strange beast there makes a man: when they will not give a doit to a lame beggar, they will lay out ten to see a dead Indian.
>
> (*The Tempest*, II.ii.27ff.)

When cultural difference is less ambiguously affirmed, it can solicit our resources not merely as spectators or consumers but also as fellow travelers. Where the Medieval explorer employed analogy and correspondence to make even the unprecedented familiar, a Renaissance ethnographer like Jean de Léry insists on an irreducible, inexpressible, but compelling residuum of difference in the lands and people he describes. After a full and evocative portrait of native Brazilians comes this disclaimer: "Their gestures and countenances are so different from ours, that I confess to my difficulty in representing them in words, or even in pictures. So, to enjoy the real pleasures of them, you will have to go and visit them in their own country."[7]

Difference draws us to it; it promises pleasure and serves as an invitation to firsthand experience, otherwise known as colonization. Where words and portraits failed, the thing itself was there for the taking. Trinculo's hypothetical Indian was something of a historical commonplace in Elizabethan London. In 1577, for example, Martin Frobisher brought an Eskimo couple back from his second voyage to Meta Incognita, later known as Nova Scotia. The captives survived in England for over a year, a lengthy duration for such ethnic "tokens" of New World Voyages. During that time, upheld by the queen's license and a skin-covered boat, the man could be seen (without charge, as far as we know) hunting the royal ducks and swans on the Thames; before her death the woman gave birth to a child who survived its parents briefly—residing at the Three Swans Tavern while alive, and the Church of St. Olave's thereafter, apparently with the grace of a Christian burial.[8]

What the period could not contain within the traditional order of things, it licensed to remain on the margins of culture: a procedure which not only maintained literal aliens like Frobisher's Eskimos, but also upheld figures of Elizabethan society such as the common players who, without a proper place of their own, were licensed to "make" any strange beast on stage, from Caliban to gentlemen and even kings. I will want to turn to the marginal status of the Elizabethan stage, to consider both its role in the representation of other cultures and, more importantly, the degree to which the popular stage occupied the position of a strange thing itself, fascinating but subject, as a consequence, to the same rituals of inclusion and exclusion as anything else that was deemed marginal, masterless, vagabond, or otherwise outlandish and out of place. For the moment, however, it will suffice to note that the line between Frobisher's Eskimos and the theatrical creations of court and popular theater was by no means a firm one; when cultural productions of the period achieved their fullest dramaturgical form, the distinction between the alien and its representation, the real and the theatrical, virtually ceased to exist—at least for a brief and studiously foreclosed period of time.

The city of Rouen provides us with an example worth considering at some length. In 1550, a meadow bordering on the Seine and located on the outskirts of Rouen was planted with trees and shrubs, some natural, some artificial, all foreign to the locale and all combining to create the semblance of a Brazilian forest landscape. From the reports of those present, it was a re-creation convincing to the knowing and well-traveled observer, both in what it revealed and in what it left concealed. The foliage was at certain points impenetrable to the eye, allowing the simulated forest to serve as habitat and refuge for the parrots, marmots, and apes that had been set at large within it. The *bons bourgeois* of the city had also constructed two authentically detailed Brazilian villages, the huts carved from solid tree-trunks at great labor but "in true native fashion." The villages themselves were stocked with over fifty Tabbagerres and Toupinaboux Indians freshly imported for the occasion. Supplementing the genuine Brazilians were some two hundred and fifty Frenchmen appropriately costumed— "sans aucunement couvrir la partie que nature commande"—and drawn from the ranks of seamen, merchants, and adventurers who had been to Brazil and knew the manners, customs, and tongues of the tribes involved. "Elle sembloit véritable," as an account published in 1551 testified, "et non simulée."[9]

The occasion was Henri II's royal entry into Rouen: an event which can hardly explain the genesis of one of the most thorough performances of an alien culture staged by the Renaissance, but does at least illuminate the pragmatic function of Brazil in the ongoing dramaturgy of city and state. A delicate negotiation of power and prestige was at once necessitated and accomplished by a monarch's passage into an early modern city of any size. In keeping with the conventions of the Roman Triumph as transformed and elaborated by the Renaissance, it had become customary for a monarch and his procession to pause outside the city gates, on the threshold of the community, at that tenuous point where royal domain shaded into civic jurisdiction. Halting made the royal visitor more spectator than actor in the drama at hand and, prompted by his gaze, a mock battle or sciamachy would commence. Oftentimes the martial triumphs thus staged would celebrate the royal spectator's own military prowess and accomplishments. A mock siege was common. A castle erected on the margins of the city would be stormed and taken: rather than lay siege to gain entry, the monarch granted an entry was entertained by the comfortably displaced spectacle of a siege, a dramatic enactment that at once represented the potential for conflict manifested by a royal visit and sublimated that potential, recasting it as a cultural performance to be enjoyed by city and Crown alike. When Queen Isabella of Bavaria entered Paris in 1389, it was only after watching Saladin and his Saracens defend a castle eventually taken by Richard Coeur de Lion; at Rome in 1492, in commemoration of the victory at Granada, Spanish troops stormed a wooden castle occupied by citizens in Moors' clothing.[10]

Henri did not witness a siege, but he did view what the Imperial ambassador described as "a sham combat illustrating the manner of fighting in Brazil."[11] Before the battle began, however, the royal party lingered for some time, delighted with the convincing performance of natives real and counterfeit as they went about their daily rounds. Such a delay marked a temporary suspension in the momentum of the king's entry—lingering on the threshold not only of the city, but also of the sciamachy which customarily manifested that threshold—but the breach in ceremonial decorum was quite understandable. The "Figures des Brasilians" (fig. 4) that accompanies the official account of the entry shows men hunting monkeys with arrows and spears, or scaling trees to gather the fruit that was either lashed in place or growing there. A group of men and women dance in a clearing, their hands joined in a circle reminiscent of European May-games. Couples stroll arm in arm through the foliage; toward the right-hand margin of the scene, a man and a woman strike a pose that recalls period illustrations of Genesis. Yet the tableau is polymorphous, overdetermined in the sense that it represents more than a single scene should be able to contain. Along with its version of Edenic pastoral it reveals a land of unbiblical license and enterprise. Some of the couples are partially obscured in the underbrush, taking advantage of the cover

F I G U R E 4. From *C'est la Déduction* . . . (Rouen, 1551). By permission of the Houghton Library, Harvard University.

to indulge in relatively unabashed foreplay; men are hewing trees, then carrying them to the river to build primitive barks. The soft primitivism of biblical tradition coexists with a harder interpretation of pagan cultures, akin to the portraits of barbaric life composed by Piero di Cosimo.[12]

What we have is a detailed mise-en-scène of Brazilian culture, re-creating even the moment of the natives' capture—on the Seine, a French merchant ship is under sail, gradually approaching the bank where a group of naked and unknowing figures awaits its arrival[13]—and the projection of European libido and myth onto that scene. The New World is both recreated in the suburbs of the Old and made over into an alternate version of itself, strange but capable of imagination. Dominating the field of the spectacle, a man and woman occupy a hammock stretched prominently between two trees. The two are naked like those below them, but even so they are invested with a regal bearing; the man holds a scepter, and both figures wear crowns that contrast sharply with the leaves and fronds worn as headgear by their savage subjects. Similarly crowned but fully cloaked in the robes of state, watching his heathen surrogate from the vantage point of a scaffold placed at the edge of the meadow, Henri must have been especially pleased to find a version of himself and his queen, Catharine de Medici, thus occupying the scene he beheld. A major theme of the day would be revealed in the final emblematic display of the entry, in the heart of the city, where Henri's father would be praised "for having restored letters and saved [Rouen] from barbarism,"[14] and Henri himself would be admonished to follow *in his* father's footsteps. It was a duty foreshadowed, its barbaric metaphor cast into more literal terms, in these figures of primitive patriarchy, raised above the savage scene they commanded, over which they ruled.

At some point, fighting broke out between the two tribes. One decimated the ranks of the other, then burned its village to the ground. On the following day victor and vanquished would trade roles, for the entire Triumph was repeated in an encore performance for Catharine's own entry,[15] during which the second village, faithfully and elaborately fashioned so as to be "le certain simulacre de la verité," was also set ablaze and reduced to ash. The re-creation of Brazil had been surprisingly detailed and complete, and its consummation followed suit. It was the age of conspicuous expenditure and ostentatious display; what was displayed in public ceremony was often, in one sense or another, used up in the process, consummation being in fact the point: what you had was most clearly manifested by how much you could afford to expend in lavish and costly celebration.[16] But the consumption of Brazil can hardly be explained by such generalities of early modern culture. What was most conspicuously expended in this instance was neither money, time, nor other indigenous resources, but an alien culture itself, at least in terms of theatrical representation. It is difficult to say which is more awesome: the painstaking expense of spirit and wealth that went into such a carefully reconstructed and authenticated verisimilitude, or the thoroughness with which it was all effaced, even though full effacement required a full-scale repetition of the entire entry.

Representation is always a form of repetition, but in the two-day course of events at Rouen both representation and re-presentation, imitation and repeated performance, conspired to achieve a paradoxical end: not the affirmation of what was thus represented and repeated, but its erasure or negation. The enthnographic attention and knowledge displayed at Rouen was genuine, amazingly thorough, and richly detailed; the object, however, was not to understand Brazilian culture but to perform it, in a paradoxically self-consuming fashion. Knowledge of another culture in such an instance is directed toward ritual rather than ethnological ends, and the rite involved is one ultimately organized around the elimination of its own pretext: the spectacle of the Other that is thus celebrated and observed, in passing. To speak of Renaissance curiosity or fascination with other cultures hardly begins to address what is odd in such an anthropology, geared not toward the interpretation of strange cultures but toward their consummate performance.[17] What we glimpse in the field outside Rouen is not a version of the modern discipline of anthropology, but something preliminary to it; not the interpretation, but what I would call the *rehearsal* of cultures.

III

A rehearsal is a period of free-play during which alternatives can be staged, unfamiliar roles tried out, the range of one's power to convince or persuade explored with some license; it is a period of performance, but one in which the customary demands of decorum are suspended, along with expectations of final or perfected form.

For us, as a phenomenon most immediately associated with the stage, a rehearsal is also fully distinct from actual performance, but such a distinction is a modern one. In Elizabethan England, for example, rehearsal referred as easily, and as often, to performance or recital—*recitare* is commonly translated as "rehearse"—as it did to some practice session preparatory to public performance. For Shakespeare and his contemporaries, to recite, rehearse, or perform were synonymous terms, fully interchangeable and appositely applied to almost any dramatic situation. The one exception, where a rehearsal was a necessary prerequisite to public performance, is an important one for our purposes, for it takes us outside a strictly theatrical arena and introduces us to a form of rehearsal dictated by jurisprudential rather than artistic concerns. A rehearsal was fully distinct from public performance when it took place at the Office of Revels, "where our Court playes have become in late daies," as Thomas Heywood wrote in his *Apology for Actors,* "yearly rehersed, perfected, and corrected before they came to the publike view."[18]

Such a rehearsal, performed under the gaze of jurisprudence for purposes of cultural review, is only coincidentally related to the history of the stage. Plays came to be rehearsed before the Master of Revels not because they were plays, that is to say, but because they attained a prominence that made them potentially dangerous (and hence, potentially useful) to reigning cultural hierarchies. Other matters, nondramatic in nature, were likewise rehearsed before the powers that be. When John Dee, accused of conjuration and rumored to be a papist, published an account of his life and studies, he named his treatise *The Compendious Rehearsal:* it was to be read by Elizabeth and the public at large, to be judged and, along with its author, either censured or given a clear imprimatur.[19] The genealogy of such rehearsals lies not with the stage but with the larger dramaturgy of power and its confrontations with the forbidden or the taboo, with all that stood outside the strict confines of authority, whether embodied in magical science, plays, or alien cultures themselves. In England, what appears to be the earliest example of cultural rehearsal in this sense comes from the reign of Edward I, whose colonization of Wales in the thirteenth century would provide a model and precedent for the foreign and subcultural excursions of sixteenth-century England. Edward first conquered Wales, then "rehearsed" Welsh culture as a necessary prolegomenon to full colonization. "We have caused to be rehearsed [*recitari*] before Us and the Nobles of our Realm," he declares in the *Statuta Wallia* (1284), "the laws and customs of these parts hitherto in use: which being diligently heard and fully Understood, We have, by the Advise of aforesaid Nobles, abolished certain of them, some of them We have allowed, and some of them We have corrected."[20]

The field cleared by the conflagration of Brazil was, of course, French to begin with; Henri occupied the position not of a judge or censor but of an appreciative and admiring spectator. In describing the Brazilian interlude at Rouen as the rehearsal of a strange culture, I mean to cast it neither as a practice session nor as the mere performance of something alien; neither do I mean to reduce it to the merely colonial, although we are obviously involved with the symbolic, socially "misrecognized" armature of the colonial enterprise of the period. We are concerned here with a cultural practice that allows, invites, and even demands a full and potentially self-consuming review of unfamiliar things. Whatever the ultimate end of such a rehearsal, whether consummation, colonization, or a less clearly defined negotiation between a dominant culture and its Others, the attention directed toward Brazilian ways at Rouen was by no means reserved for New World cultures. "The 'ethnicks' of the Americas," notes J. R. Hale, "had a special, though delayed, power to jolt the Europeans into taking fresh stock of themselves."[21] Of themselves or, more accurately, of those "ethnicks" they could call their own. In the sixteenth century, a commonly drawn analogy articulated a certain equivalence between inquiries into newly discovered cultures of the Western hemisphere and the increasingly important subcultures of the Old World. "We have Indians at home," one Englishman observed, "Indians in Cornwall, Indians in Wales, Indians in Ireland."[22] Europe had begun to mind its own, to take note of its rural and suburban populations, to review their customs and rituals, their ways of speech and community. "Their languages, names, surnames, allusions, anagrams, armories, monies, poesies, epitaphes," to quote from the title of Camden's *Remaines concerning Britaine* (1614).

The late sixteenth century stands as an odd interregnum in history. The impressive but ineffectual body of Elizabethan poor laws began, at this time, to compose its growing list of peddlars, wandering scholars, unlicensed players, sturdy beggars, and the like, all brought together as "vagabonds," assembled, like the marvels of a wonder-cabinet, to await the disposition of a later age—in this instance, to wait nearly one hundred years before the early modern state articulated itself well enough to create a bureaucracy capable of implementing the Vagabond Acts. Madness was confined and maintained during the period, but not excluded from public view or shut away from the light—of day or of Reason—as it would be during the Enlightenment. Rather, Folly in all its variety was gathered together so that it could be fully licensed for display, made more accessible and given greater currency than had ever been the case in the Middle Ages, when madness was free (or subject) to wander. Throughout Europe, writes Michel Foucault, "a new and lively pleasure is taken in the old confraternities of madmen, in their festivals, their gatherings, their speeches."[23] In England, Bedlam Hospital was operated as a concession under its Tudor administration, a playhouse of Folly that served as much to showcase madness and oversee its performance as to confine or control it.

The theatrical metaphor is hardly inappropriate, if it can be called a metaphor at all. We find the same audience, the same suspension of cultural decorum and blurring of xenophilia and phobia, in attendance at madhouses, royal entries, and wonder-cabinets as we find at the popular playhouses of Elizabethan London. When we do turn to the popular stage, however, its place in this larger cultural review proves to be a fully ambivalent one. According to Muriel Bradbrook, a great many "social and customary forms might have passed relatively unobserved" if the popular stage had not recorded and transformed them into drama, if Marlowe and Shakespeare had not cultivated a language and a stagecraft capable of sustaining such a *bricolage* of other cultures—New World, European, and most importantly, popular. "Country pastimes too might have vanished . . . leaving no signs other than those to be disinterred by the social historian."[24] While a great deal of what we know about country ways and pastimes does indeed come from the stage, rural and folk customs were not merely vanishing, however. Far from being neglected in Elizabethan England, they were being accorded an unprecedented degree of attention. In his archaeological quest for pastime, the modern social historian turns to a quite full archive, made up of sermons such as Lattimer's attack on May-games, Puritan tracts detailed in the objects of their revulsion, city ordinances and Statutes of the Realm protecting the Sabbath, exiling or branding rogues, vagabonds, and other masterless men, banning and regulating country pastimes, festivities, and of course, plays themselves. Documents of criticism, as E. K. Chambers called them, and documents of control.

Such documents were designed to be read by as large an audience as possible; some even became works of popular literature in their own right, read with as much delight as Hakluyt's *Voyages* or Peter Martyr's *Decades*. It is customarily regarded as one of the ironies of history that works such as Phillip Stubbes' *Anatomie of Abuses* (1583) provide us with our fullest account of the country, alien, heathen, or otherwise strange ways they would see repressed but must first review or rehearse at some length. Indeed, repression may be too crude a mechanism to describe the paradoxical process involved. Stubbes, for example, charges that stage plays "maintaíne bawdrie, insinuat folery, and revive the remembrance of hethen idolytrie," but is himself forced or otherwise compelled to stoke the popular memory with detailed descriptions of the "babblerie" and pastimes he would see abolished:

> Against *May, Whitsonday* or other time, all the yung men and maides, olde men and wiues, run gadding ouer night to woods, groves, hills, & mountains, where they spend all night in pleasant pastimes; & in the morning they return, bringing with them birch & branches of trees,

to deck their assemblies withall. And not meruaile, for there is a great Lord present amongst them, as superintendent and Lord ouer their pastimes and sportes, namely, Sathan, prince of hel. But the cheifest iewel they bring from thence is their May-pole, which they bring home with great veneration, as thus. They haue twentie or fortie yoke of Oxen, euery Oxe hauing a sweet nose-gay of flouers and hearbes, bound round about with strings from the tope to the bottome, and sometime painted with variable colors, with great deuotion. And thus beeing reared vp with handkercheefs and flags houering on the top, they straw the ground rounde about, binde green boughes about it, set vp sommer haules, bowers, and arbors hard by it; And then fall they to daunce about it, like as the heathen people did at the dedication of the Idols, wherof this is a perfect pattern, or rather the thing it self. I haue heard it credibly reported (and that *viua voce*) by men of great grauitie and reputations, that of fortie, threescore, or hundred maides going to the wood ouer night, there haue scaresly the third part of them returned home againe undefiled.[25]

Stubbes recreates the May festival for us and draws us into it with his conspiratorial air (*viva voce*). To a degree, the need for such detail stems from the audience for which Stubbes composed his *Anatomie*. The work poses as a description of a foreign land and its customs, a *Discoverie*, as Stubbes calls it, of "a very famous Ilande called Ailgna." Thomas Platter's *Travels* is of the genre imitated; the country visited is England, but Stubbes' fiction of traveling to a distant land was, as C. L. Barber writes, "not altogether inappropriate, for Merry England was becoming foreign to the pious tradesman's London for which Stubbes was the spokesman."[26]

But it is not merely cultural alienation or distance that accounts for Stubbes' apparent fondness for detail. When the Church sought to put down pagan customs, it did so with circumspection, making sure the customs it proscribed could not be recreated from the description it gave. Jean-Baptiste Thiers described magic rituals in his *Traité des superstitions qui regardent les sacramens*, but he suppressed certain signs and words, marking the deletions with ellipses, in order to insure that his readers would not be able to try out the spells he denounced.[27] In Stubbes we encounter no analogue to such caution. In place of a more elliptic depiction we find, if not a perfect, then a fully fleshed portrait of "the thing itself." We could recreate the May-games, thanks to Stubbes, with as much verisimilitude as we encountered in the re-creation of Brazil. Remembrance is at any rate renewed by such a rehearsal of culture; Stubbes' treatise is an exercise in cultural mnemonics, an effort to displace or recreate cultural memory. The question, for pastimes and for us, is what it means to be attended to in such fashion.

An answer is suggested by Sir Thomas Browne. "Knowledge is made by oblivion," Browne writes in *Pseudodoxia Epidemica*,[28] "and to purchase a clear and warrantable body of Truth, we must forget and part with much we know." Browne's work, otherwise known as *Enquiries into Vulgar and Common Errors* (1649), is a collection of proverbial and country wisdom compiled for a learned audience, many of whom had never heard the folk sayings he would have them forget. Forgetting becomes a more arduous task when its first stage is the review or remembrance, even the initial learning, of what is to be consigned to oblivion. The paradox requires Browne to compose "a long and serious *Adviso*, proposing not only a large and copious List, but from experience and reason attempting their decisions [from *decidere*, to cut off]." Although collections of proverbs existed throughout the medieval period, Browne's work belongs to a new genre, as characteristic of its age as wonder-cabinets were. Laurent Joubert's *Erreures populaires* (1578) is the earliest of such anthologies: forays by the learned into the new-found land of popular culture, in which "vulgar" thought and customs were recorded and collected as Error. Such collections were made for the sake of posterity, but it was a posterity that would only be achieved if the errant proverbs and pastimes thus gathered together were not included in it. As Natalie Davis has shown, the aspirations of French and English collectors of proverbs were at best contradictory. On the one hand, the recording of popular thought marked an effort to enrich the vernacular by absorbing folk and country sayings into the learned discourse of the mother tongue; on the other, there was an effort to purify the vernacular, to control and correct popular thought—also by collecting it.[29]

Although the aims seem mutually exclusive, they were often announced by one and the same collector; purification could only come after all that would ultimately be banished from the language was first worked through, in full. The rhythm is one of exhibition, followed by exclusion or effacement; a rehearsal of popular culture, with a self-consuming end in mind. The process of observation and review does not merely precede the subsequent revision, where a rehearsal of culture is involved. As with the Brazilian interlude at Rouen, the exhibition of what is to be effaced, repressed, or subjected to new and more rigorous mechanisms of control can be a surprisingly full one. It is a form of exhibition, in fact, that recalls one of the more archaic uses of the word. "Exhibition" once referred to the unveiling of a sacrificial offering—to the exposure of a victim, placed on public view for a time preliminary to the final rites that would, after a full and even indulgent display, remove the victim from that view. Early modern collection was not merely an idle assembly of strange and outlandish things: such collection was a ritual process, a rehearsal of cultures which can be glimpsed in a number of settings and forums, and which comes into clearest view on the Elizabethan stage.

The juxtaposition of Elizabethan playhouse and the more explicit collective activity of the period takes us back to Thomas Platter—who was, at least implicitly, the first to relate such apparently distinct cultural phenomena. Before visiting Cope's apartments, Platter crossed the Thames to sample the entertainments of Bankside: a bullring, a bear-baiting and a cockfight, the taverns of Southwark (where women drinking freely alongside their husbands or lovers proved as astonishing a sight as any other spectacle of the day), and one of the first performances in the recently constructed Globe—a version of *Julius Caesar*, almost certainly Shakespeare's. The phenomenon of the Elizabethan play was as striking and unfamiliar to Platter as Cope's collection is to us; unfamiliar enough, at any rate, to require some explanation, as *Wunderkammern* did not. "With these and many more amusements the English pass their time, learning from the plays what is happening in other lands; indeed, men and women visit such places without scruple, since the English do not travel much, but prefer to learn of strange things [*frembde* (sic) *Sachen*] and take their pleasures at home."[30]

Platter surveys and samples London's Liberties quite thoroughly, failing only to note what a foreign visitor could not know: that the stage he visits and finds to be a dynamic and dramatic exhibition of "strange things" was itself a recent cultural phenomenon, fully contemporaneous with wonder-cabinets and the like. As Platter's brief observation suggests, the popular stage did indeed serve as a glass in which Elizabethan culture could find the objects of its fascination represented and reflected; yet that stage was also, like Cope's feathered Madonna, a strange thing in and of itself. Shakespeare's contemporaries did not take their pleasures quite at home. The journey across the Thames, from the city to the Liberties, was a short but considerable one: a passage into a domain of cultural license as diverse as any wonder-cabinet, a field of ambivalent cultures and marginal pastimes lodged, like Rouen's Brazil, on the margins of order and community. At once native and strange, the popular stage also stood enough outside the dominant culture of its time to be capable of some reflection on what it meant to be thus maintained, as something Other— to be upheld for a while, as Hal says early in *1 Henry IV,* when he moves to the edge of an extraordinary career collecting and rehearsing strange ways, tongues, and of course, companions.

IV

Thomas Platter speaks only of the "pleasure" of learning strange
things after his encounter with an Elizabethan play; few of Shakespeare's contemporaries (Elizabethan or modern) have more to tell
us. Warwick in *2 Henry IV* is a significant exception.[31] It is an unfamiliar
process of education, a theory of learning unformulated in any contemporaneous text I know, that Warwick articulates when he endeavors, late in both the play and the history of the King's doubts, to
convince Henry IV that his prodigal son will soon sequester himself
from open haunts and popularity, cease to be the royal familiar of
Eastcheap's taverns and brothels, and most notoriously, will cut short
his tutelage with that immensity known as Falstaff:

> The prince but studies his companions
> Like a strange tongue, wherein, to gain the language,
> 'Tis needful that the most immodest word
> Be look'd upon and learnt; which once attain'd
> Your Highness knows, comes to no further use
> But to be known and hated. So, like gross terms,
> The prince will, in the perfectness of time,
> Cast off his followers . . . .
>
> (*2HIV*, IV. iv. 68–75)

By this point in the Lancastrian tetralogy, we are strangers neither to
the situation nor the import of Warwick's words. The cycle of doubt
and reassurance has been repeated more than once since Henry first
linked riot and dishonor to the name of his young Harry (I.i.80–90);
Hal himself announces his reasons for misrule at his first opportunity,
as if to allay our own doubts about his character, and Warwick's tone
("Your Highness knows . . .") lends a familiar air to the scene. Like
the prince himself, Warwick speaks to what is intentional in Hal's
prodigal career. Hal has planned to attain propriety and respectability
through a sort of *via negativa*, a self-conscious rite of passage that will
carry him from the stews of Eastcheap to the halls of Westminster,
from ritual defilement to purification in the public eye. "He is getting
to know the seamy side of life," as Jonas Barish paraphrases the
passage, "acquainting himself with vices *so as* to hate and shun them,
as men learn foul words in foreign tongues *in order to* purify their
vocabularies."[32]

The paraphrase is an accurate one, perhaps too much so. It repeats
not only Warwick's meaning but his tone as well. But is the language
lesson Warwick describes such a commonplace affair? It would be
one thing to say that we inevitably acquire immodest words and gross
terms in the process of learning a strange tongue, that only when we
attain some mastery of the language are we in a position to recognize

what is gross as gross, and eliminate it from our discourse. It is quite another thing to say, as Warwick does, that gross or obscene words are learned *because* they offer material for future reformations, that they are acquired *in order that* we may purify our vocabularies by casting them off, after a period of what Barish calls an "immersion in an alien element." Such a language lesson, described in terms proper to ritual exclusion and sacrifice, would have been no more familiar to its original audience than it is to us. It would, however, have registered in a more immediate and highly charged context, considering the ambivalence attached to "strange tongues," foreign or domestic, during the sixteenth century. Warwick's comment comes at a time when learned culture was in the midst of an extraordinary and awesome linguistic shift, a shift from Latin to the competing dialects, idioms, and grammars we generalize into something singular enough to be called *the* vernacular.

Earlier in the century, in 1535, Henry VIII had addressed the problem of linguistic variety with characteristic bluntness when he outlawed Welsh, finding that "great Discord Variance Debate Division Murmur and Sedition" had arisen, due to the fact that the Welsh "have and do daily use a Speech nothing like, nor consonant to the natural Mother Tongue within this Realm" (*27 Henry 8*, c. 26).[33] But as that mother tongue came into more universal use, its "naturalness" proved the sign of its inadequacy and lack of eloquence rather than the mark of its pure self-sufficiency. Even in the earlier half of the century, when compared to other European vernaculars, English was found wanting. It was judged to be "rude, base, unpleasant, grosse, and barbarouse."[34] The mother tongue was in need not of protection but of supplementation from other languages; English itself began to study strange tongues. Richard Foster Jones has traced in detail the long debate that the vernacular carried on with and about itself throughout the sixteenth century,[35] gradually coming to justify the importation of "straunge termes" and foreign phrases, licensing, against all precedent, a principle of linguistic change that Richard Mulcaster exuberantly proclaimed to be the "*prerogative,* and libertie" of all languages.[36]

One of the results was Elizabethan English, a language "which combined both a vast range of reference—social and natural—with a unique freedom of *epiphora*, a freedom, that is, to transpose, a liberty of transference and application."[37] The vernacular was not a fixed linguistic system so much as a linguistic crossroads, a field where many languages—foreign tongues, local dialects, Latin and Greek—intersected; as the vernacular transposed and assimilated words and phrases from other languages, it came more and more to be a "gallimaufray, or

hodgepodge of al other speeches."[38] The medieval world had been
structured around a dual language hierarchy: on the one hand, a stable
and monolithic Latin for learned and official society, and on the other,
the metamorphic, plural, and largely oral vernacular, a plethora of local
dialects, idioms, and jargons that was the province of popular culture.
As that hierarchy broke down, however, the linguistic worlds that had
formerly been held apart, as distinct and separate entities, came into
increasing contact with one another. The European vernaculars came
to inhabit the boundaries of other languages, to import values, concepts, and ideologies from strange tongues both foreign and domestic.
The literary and linguistic vitality of the Renaissance was born in the
space of such contact and assimilation, where a certain capacity for linguistic self-estrangement was possible—a capacity, as Mikhail Bakhtin
says of Rabelais' linguistic world, to stand outside one's own mother
tongue, to cultivate it as one would the tongue of another:

> The primitive and naive coexistence of languages and dialects had come
> to an end; the new consciousness was born not in a perfected and fixed
> linguistic system but at the intersection of many languages and the
> point of their most intense interorientation and struggle. Languages
> are philosophies—not abstract but concrete, social philosophies, pen-
> etrated by a system of values inseparable from living practice and class
> struggle. . . . The language of the sixteenth century, and especially the
> language of Rabelais, are sometimes described as naive even today. In
> reality the history of European literature presents no language less
> naive. Rabelais' exceptional frankness and ease are anything but that.
> The literary and linguistic consciousness of his time was aware of its
> media not only from the inside but also from the outside, in the light
> of other languages.[39]

When we are dealing with learned society, we must remember that
the vernacular in and of itself was a strange tongue. Montaigne learned
Latin before French, and despite neglecting the former for nearly
forty years—avoiding Latin altogether in speech and only rarely employing it for writing—it remained his "naturall" tongue, surfacing
immediately in times of crisis or anxiety. "In some extreame emotions
and sudden passion," he reports, "I have ever, even from my heart
uttered my first words in Latine: Nature rushing and by force ex-
pressing itself, against so long a custom."[40] When the translators of
the 1611 Bible compared their work with other translations "both in
our owne, and *other* [my emphasis] forreigne languages," they identified, with their eloquent and inclusive "other," a state of linguistic
alienation characteristic of the Renaissance. It was a period when the
shift to the vernacular meant speaking and writing daily in a language
regarded as one's own mother tongue and as a barbarous language.

This is most emphatically the case where English was concerned. English was neither Greek, Hebrew, nor Latin, but rather "the rudest countrie, and most barbarous mother language."[41] The voice of the Other, of the *barbaros,* sounded in the throat whenever the mother tongue was spoken; one's own tongue was strange yet familiar, a foreigner within, a quite literal internal *émigré.*

English manifested an extreme inadequacy and barbarity for sixteenth-century Englishmen; no other European vernacular met with such ambivalence from its native speakers. According to Richard Carew, however, the poverty and strangeness of the English language were not to its disadvantage. Rather, they were the sign of its potential, a sign, in fact, of power. Growing up with a mother tongue that was itself barbarous and strange, to be likened to "other forreigne languages," made linguistic chameleons of the English, developing in them a capacity to adopt and assimilate foreign cultures as if they were their own. It is such a capacity which Carew praises as "The Excellencie of the English Tongue":

> a Stranger, though never so long conversant among us, carrieth evermore a Watchword upon his tongue, to descry him by; but turn an *Englishman* at any time of his Age into what Country soever, allowing him due respite, and you shall see him profit so well, that the imitation of his Utterance will in nothing differ from the Pattern of that native language, the want of which towardness cost the *Ephraimites* their skins.[42]

Carew also praises English for the forcefulness of its metaphors ("our speech doth not consist only of words, but in a sort even of deeds") and for the many puns and equivocations open to it in its expansiveness. What he calls the "towardness" of the language—a resource native to Englishmen, wanting in the Ephraimites—is a kind of linguistic sympathy, a capacity for imitation that allows the Self and the Other to speak the same tongue, indistinguishably. It is an imaginative sympathy that allows alien voices and ideologies not merely to be recorded or studied, but entered into and enacted quite fully: a theatrical capacity, then, with which boundaries between nations, tongues, and classes can be crossed with liberty.

It is just such a quality of "towardness" that Shakespeare's Prince Hal relies upon and displays so brilliantly in his antithetical rise to power. His time in the taverns of Eastcheap is a literal as well as a figurative language lesson; although the tenor of Warwick's simile concerns Hal's companions, studied like a strange tongue, the comparison is also something of a two-handed engine. In the context of *Henry IV* it is fully reversible, since the language lesson deployed as an analogy also acts as a literal and quite apposite description of Hal's marginal pursuits. Shakespeare's prince studies strange tongues (En-

glish in its various dialects and idioms) *as* he learns his companions—
that is, in the same fashion and at the same time:

> Sirrah, I am sworn brother to a leash of drawers, and can call them
> all by their christen names, as Tom, Dick, and Francis. . . . they call
> drinking deep "dyeing scarlet," and when you breathe in your watering
> they cry "hem!" and bid you "play it off!" To conclude, I am so good
> a proficient in one quarter of an hour that I can drink with any tinker
> in his own language during my life. (*1HIV*, II. iv. 6ff.)

In Elizabethan legend, Henry V first acquired the English language
during his prodigal youth in the inns and alehouses of London. He
went on, once he assumed the throne, to make the King's English—
a phrase that originates with the reign of Henry V—the official language of the Court.[43] Shakespeare's Hal likewise descends from "a
prince to a prentice" (*2HIV*, II. ii. 174), but with a difference. Shakespeare does not repeat history but instead displaces it into his own
present. The English that Hal acquires when he sounds the base string
of humility is not Chaucer's but Shakespeare's English; he does not
learn the mother tongue for the first time, but he does immerse
himself in the native yet alien element of country dialects and "rude"
words with which Shakespeare's dramatic language abounds—in which
the two parts of *Henry IV* are most significantly immersed.

Learning tinker's tongues, Hal also acquires their tastes, becoming
"so loosely studied as to remember so weak a composition" (*2HIV*, II.
ii. 7–8) as small beer, and to desire it with an unprincely appetite.[44]
It is an appetite that ranges from the tongues of the taverns to the
items on Falstaff's sack-heavy shopping list—"What there is else keep
close, we'll read it at more advantage" (*1HIV*, II. iv. 534–35)—and
the easily mastered comings and goings of an apprentice like Francis;[45]
an appetite for the unfamiliar details of popular culture, for the
manners and morals, the ways of speech and material conditions of
life on the margins of society, among the masterless men, bawds,
bankrupts, wayward apprentices, and refugees from country reforms
whom Falstaff sums up as the "tattered prodigals" of the land. From
the vantage point of Henry IV, of course, the prince's marginal pastimes are merely "vile participation" in a cultural domain removed
from the province of proper authority or efficacious rule. Such participation in the life of the taverns removes the prince from his place
in the hierarchy of state and makes him "almost an alien to the hearts /
Of all the court" (*1HIV*, III. ii. 34–35). As far as Henry is concerned,
the prince is in his errancy: a prodigal son.

It is a point of view with which Shakespeare's audiences expected
to occupy themselves when they ventured beyond the confines of
sixteenth-century London to see the first part of *Henry IV*. They

came to see a familiar and well-known story. As Richard Helgerson has shown, the parable of the prodigal son was deeply engrained in the cultural imagination of Elizabethan England; its rhythm of exorbitance and recovery, of wayward youth succeeded by mature responsibility, held such great appeal for Elizabethans that men whose adolescence was relatively staid and well-mannered often depicted their youth as a time of license and riot, projecting back upon the past the contours of a prodigality never experienced yet nonetheless remembered and recounted as real.[46] The two versions known to the full spectrum of Elizabethan society were the biblical parable itself and the much-mythologized story of Henry V's wild adolescence. Hal's initial appearance on stage—bantering with Falstaff and Poins, baffling the former with unsavory similes and plotting Gadshill with the latter—would have met with immediate and self-gratified recognition from the audience. Immediate, yet pointedly short-lived:

> I know you all, and will awhile uphold
> The unyok'd humour of your idleness.
> Yet herein will I imitate the sun,
> Who doth permit the base contagious clouds
> To smother up his beauty from the world,
> That, when he please again to be himself,
> Being wanted he may be more wonder'd at
> By breaking through the foul and ugly mists
> Of vapours that did seem to strangle him.
> If all the year were playing holidays,
> To sport would be as tedious as to work;
> But when they seldom come, they wish'd-for come,
> And nothing pleaseth but rare accidents:
> So when this loose behaviour I throw off,
> And pay the debt I never promised,
> By how much better than my word I am,
> By so much shall I falsify men's hopes. . . .
>
> *(1HIV,* I. ii. 190ff.)

Hal alienates himself from the audience in an unexpected sense—falsifying *their* hopes—when he steps aside from his prodigal career to discourse on its strategic potential. Moving forward to deliver his opening soliloquy, he moves beyond the confines of audience expectation to reveal a strange and unfamiliar visage: not a prodigal youth given over to vile participation but a prince who plays at prodigality, and means to translate his rather full performance into the profession of power.

Henry continues to see only a prodigal son, but for the audience Hal's participation in the taverns represents a prodigality of a different order—the sign not of errant youth but of power, making a far from traditional passage through the margins and subcultures of its domain. As a result of that passage, the taverns of Eastcheap are difficult to navigate without a copy of Tilley's *Proverbs* as a guidebook: they comprise a kind of wonder-cabinet themselves, composed not of strange artifacts but of country proverbs, idiomatic expressions drawn from local dialects, and phrases of popular jargon, many of which would have gone unrecorded if they had not appeared in these plays, the richest in Shakespeare's corpus for popular speech. Some expressions remain as inaccessible to us as the Welsh we assume was spoken by Glendower and Lady Percy in *1 Henry IV* (III. i. 185ff.), and may have been equally inaccessible to a large part of Shakespeare's audience.[47] Others are relatively clear:

> By the mass, here will be old utis; it will be an excellent strategem.
> (*2HIV*, II. iv. 19)

The drawer's exclamation to Francis anticipates the prince and Poins dressed in jerkins and leather aprons, playing prentices to Falstaff's disadvantage. In the dialect of Worcester, "utis" meant noise, confusion, or din; yet "utas" is also a corruption of "octave," the traditional term for the eighth and final day of a festival, and generally used for any period of festivity or customary celebration. " 'Utis' is either," writes Humphreys in his gloss on the passage above, "or both": a high old time, but not without a certain disorder, an attendant ambivalence.[48] Ultimately, however, the most authoritative gloss comes from Hal himself—when Hal, no longer himself but the newly crowned Henry V, puts his apprentice days behind him and redefines, in retrospect, the world of festivity and popular pastimes as mere confusion and disorder, to be banished like the gross terms and immodest words of any strange tongue.

Learning strange tongues or collecting strange things, rehearsing the words and ways of marginal or alien cultures, upholding idleness for a while—these are the activities of a culture in the process of extending its boundaries and reformulating itself, and they embody a form of license, a suspension of customary limits, taboos, and other modes of cultural definition, that can only be temporary, a thing of passage. To speak of the sixteenth century as a period of transition is, of course, nothing new. But the shock we continue to feel at the end of *2 Henry IV*, when Hal achieves his own transition, suggests that we have yet to comprehend the cultural process by which a moment such as this is made inevitable—as inevitable, in its way, as the consummate Brazilian performance we encountered outside of Rouen:

> *Falstaff:* My King, my Jove! I speak to thee, my heart!
>
> *King:*   I know thee not, old man. Fall to thy prayers.
>   How ill white hairs becomes a fool and jester!

> I have long dreamt of such a kind of man,
> So surfeit-swell'd, so old, and so profane;
> But being awak'd I do despise my dream.
> Make thy body hence, and more thy grace;
> Leave gourmandizing; know the grave doth gape
> For thee thrice wider than for other men.
> Reply not to me with a fool-born jest;
> Presume not that I am the thing I was;
> For God doth know, so shall the world perceive,
> That I have turn'd away my former self;
> So will I those that kept me company.
> When thou dost hear I am as I have been,
> Approach me, and thou shalt be as thou wast,
> The tutor and feeder of my riots.
> Till then I banish thee, on pain of death.
>
> (*2HIV*, V. v. 46ff.)

At Westminster Abbey, Falstaff and his companions are the only gross terms to be literally cast off. The old knight presents a rather large figure, however: he is a medieval Vice, a decadent noble and coward, an irrepressible spirit of wit, a religious rebel, a quite substantial embodiment of the festive impulse. "It is hard," as Empson said, "to get one's mind all round him."[49] And despite all the anticipations of the promised end, as well as all that has been written on the topic since Morgann, the banishment of Falstaff also remains hard for criticism to comprehend or encompass. It still takes us somehow by surprise, and can prove discomfiting. According to C. L. Barber, it is the playwright's aesthetic failure that makes us uneasy; at the point of Falstaff's rejection we slip from the world of festive comedy back into untransformed ritual, and Shakespeare slips with us.[50] Jonas Barish records a more significant rupture in the scene, a forcible and even violent displacement of play and audience "from the domain of comedy to the grimmer realm of history."[51] Yet *Henry IV* never was a comedy; its genre like its language is mixed throughout. What surprises us is not the event itself but the fact that the world being cast off has been so consummately rehearsed: so fully represented to us, and consequently so fully foreclosed. We do not move into history at the end of the play so much as we feel the abrupt shock of history on the move, transforming itself and its direction, taking over rhythms proper to ritual and imbuing them with a new morality and an unprecedented purpose. The ritual course of language identified in Warwick's simile does not merely reflect back upon Hal's career, his character, or his intentions, whether good, bad, or politic; nor does it merely look forward to the end so often anticipated, to prepare us once again for the banishment we always knew was on its way. Rather,

Warwick's gloss on the play opens out onto a dramaturgy much larger than Shakespeare's tetralogy, one being performed, as it were, by history itself.

The course of instruction is a curious one—a passage through certain aspects of the vernacular, strange tongues and the companions who speak them—yet it is an apt description of our experience of *Henry IV* and of the historical moment which produced it. It is a course Natalie Davis has also charted in her study of the raids upon popular culture being made by French collectors of proverbs during the same period. In French, too, the gross or vulgar—terms which were themselves in the process of acquiring the moral opprobrium they carry today—were being for a while upheld, entertained, to an extent assimilated, and then cast off. "As the language perfected itself," Davis writes, "it pulled away from the proverbial style and rejected with disdain all words that were lowered by passing too often through the mouths of the people."[52] In Elizabethan England, such disdain was increasingly focused on the popular stage—a collection of strange things, marginal pastimes, and subcultures, to be sure, but one that was itself lodged on the tenuous margins of its society, as much an object of ambivalent fascination as any of the other extravagant and extraneous cultural phenomena being maintained and, for a while, upheld by the period.

A new sense of propriety was in the wings, listening to the language of the stage with an ear attuned to the gross and improper. Words "fetched from Latin inkhorne or borrowed of strangers seldom are pleasant," according to Puttenham,

> saving perchaunce to the common people, who reioyce much to be at playes and enterludes, and besides their natural ignoraunce, have at all times their eares so attentive to the matter, and their eyes upon the shewes of the stage, that they take little heede to the cunning of the rime and therefore be as well satisfied with that which is grosse, as with any other finer and more delicate.[53]

Shakespeare could hardly have been unaware of the fragility of the social and cultural conditions that made possible the range of language, character, and ideology that we properly locate at the heart of his dramaturgy. He was an Elizabethan playwright, which is to say that he was continually reminded of the potential (if not inevitable) consummation of the cultural license enjoyed by popular drama. His company was annually rehearsed by the Court and barely tolerated by a city which, quite against its own will, also provided its livelihood. London annually threatened that livelihood, but in 1597—the year of composition for *1 Henry IV*—it seemed on the verge of translating threat into reality for the first time in nearly fifty years. The city had won an unprecedented order from the Privy Council, calling for "the present staie and fynall suppressinge of . . . stage plays, as well at the Theatre, Curten, banckside, as in all other places in and about this Citie."[54] It is difficult today to say why the order had such little effect; it was impossible to predict at the time that it would not severely constrict the world Shakespeare inhabited—the world so amply represented in the "prodigally lavish" economy of *Henry IV*, and so fully proscribed at its close.

V

History moves at a different pace than drama does, as Shakespeare's histories always remind us; the world that felt threatened in 1597, the world being rehearsed and maintained by the dominant cultures of early modern society as they redefined themselves and their domains, was upheld for a while longer. When history does move, however, it moves along the lines intimated by Shakespeare's second tetralogy: toward the regulation of the vernacular into a clear and ordered discourse, and toward the suppression of popular ritual and pastimes that Weber christened as "the disenchantment of the world."[55]

In England, the disenchantment was more abrupt, the shock of history on the move more pointedly dramatic; as a result, the paradoxical process by which such a conclusion is achieved or made inevitable also comes into clearer focus. An anecdote from the Commonwealth reveals in miniature the outlines of that process.[56] In 1649, a Parliamentary soldier entered a village church in Surrey, at the moment when evening services were drawing to a close. He bore a lantern in one hand and four candles in the other, and declared that he carried a message from God, to be delivered to the parishioners. Denied the use of the pulpit, he went into the churchyard to make his message known. His vision consisted of five points, each an example of what was "merely ceremonial" in the church, and to be abolished: the Sabbath, tithes, ministers, magistrates, and finally the Bible itself, which was to be rejected as a repository of ceremonies and practices no longer necessary, "now Christ himself is in Glory amongst us." But the abolition of all ceremony was ceremoniously conducted. For each of his cardinal points, the soldier lit a candle from the lantern; describing the ceremony to be abolished, he extinguished the corresponding flame and declared the feat accomplished. When he reached the Bible he set fire to its leaves, allowed it to be fully consumed, then put out the lantern itself, declaring, "And here my fifth light is extinguished." What he performed was a working through of Church ceremony, a last rite for Christian ritual. That he employed ceremony to extinguish ceremony was a contradiction, but just such a contradiction was fundamental to the recreation of early modern culture: a process that begins in the adoption of the strange, and that ends with a full entrance into and performance of alien and residual cultures, consummately rehearsed and thus consummately foreclosed.

It is a process that Hal first performs proleptically when he steps forward to announce the shape of his future "reformation." He steps out of the play that is at once his context and his vehicle, and in a sense he steps into a historical moment that does not yet exist, except on the stage he occupies. It is a position that allows the gross terms and improprieties of Shakespeare's language to be observed, as if in retrospect; for all the attacks on the stage, it is a form of observation or surveillance, a view of the strange or gross as Error, that Dryden, looking back on Shakespeare from the stage of history itself, associates with the Restoration:

> Neither would I be understood, when I speak of impropriety of language, either wholly to accuse the last age, or to excuse the present; and least of all, myself; for all writers have their imperfections and failings; but I may safely conclude in the general, that our improprieties are less frequent, and less gross than theirs. One testimony of this is undeniable; that we are the first who have observed them; and, certainly, to observe errours is a great step to the correcting of them.[57]

Our course through the rehearsal of cultures in the Renaissance suggests that the observation of Error is a more complex and paradoxical process than Dryden's self-satisfaction can quite comprehend. If Dryden's language is, in his terms, less gross or improper, this is only because Shakespeare's language was what it was. The first stage of Dryden's observation was not passive, but an active participation in all that passed for the gross, the improper, the anomalous, the strange.

The terms are ones Shakespeare rehearses once again, in the last play of the Lancastrian cycle. Against Dryden's retrospective on the state of Shakespeare's language, we should juxtapose the playwright's own rearward glance at the improprieties that occupied the ambivalent center of Hal's prodigality. I began with a list of strange things gathered together in an Elizabethan wonder-cabinet, and would conclude with another list, a strange wonder in its own peculiar way, as recited by Katharine of Valois:

> Le foot, et le count? O Seigneur Dieu! ils sont les mots de son mauvais, corruptible, gros, et impudique, et non pour les dames d'honneur d'user. Je ne voudrais pronouncer ces mots devant les seigneurs de France, pour tout le monde. Foh! le foot et le count! Néanmoins je

reciterai une autre fois ma leçon ensemble: d'hand, de fingre, de nails,
d'arm, d'elbow, de nick, de sin, de foot, le count. (*Henry V*, III.iv.52ff.)

Marx notoriously suggested that the major events of history occur
twice: once as tragedy, and again as farce. Tragedy may be too strong
a term for the catastrophe of Hal's language lesson, but Katharine's
scene of instruction is indeed borrowed from French farce, and as
such is nearly unique in Elizabethan drama.[58] What we have is a fully
staged language lesson, conducted in one strange tongue and concerned with another; quite literally, Katharine's list is a recital or
rehearsal of gross terms. Most striking after *Henry IV* is the ease with
which Katharine first rejects what is gross and dishonorable and then
revisits it, repeats it, recites it anew. The sign of that ease is "néanmoins": once the strange has been proscribed as gross Error, it can
be allowed to return, but in a much reduced and vitiated form. Like
Katharine's gross terms, Falstaff and his companions will return, or
so we are promised—but not until "their conversations / Appear more
wise and modest to the world" (*2HIV*, V. v. 100–101). The old knight
passes with a great deal less ease than Katharine's gross terms; his
rehearsal reaches its final conclusion offstage, and "néanmoins" is the
word missing from his babbling end. Nevertheless, as Katharine would
say, he returns to the stage in *The Merry Wives of Windsor*, where he
will "speak like an Anthropophaginian" (IV.v.8): still an emblem of
strange tongues and unsavory cultures, but reduced to the only stage
provided for such repeat performances—that of farce.

4

Apprehending Subjects, or the
Reformation in the Suburbs

I

In March of 1500, Remirro de Orco was appointed lieutenant general of the Romagna, recently conquered but not yet subdued by the duke of Valentino, more familiarly known as Cesare Borgia. De Orco's task was to reduce the land to submission if not obedience, and within a period of two years he had succeeded, largely through the brutal and vigorous elimination of all opposing factions. Borgia's use for his lieutenant did not end, however, with de Orco's success. "The recent harshness," as Machiavelli recounts with characteristic understatement, "had generated some hatred."[1] In order to win the hearts and minds of the people, Borgia needed a device to make clear to them that the reign of terror was at an end, a device that, more crucially, would "purge their spirits ... and make plain that whatever cruelty had occurred had come, not from him, but from the brutal character of the minister." On December 26, 1502, the townspeople of Cesena awoke to discover such an emblem or device decorating their public square, in the form of a human body neatly cut in two and framed by a length of wood and a bloody knife. The body, of course, was de Orco's; the people, Machiavelli tells us, were both stunned and satisfied by the scene, "satisfatti e stupidi."

There was no trial, no procession through the streets, no public reenactment or charting of the condemned man's misdeeds—and I would add, in order to emphasize the pristine and almost surgical acuity of Borgia's mise-en-scène, no disembowelment *in vivo* or any of the other protracted rites of death which characterized juridical executions of the period. Such a show of legality could have been staged, even with an understandably recalcitrant de Orco, but at the obvious risk of straining the credulity of the populace. No one could have thought that de Orco's rapaciousness was unlicensed, that Borgia had saved them from anything other than his own designs—designs that included, moreover, their carefully timed and orchestrated salvation—and Borgia does not ask for such belief. If anything, he disposes of his lieutenant in a manner that accentuates his unseen hand, acknowledging rather than denying his controlling offstage presence, but in a manner that also fosters a certain complicity with his subjects. He presents the town with a body but denies access to and observation of its progress toward death. De Orco's death violates customary proceedings, both juridical and ritual; it withdraws from the public eye, but only to expand and occupy a larger and more significant realm in the public imagination. Stunned by the grisly scene to which they awake, provided with no commentary or explanation, the people must supply what is missing, make of de Orco's body what they will; their interpretation and response occupy center stage along with that body, which thus precipitates a vicarious participation and investment in the scene. In their satisfaction, the people are not so much deceived as induced to suspend their disbelief willingly, to accept and enter into their self-deception, prompted by the allure of a convenient object for their hatred and fear, a much-desired catharsis that would "purge their spirits"—a scapegoat who, like any scapegoat, is effective because he is at least a partial fiction, a symbolic object constituted as such by an entire community. The duke supplies a body, bisected and emblematically arrayed; the people in turn supply a defining and hence comforting narrative sequence, a historical drama that structures their recent experience and encourages them to fix what has transpired as past and to project, out of their own hopes and fears, a more promising future. A body, a club, a bloody knife: the time of brute force is past, the blunt and indiscriminate reign of the club has been supplanted by a power that would, as Escalus says in *Measure for Measure,* "be keen, and rather cut a little, / Than fall, and bruise to death" (II.i.5–6). The import of the tableau was manifest to all, not so much believed as *credited* by all— in part because the townspeople had invested their own imaginations in it, because they had, to a certain and telling extent, been induced to create it themselves.

In the sixteenth century, Borgia's manipulation of the hearts and minds of his subjects achieved a notoriety that extended far beyond the boundaries of the Romagna. Machiavelli not only accords it a prominent place in *The Prince,* presenting the incident as "worthy of special note, and of imitation by others," but also recapitulates it at least twice in his letters; Innocent Gentillet returns to it obsessively in his so-called "contra-Machiavel,"[2] and a little over a century after de Orco's death it would be restaged again in a different forum and an altered but resonant fashion. Another duke, faced not with a new conquest but with an increasingly unruly populace, would appoint a lieutenant to strike "in th' ambush of [his] name" and to impose what he confesses will be a repressive tyranny; like Borgia, this ruler would also show his hand at the right moment, "save" his subjects from the repression he had visited upon them, and dispose of his surrogate in an appropriately public and effective fashion. True, Duke Vincentio only *threatens* his scapegoat and substitute with death; the only dismembered body to appear on the stage of *Measure for Measure* is that of Ragozine the pirate, beheaded after a convenient demise from natural causes. But Shakespeare's Duke is nonetheless a figure far removed from the detached symbol of justice found in the canonically accepted sources for the play—removed enough that at least one critic has found that he bears an uncanny family resemblance to Machiavelli's duke. Tracing similarities between Shakespeare's play and Gentillet's account of Borgia's actions, Norman N. Holland has argued that Shakespeare not only read Gentillet but also read *through* his moralizing, anti-Machiavellian platitudes (while reproducing many of his misreadings) to recover the essence of Machiavelli. In a credible act of close reading, Holland suggests that Shakespeare's reliance on and divergence from Gentillet reveals Borgia as a sort of spiritual father to Duke Vincentio, Machiavelli and his "shrewd awareness of the need for dramatic effects in government" as something of a ghostly, indirect source for Shakespeare.[3]

Source study, even at its best, typically goes no further. Writing at a time when criticism commonly portrayed Shakespeare's Duke as an emblem of divine justice, Holland sought to cloud the assurance of such readings by casting a Machiavellian shadow over *Measure for Measure,* and in this effort he succeeded admirably. He establishes a convincing relationship between the two texts, but assumes the significance of that relationship is obvious—that our awareness of a certain passage from *The Prince* will, insofar as our awareness was shared by Shakespeare, interpret the play for us. However convincing in its details, such an approach to two highly problematic and historically determined texts necessarily strips them of their particular cultural contexts to establish a strictly linear and narrowly literary relationship between them. At best, such a perspective fails to allow for a more searching and historically significant ambition in Shakespeare's return to Machiavelli; at worst, it collapses a century of tumultuous history into a case of literary influence—a century which, for Shakespeare, included not only

Machiavelli but also the emergence of a thriving theater with its own capacities to stun and satisfy. Even the theatricality with which Duke Vincentio manages his various subjects in the final act of the play is, in Holland's account, attributed to Machiavelli—as if Shakespeare, at this point in his career as a playwright and an English subject, needed such a tutor in either the theatricality of power or in the power of the theatrical, as if "dramatic effect" could adequately address the theater of subjection staged in either Machiavelli's Romagna or Shakespeare's Vienna.

In the Romagna, as I have already suggested, Borgia in fact eschews much of the attendant "drama" the populace might have expected. Rather than present the town with a familiar juridical ritual—one that in the given circumstances would register as a patent and unconvincing fiction—Borgia provides instead a stark and emblematic representation, a shocking *tableau mort* capable of drawing the townspeople into it, both as interpreters and as subjects—as subjects produced and reconstituted, in fact, by their interpretive investment in the scene. Whether sacred or secular, ritual relies upon and produces a certain consensus of belief; although highly dramaturgical, it functions effectively only in a relatively stable hierarchical society. Seeking to destabilize and redefine hierarchy, Borgia's disposition of his lieutenant displaces ritual toward the province of what would properly be called the theatrical. "The theater," as Stephen Greenblatt has recently remarked, "elicits from us complicity rather than belief,"[4] and as Greenblatt would be the first to acknowledge, the inducement of such complicity in the sixteenth and seventeenth centuries was not limited to the theatrical institution itself. In recent criticism, however, the theatricality of early modern power has become something of a catchphrase, enough so that it is in danger of being emptied of all meaning as it is applied indiscriminately to any public cultural performance staged by the powers that be. Greenblatt's distinction between theater and ritual is a crucial one, not only for distinguishing the power of the stage from the dramaturgical effects of customary ritual but also for aligning the stage with other cultural forums in the period, in which customary ritual and spectacle were being displaced to achieve a vicarious sense of complicity in the subject, a theatrically induced investment in the dramaturgy of state.

Leo Salingar once observed that passing from Shakespeare's early comedies to *Measure for Measure* was "like passing from the Renaissance to the Reformation;"[5] it is such a passage that I want to explore—that I believe Shakespeare's play explores in some depth—but I begin as I have in order to remind us of another, less

benign version of the Renaissance than Salingar had in mind, and
one which has a clear bearing not only on Duke Vincentio's own
manipulations of princely surrogates and subjects but also on the
cultural situation of the popular stage in Shakespeare's time. I want
to suggest, in other words, that Machiavelli is less a literary source
for Shakespeare than a cultural locus, recollected in order to define
a historical continuum whose origin is assigned to *The Prince* and
whose culmination is, in *Measure for Measure,* located on the boards
of the English popular stage. No less than Machiavelli's treatise,
Measure for Measure is, in its brief scope, an encyclopedic exploration
of the workings and limits of exemplary power, or more accurately,
a compressed history and genealogy of such power and of the
cultural pressures that would, in the course of the sixteenth century,
necessitate its increasing theatricalization. Among those pressures,
Shakespeare's play encompasses, of necessity, a great deal that Machiavelli could not address—including the most significant displacement of customary ritual and spectacle experienced by the period,
which is to say, the Reformation itself.

II

Any culture defines itself in terms of its Others, whether imaginary
or real; what a given culture excludes as alien can, however, come
back to haunt it. Having divorced themselves from Rome but not
supplanted it entirely, the Protestant countries of early modern
Europe were not only confronted with an ongoing and tenuous
struggle for political and religious stability; they were also confronted with the continuing presence of what was, for them, their
own past. Whether they made the journey in person or in print,
English travelers to the Continent in the late sixteenth and early
seventeenth centuries were well aware, sometimes acutely so, that
they were traveling in time as well as space, viewing cultures that
were, in a certain sense, living fossils of themselves, that might have
been themselves had their own culture not reconstituted or reformed itself so radically. Thus, for John Aubrey, the vicarious
experience of Europe provided by Edwin Sandys' *Europae Speculum*
results not in a reflection on the current state of affairs on the
Continent but rather in a retrospective speculation upon all that
England had relegated to a dead past. The mirror of Europe was
a glass in which to view the way things had and might have been:

> Then the Crusado's to the Holy War were most magnificent and
> glorious, and the rise, I believe, of the adventures of knights errant

and romances. The solemnities of processions in and about the fields, besides their convenience, were fine pleasing diversions: the priests went before in their formalities, singing the Latin service, and the people came after, making their good-meaning responses. The reverence given to holy men was very great. Then were the churches open all day long, men and women going daily in and out hourly, to and from their devotions. Then were the consciences of the people kept in so great awe by confession, that just dealing and virtue was habitual.[6]

That Aubrey's pre-Reformation utopia never existed does not mean it did not occupy a significant place in the cultural imagination; nor was such a vision limited to expressions of sheer conservatism or cultural nostalgia for the past we have lost—for what is, in the passage above, a religious variant of the period's sheerly mythic recollection of "merrie old England."

For an early reformer like William Tyndale, the ability of the Roman Church to weave itself into the social fabric of everyday life was without qualification pernicious. Blaming the Peasants' Revolt of 1525 on the "bloody doctrines of the pope" himself, Tyndale could complain that "we have sucked such bloody imaginations into the bottom of our hearts, even with our mother's milk."[7] By the early seventeenth century, however, the efficacy of Catholic ritual and practice could evoke not only the expected fear and loathing but also a grudging and politic admiration. Here, for example, are William Bedell's reflections on the discipline of mother's milk, prompted by his observation of children's games in Venice circa 1608:

noe sooner doe their Children almost creep out of their Cradles, but they are taught to be Idolators. They have certain childish processions, wherein are carryed about certain puppets, made for their Lady, and some boy that is better Clerke than his fellows goes before them with the words of the Popish litany; where the rest of the fry following make up the quire. A great tyrant is custome, and a great advantage hath that discipline which is suck'd in with the mothers milke. But to convey superstition into the minds of that tender age under the form of sport, and play, which it esteemeth more than meat and drinke, is a deeper pointe of policy, and such as wise men would profitably suck somewhat out of it for imitation to a right end.[8]

As his tone suggests, Bedell was hardly a papal sympathizer; indeed, he was in Venice as something of an agent provocateur, seeking to turn the city's dissatisfaction with Rome into a cause for secession, and he even entertained serious if misguided hopes that the independent state thereby created would be a Reformed one. What moves him to reconsider the efficacy of ritual practice, the policy of sport and play, are not ideological second thoughts but rather a nagging sense that, in strategic terms, the Reformation may have succeeded all too well.

"Power can neither see, work, nor devise," as Fulke Greville notes in *Mustapha,* "Without the people's hands, hearts, wit, and eyes" (*Chorus Secundus,* 207–8).[9] It is an astute anatomy, born as it is of the recognition that power is never merely a coercive or repressive force, that it must not be limited to acting upon its subjects but must instead, to be effective, act through them as well, inducing them to participate and even to become the primary actors in the ongoing drama of their own subjection. From a Protestant perspective, however, such a recognition was also inescapably double-edged; it is in Venice, not in London, that Bedell finds the fullest manifestation of such an incorporative power in action, seeing, working, and devising through even toddlers' hands, hearts, wit, and eyes. The customs and practices that the Reformation excoriated as idolatrous fictions were no less powerful for being branded as fictions or, to use the period's terminology, as theater; the image of the Church that the Reformation had defined itself against— that of a tightly organized and monolithic power structure, ruling from within the minds of kings and paupers alike, quelling or otherwise managing all forms of internal dissent—was in itself partly a fiction, but it was one that projected onto the enemy the capacity to resolve and even to preempt social and political dilemmas at their source, and by means of a process of ideological inscription that a country like Elizabethan England had denied itself.[10] In a time of unprecedented cultural change and social mobility, Bedell was hardly alone in feeling the need for a greater and more affective access to the hearts and minds of the people. "In times past," writes George Whetstone in *A Mirrour for Magistrates,* "a Proclamation, would keep men in awe; and nowe, an Example of Justice, scarce makes the wicked change their countenaunce."[11] Rome got obedience; England could scarcely succeed in making its subjects blink. Lacking the bureaucracy necessary for the policing and surveillance of its populace, early modern England was forced to rely upon a system of exemplary justice, of public and often spectacular punishment, that sought to instill the proper degree of awe and fear in the minds of the people but was at best inadequate to the task—if not contrary to it. "We have found by wofull experience," as Coke himself observed, "that it is not frequent and often punishment that doth prevent like offenses. . . . Those offenses are often committed that are often punished, for the frequency of the punishment makes it so familiar as it is not feared."[12]

Punishment makes familiar both the crime and its consequences, but with a crucial difference. Frequent punishment advertises the taboo or the forbidden as a common occurrence, and at the same time inures its audience to the spectacle of the law taking hold of and inscribing itself upon the body of the condemned. Exemplary power not only fails to deter, it even produces and promulgates the very transgressions it acts upon—by the mere fact that it must act upon them, giving them a currency or circulation they would not otherwise possess. Coke is not, I should hasten to add, mounting an argument against corporal punishment. If punishment is no deterrent of crime, if the two are locked into an exponentially expanding and vertiginous cycle of reciprocity, this does not mean that crime should be allowed to act as a deterrent upon punishment. For Coke as for Michel Foucault, sovereign power exists only to the degree that it makes itself manifest; the paradoxical effects of its manifestation do not argue against its operation, but they do underline the need for a supplement, a less spectacular and more incorporative form of power—one that would augment the discipline of patriarchal authority with something like the discipline of mother's milk, such as William Bedell would glimpse in the deeper policy of Venetian sport and play.

Taken together, Bedell and Coke define a significant rent in the social fabric, an opening in the cultural and political landscape that produced, to say the least, considerable anxiety and controversy. In another but no less anxious or controversial sense, however, it was also an opening necessary for the emergence of popular drama in Elizabethan and Jacobean England. Like any emergent cultural phenomenon that is marginal to the dominant hierarchy of its times yet also achieves a significant viability, the popular stage was born of the contradictions of the culture that produced it; insofar as it manifested those contradictions it was perceived, and rightly so, as an illegitimate product at best, an embarrassment if not a threat. And yet the stage also claimed to provide something like the deeper policy Bedell had in mind, to be not merely an embodiment but also a resolution of the period's internal contradictions, a potent forum for the reformation as well as the recreation of its audience. Whatever we make of such claims—and I will want to take them seriously here—it must be acknowledged that the emergence of popular drama in Renaissance England was not merely or even primarily a literary phenomenon. In an age of limited literacy and restricted access to knowledge, that emergence represented a sig-

nificant expansion of what might be called the symbolic economy
of the period—by which I mean the entire repertoire of cultural
forces, official and unofficial, that shaped the ideological subject
and defined his or her place in the cultural community. In its official
domain, the symbolic economy of the period ranged from the pulpit, press, and other forums for the controlled dissemination of
knowledge to the various cultural performances through which
officially sanctioned images of power and community were placed
in circulation, displayed, and performed before the populace. The
Reformation severely restricted this official domain, and at a time
of expanding social and political demands upon the dominant hierarchy. The Tudor state sought to compensate for such a restric-
tion and address such demands, but its efforts could not escape a
contradiction fundamental to the operation of sovereign power
within a relatively closed symbolic economy. Coke's dilemma—that
even officially sanctioned and adroitly staged manifestations of sovereign power could produce contrary and unexpected effects—
clarifies the vulnerability of such power as it was forced to enlarge
its profile, to familiarize its spectacular operation, to open itself up
to an enhanced scrutiny and observation it could neither fully control nor shape to its own designs.

For both Elizabeth and James, such vulnerability was the sign of
a discomfiting theatricality. "We princes," Elizabeth told a deputation of Lords and Commons in 1586, "are set upon stages in the
sight and view of all the world."[13] Out of context, her pronouncement can easily be given an air of bold assertion, of a power over-
coming its inadequacies to achieve a full and even exultant mastery
over the dramaturgical demands upon it. In context, however, Elizabeth's assertion was in fact a rather vexed and apprehensive complaint. The deputation of Lords and Commons were demanding
that she sign a death warrant for Mary Queen of Scots; Elizabeth
wanted the execution to go forward, but without her explicit order
for the death of a sister-monarch and kinswoman.[14] What sets Elizabeth on stage is one of the more momentous genealogical crises
of authority in the sixteenth century; her visibility is not a sign of
sovereign potency but of her own discomfiting subjection to the
sight and view of all the world, and her apprehension over what
that world would make of her hand in Mary's death. At the beginning of the controversy, Elizabeth had declared, "I know what it is
to be a subject, what to be a Soveraigne;"[15] by its end, when an-
nouncing her stage presence, she had discovered what it was like
to be both at once.

In the course of her reign, Elizabeth would adjust with remarkable dexterity to the theatrical apprehension of sovereign power—to a form of theatricality not so much commanded by her as visited upon her. Her successor learned his lesson with less grace, but even before his ascension to the English throne he had registered the constraints that conditioned sovereign power once its image entered into circulation. Cautioning his son that the royal countenance must be made public only with great care and on limited occasions, James wrote that "a King is as one set on a skaffold, whose smallest actions and gestures al the people gazingly doe behold."[16] Even a king with James' absolutist ambitions had to recognize that a certain power resides in the eye of the beholder—that the power wielded by the monarch, the power he was invested with, was to a large degree invested in him by the gaze of his subjects. The royal image and identity were not wholly at the king's command but were in part the projection and hence the product of those subjects. Power can neither see, work, nor devise without the people's hands, heart, wit, and eyes.

In later editions of *Basilicon Doron*, James would emend the ambiguous "skaffold" to "stage"—a response, as Stephen Orgel has suggested, to "the danger James must have felt to be inherent in the royal drama" of the English popular stage, where monarchs brought on the dramatic scaffold often ended their careers on its juridical counterpart.[17] The emendation serves to remind us that the symbolic economy of the period was not limited to the official or dominant hierarchy but was increasingly open to unofficial and at least partly illicit cultural phenomena. Most prominent among them was the popular stage, occupying a cultural and ideological ground made available to it by the Reformation in England and claiming to foster a reformation of its own—a reformation of the political and ideological subject, of the eye and mind of the beholder to which Elizabeth and James found themselves subject.

III

Like most of its predecessors, Thomas Heywood's *Apology for Actors* is not primarily a moral defense of the stage; rather, it is a political and sociological treatise, pointedly addressed to anxieties produced by the Reformation itself. Thus Heywood presents the stage as a powerful and much-needed instrument of policy, both foreign and domestic. As an ornament to the city, a viable theater serves to attract and impress visitors from other realms; as a forum that is at once literary and social, it provides a laboratory for the further refinement and promulgation of the vernacular; and last but not least, drama offers an exemplary and effective form of social control, one that can, in Heywood's terms, instruct the illiterate, teach the unlearned, and make "the ignorant more apprehensive." By making men "see and shame at their faults," drama induces them to reform themselves "lest they should happen to become the like subject of general scorne to an auditory."[18]

Describing the theater in such terms, Heywood locates it at a significant threshold of the early modern period, a threshold that is at once linguistic and social. The stage is a theater of apprehension in both the traditional sense of that term, which up until the early seventeenth century referred to the relatively neutral process of mentally grasping or comprehending something in its entirety, and in the modern sense of self-reflexive shame, dread, or anxiety—a sense that is both new to Heywood's generation and that makes its earliest recorded appearances on the Elizabethan stage. I will want to return to this notion of an apprehending, and consequently apprehensive, audience; for the moment, I would note that when confronted with such a claim—that dramatic recreation contributed to the re-creation or reformation of its audience— modern criticism has tended either to discount it entirely or to embrace it too immediately. Responding to the echoes of an archaic tradition, that of the morality play, which indeed pervades such defenses of the stage, we regard those echoes as irrelevant or not depending on how we view the drama in question—as either an ambivalent and potentially subversive phenomenon or as one that served primarily to reinforce and reflect well-established cultural norms and dominant ideologies. The period was forced to take Heywood's claim more seriously, however, and in quite different terms. The affective powers of the stage were a source of apprehension for the learned as well as the ignorant; at least where the antitheatrical opposition was concerned, those powers were neither doubted nor embraced, but were instead branded as illegitimate, unlawful, even sacrilegious. "Players," as I.G. framed the issue in his response to the *Apology*, "assume an unlawfull office to themselves of instruction and correction."[19] It was an office usurped not only from God's appointed magistrates, but also from his duly anointed ministers:

> God gave authority to instruct and preach, to correct and anathametize, which is the keyes of heaven, only to the Apostles and their successors, and not to Players. . . . it were most impious . . . to mixe Divinity with scurrility on the stage.[20]

The specter Heywood has raised with his talk of shame and apprehension before a judgmental auditory is a considerable one; what I.G. fears is a return, in a dramatically altered but all the more demonic form, of the ghostly practice the Reformation sought most strenuously to suppress—the *psychotyrrani* of auricular, sacramental confession, through which the Church exercised its power to "sit in the consciences of men."[21]

Although the association is not an uncommon one in the antitheatrical literature of the times,[22] it is nonetheless a curious one. Indeed, it is hard to imagine two cultural phenomena with less in common than the playhouse and the confessional. It is not the confessional that is at issue, however—not, at any rate, the darkened, private, compartmentalized enclosure in which confessor and penitent sat, separated by a partition with the familiar mesh-grille. Such a device was the product of the Counter-Reformation, and did not appear in England until long afterwards; designed and popularized by Cardinal Borromeo in the late sixteenth century, it provided, for the first time since the institution of mandatory annual confession by the Fourth Lateran Council, the penitential technology necessary to insure a genuinely private and verifiably chaste examination of the soul. (To insure that the examination would be of the soul and not the body, Borromeo went so far as to specify that the holes in the grille were to be "about the size of a pea," small enough to prevent the smallest appendage from passing through; presumably the appendage that Borromeo had in mind was the confessor's little finger.)[23] Prior to the introduction of the cardinal's box, however, confession was hardly such a discreet affair. Qualified confessors were few, and the demands upon them as the end of Lent drew near were such that the privacy of confession was at best a euphemism. "It occurred," as John Bossy suggests, "once a year, in the not-so-remote presence of a large number of neighbors."[24] Indeed, judging from what we know of the behavior of sixteenth-century churchgoers during services, their behavior while waiting for confession must have had its entertaining aspects.[25] We must imagine a substantial gathering, composed of both men and women and filling a moderately large hall; despite a certain rowdiness—a game of dice in one corner, a bargain being struck, bawdy jokes making their rounds—the attention of those present would have been focused on the two figures at the front of the gathering, engaged in dialogue and apparently oblivious to, although not necessarily beyond the hearing of, the spectators and auditors waiting to perform their own annual Christian duty.

Whatever the social drama or carnivalesque atmosphere that may have attended annual confession for the majority of the populace, however, sacramental confession was still largely an internal drama, one staged within the soul but also performed before a judgmental authority, at times harrowingly silent, at times sharply inquisitorial. The confessor's silence, like his questioning, produced further self-scrutiny, an internal dialogue in which, as Michel Foucault has suggested, the penitent was induced to take on at one and the same time the roles of subject, object, and inquisitor.[26] The process may not always have produced the paralyzing psychological tyranny that figures like Luther felt,[27] but it was certainly a more acute experience than the general Protestant confession that replaced it. The Reformation had sought to eliminate the apprehensive powers of confession, and for a man like William Tyndale such powers were no mere psychological or spiritual threat; they made sacramental confession a politically dangerous forum where nothing is secret, where the state and the family alike are an open book:

> All secrets they know thereby. . . . The pope, his cardinals and bishops, know the confession of the emperor, kings, and of all lords: and by confession they know all their captives. If any believe in Christ, by confession they know him. Shrive thyself where thou wilt, whether at Sion, Charterhouse, or at the Observants, thy confession is known well enough. . . . Wonderful are the things that thereby are wrought. The wife is feared, and compelled to utter not her own only, but also the secrets of her husband; and the servant the secrets of his master.[28]

By contrast, no one in the period could feel fear or anxiety, whether psychological or political, over the Protestant alternative. "Our protestant confessions," as Archbishop Bramhall complained, "are for the most part too general; we confess that we are sinners, and that's all. . . . and [we are] a little too careless, as if we were telling a story of a third person, that concerned not us."[29] Confessing one's sinful state in such general terms, and with such a lack of care and anxiety that one might as well be "telling a story of a third person," is quite different, however, from watching and listening to the story of a third person, dramatized in such a manner as to invite and even demand projection and identification. The former could only serve to reinforce the boundary between the self and a judgmental Other (in the case of Protestant confession, neither a minister nor a congregation, but God); the latter, in which the subject is not only viewing, enjoying, and judging but is also projecting his or her self into an ensemble of fictional characters, the subjects of their vicarious apprehension, does not so much dissolve that boundary as internalize it.

For us the latter experience is a familiar one, but for a period accustomed to a more abstract mode of dramatic representation, to the personification of absolute states of being—Vice and Virtue, Sedition and Youth, ad infinitum—rather than the individualized and concrete characterization of dramatic subjects, it was a compelling novelty. Enough so, that the language had to evolve to accommodate it, and by 1600—when the popular stage had achieved its full prominence—this new mode of characterization had necessitated a new term to describe it.[30] Here is Heywood again, registering the new art of playing, or rather, of "personation":

> What English blood seeing the person of any bold English presented and doth not hug his fame and hunny at his valor, pursuing him in his enterprise with his best wishes and as being wrapt in contemplation, offers him in his heart all prosperous performance, as if the performer were the man personated? so bewitching a thing is lively and well-spirited action, that it hath power to new mould the hearts of the spectators.[31]

Observing artificial others in such a fashion requires and induces enhanced powers of identification and introjection; such a form of apprehension, even in the older, strictly conceptual meaning of the term, necessarily blurs the boundary between the observing subject and the dramatic subject. From our distance it is difficult to grasp the full impact of such a theatrical transaction upon an audience for whom it was powerfully new, but we can at least agree with Robert Weimann's speculation that the new mode of characterization was a significant aspect of what he calls the "civilizing function" of the popular stage in society.[32] And we can go further, by recognizing that the stage was one of many cultural forces reshaping the self in early modern society.

As Norbert Elias has shown in his detailed and still invaluable studies of behavior manuals from the period, the social self began to be observed in new ways, to be shaped by cultural forces that fostered an enhanced degree of self-scrutiny, one that was wholly secular but all the more powerful. Sacramental confession, in which a subject spoke in great detail about his or her own life to a ghostly and judgmental authority, had also been organized around an acute process of self-observation and self-scrutiny, but its powers of inquiry had also been rigorously delimited, confined not only to the realm of sin but also to particular types and varieties of sin. (Prostitutes, for example, were exempt from annual confession, on the

assumption that they could not be sincerely penitent about a trade
they intended to return to—a trade, moreover, to which the Church
had granted a de facto if grudging license.)[33] The development
Elias has traced in the period represents, on the one hand, the
secularization and extension of the realm of scrutiny from that of
sin to the minutiae of everyday life, and on the other, the incorporation of judgmental authority within the self. The result was
an expanded threshold of shame and apprehension, created by
complementary processes of internalization and socialization:

> The conflict expressed in shame-fear is not merely a conflict of the
> individual with prevalent social opinion; the individual's behaviour
> has brought him into conflict with the part of himself that represents
> social opinion. It is a conflict within his own personality; he himself
> recognizes himself as inferior.[34]

For Elias, this conflict within the self marks an expansion of the
social and psychological domain of the superego; produced as it is
by an imaginary identification with an Other whose perspective is
both incorporated within and turned upon the self, now viewed as
an inferior entity, it amounts to something like a cultural mirror-
stage—a mirror-stage in which the subject is not initially constituted
but rather reconstituted, reformed in a manner intricately involved
with the Reformation itself. In less global terms, the expanded
threshold of self-apprehension and shame in the period is the product of an induced division or splitting within the self, an internal
distantiation that creates a theater of and within the subject, in
which one views oneself as if on a stage, through the eyes of a
judgmental and imaginary Other.

The actual theater locates itself within this "civilizing process"—
a phrase, I should note, that Elias uses with a fine irony—when it
argues that plays "encrease the discipline of good manners;"[35] coming late to the controversy over the stage, Heywood gives us the
clearest portrait of the combined powers of identification, displacement, and incorporation that could produce in the subject a full
sense of apprehension. It is a sense of dread or shame, but also a
sense of being observed—as was indeed the case, insofar as the
drama that developed in the late sixteenth century fostered a vicarious participation and identification that made the spectators,
in an imaginary but potent sense, the object of their own gaze.
They "see and shame at *their* faults," meaning both their own and
those of their fictional counterparts; they incorporate and turn
upon themselves this combined perspective of self and other, "lest
they should happen to become the like subject of general scorne

to an auditory." I would agree with Stephen Greenblatt, however, when he argues that the affective powers of the Renaissance stage extended far beyond the realm of vice and virtue which, of necessity, defined a certain horizon of discourse for writers like Heywood:

> the mode of drama, quite apart from any specific content, depended upon and fostered in its audience *observation*, the close reading of gesture and speech as manifestations of character and intention; *planning*, a sensitivity to the consequences of action (i.e., plot) and to kairotic moments (i.e., rhetoric); and a sense of *resonance*, the conviction, rooted in the drama's medieval inheritance, that cosmic meanings were bound up with local and particular circumstances.[36]

The shift from the morality tradition, with its abstract representation of states-of-being, to a new mode of characterization—one in which, in Louis Montrose's terms, "the social dialectic, the syntax of interacting human characters, promotes the coherence and integrity of a fictional world"[37]—altered the threshold not only of dramatic representation but also of self-representation, not only of the fictional construction of character but also of the social construction of the self. The Renaissance stage does not merely reflect the larger civilizing process of its times; the destabilizing dialectic between self and other, audience and play, social and psychological constitutions of the subject which defined the complex theatrical transaction we know as Elizabethan and Jacobean drama was in itself an influential forum and laboratory for the production of the modern subject.[38]

We do not know, as far as I have been able to ascertain, what William Bedell thought of the policy of sport and play that developed on the Renaissance stage; for the antitheatrical opposition, popular drama was without doubt an imitation and pernicious resurgence of idolatrous practices, but hardly "imitation to a right end." It was not only the opposition, however, who perceived an analogy between the power of dramatic *quaestio* and that of pastoral inquiry, between the theatrical determination of the self and the intrusive, mediating, and detailed scrutiny of the soul that was at once performed and fostered by a priestly confessor. In *Measure for Measure*, Shakespeare not only raises such an analogy but also explores it quite thoroughly, in a play that also explores the relationship between the affective powers of the stage and the theatricality of power in Jacobean England.

IV

"Thoughts are no subjects," argues Isabella, kneeling before the Duke at the city gates of Vienna, "Intents, but merely thoughts"

(V. i. 451–52).[39] Although her suit proves unprofitable, it does not exactly fall on deaf ears. As she has just learned, the patriarchal figure before her is also the ghostly father she knows as Friar Lodowick, and in the course of the play his ears have become well-attuned to the thoughts and desires, sins and stratagems of his subjects; as she is about to learn, her plea for mercy is itself a manifest demonstration of the degree to which her thoughts have indeed become subjects, under the sway of a ruler who has adroitly if illicitly combined the powers of secular and ghostly patriarchy.

As Leonard Tennenhouse has demonstrated, *Measure for Measure* belongs to a genre of disguised-monarch plays which began to appear during the early plot- and plague-ridden reign of James I; like its brethren, it employs a fictive ruler's withdrawal from and return to power as a device for negotiating or managing the cultural anxieties attending the actual monarchical transition, and for exploring the shape of things to come.[40] And as Jonathan Goldberg has shown in his analysis of the style of Jacobean power, the play is acute not only in the degree to which it reveals the sustaining contradictions of James' rule, but also in the way it incorporates and appropriates those contradictions, making *Measure for Measure* "the clearest emblem for the relationship of literature and politics in the Jacobean period."[41] Among disguised monarchs of the Jacobean stage, however, Shakespeare's Duke is unique in the disguise he adopts: he takes off one mantle of authority to put on another, one which allows him not only to "visit both prince and people" incognito and spy into their overt deeds and expressed sentiments, but also to visit, as a ghostly father, the inner recesses of their souls. When he stages his return, he does not relinquish the power he has enjoyed as a confessor—to Isabella, Mariana, Claudio, and even, or so he claims, to Angelo—but rather translates that power into a new form and forum. Having "coined heaven's image / In stamps that are forbid"—Angelo's charge against illegitimate procreation is as fitting for the Duke's disguise as for Claudio's crime—the Duke allows the counterfeit to be exposed, but only at the point where the issue of his defrocking will be a new and inescapably theatrical economy of awe and apprehension.

Unrelated to anything in Shakespeare's sources or to other disguised-monarch plays of the period,[42] the Duke's disguise is unique in another sense as well: it is one of the few aspects of Vincentio that has not been viewed as an allusion to, comment upon, or reflection of James I. James did not, of course, don clerical robes himself, other than rhetorically ("your office," he told his son, "is likewise mixed, betwixt the Ecclesiastical and the civill estate: For

a King is not *merè laicus,* as both the Papists and Anabaptists would
have him");[43] he did, however, style himself as a monarch who had
a special capacity to peer into the secrets of state and subject alike,
and even before he ascended the English throne such claims had,
in conjunction with his actions, precipitated some concern in England. Writing from Kelston in 1603, Sir John Harrington mourned
the passing of Elizabeth and viewed, with a mixture of scorn and
apprehension, the passage of her successor towards London:

> Here now wyll I reste my troubelde mynde, and tende my sheepe
> like an Arcadian swayne, that hathe lost his faire mistresse; for in
> soothe, I have loste the beste and faireste love that ever shepherde
> knew, even my gracious Queene; and sith my good mistress is gone,
> I shall not hastily put forthe for a new master. I heare our new Kynge
> hathe hangede one man before he was tryede; 'tis strangely done:
> now if the wynde blowethe thus, why may not a man be tryed before
> he hathe offended [?][44]

Cast as it is in terms of pastoral elegy, Harrington's grief registers
the dexterity with which Elizabeth had adjusted to what I previously
defined as the theatrical apprehension of sovereign power. She
maintained her tenuous position as the female ruler of a patriarchal
state, in fact, by eliding the vulnerability of power with the vulnerability of gender and turning both to her own advantage, styling
herself as the unattainable, hence endlessly pursued, Virgin Queen,
adapting the conventions of pastoral romance to restructure and
manage the shape of her subjects' sexual as well as political desires.[45]
What Harrington mourns is the passing of a certain style, even a
genre of power, made all the more remarkable by the contrast with
what was evidently to come.

The hanged man was a cutpurse, taken in the act as James'
retinue was passing through Newark-Upon-Trent; the remainder
of the town's prisoners were granted a royal pardon and released
from jail. According to the official account of the king's progress,
the incident was an exemplary display of Justice and Mercy, em-
blematizing not only the penetrating scrutiny and swiftness of James'
power but also the evenhanded rule that he would bring to the
English throne. The omission of the well-established English custom of a trial somewhat marred the royal countenance James sought
to project, but it is not merely the violation of juridical process that
troubles Harrington. James' intrusive display of sovereign authority
suggests a monarch who does not recognize limits to his power or
his domain, who might pass judgment as readily on his subjects'
thoughts and intentions as on their deeds—a view to which the
royally licensed account unwittingly but ominously gave credence.

"For this is one especiall note in his Majestie; Any man that hath ought with him, let him be sure he have a just cause, For he beholdes all mens faces with stedfastnesse, and commonly the looke is the window for the heart."[46] The remarkable discretion and insight praised here is what Harrington views, with both disparagement and anxiety, as an intrusive and inquisitive power, exercising itself not only in response to men's deeds and upon their bodies but also upon their hidden thoughts. "Now if the wynde blowethe thus, why may not a man be tryed before he hathe offended?"

James would later show greater finesse in adapting the exercise of sovereign power to its theatrical conditions of possibility—most notably in his disposition of the so-called Ralegh conspirators in 1603–4. With Ralegh watching from his prison window, Markham, Grey, and Cobham were brought to the scaffold in succession. On the verge of death, Markham was told he was insufficiently prepared and returned to his cell; Grey was brought out, allowed his final words, then informed that the sequence of execution had been changed; Cobham next mounted the scaffold, said his prayers and his last dying speech, but on the verge of execution the proceedings were halted so that his fellow condemned could join him. "Now all the actors," as one account put it, were "together on the stage (as use is at the end of a play)," and the sense of theater was not lost upon the men themselves; they "looked strange one upon the other, like men beheaded and met again in the other world."[47] Again they prepared themselves for death and were even induced to acknowledge the justice of their fates, at which point they were informed that the king had granted them their lives. This time the audience responded as James expected—as they would, that is to say, at the dénouement of a well-crafted tragicomedy, which is after all what they had just enjoyed:

> There was no need to beg a *plaudite* of the audience, for it was given with such hues and cries, that it went from the castle to the town, and there began afresh, as if there had been some such like accident. . . .[48]

Thoughts *are* subjects; since his progress from Scotland, James had learned that they are most effectively constituted as such not through the sheer display of sovereign power but through its theatrical displacement—by aligning the scaffold of execution with its theatrical double, the power of the law with the power of fiction.

The actual execution the year before had not only failed to convey its exemplary message but had also raised the specter of Jacobean rule as a sort of *psychotyranni;* in Vincentio's disguise as a ghostly father, Shakespeare gives that specter a local habitation and a name. Obviously this does not make *Measure for Measure* a political allegory. As a play intimately engaged with the transition of power that had recently been enacted on the stage of history, however, it is a searching exploration of the shape a more intrusive form of power might take, an imaginary projection of a transition from one genre of government to another—from one structured along the lines of pastoral romance to one structured along the lines of pastoral inquiry and its theatricalization.

This utopian dimension of the play is set in the context of an extensive repertoire of historically available forms of exemplary power, and it gives the play a slightly distanced perspective, a kind of internal distantiation, on both the ideology and the limits of such power. Angelo recognizes those limits to a degree but also misrecognizes or mystifies them when he speaks of the task before him, of the need to make an example of Claudio:

> We must not make a scarecrow of the law,
> Setting it up to fear the birds of prey,
> And let it keep one shape till custom make it
> Their perch, and not their terror.
>
> (II. i. 1–4)

He acknowledges here the necessarily protean nature of exemplary power, its need to be constantly redefining and resituating itself, but he also speaks as if there were some alternative to making a scarecrow of the law, some way to control or fully determine its effects. Like any form of cultural representation, however, the manifest spectacle and decrees of the law can be neither unilaterally contained nor fully controlled once they are put into circulation. The language of the law is itself subject to appropriation in this play, as Elbow unwittingly demonstrates in a series of malapropisms that are never mere misprisions but always full inversions of meaning—"respected" for "suspected," "benefactor" for "malefactor," and so on. He has indeed been a constable for too long, for he seems to have picked up the local idiom of the stews without realizing it; the logic of his malapropisms is the logic of Elizabethan thieves' cant, which customarily appropriated and inverted the official terms of authority in order to create an unauthorized but useful counterlanguage, one that could be spoken openly to hatch plots and devise stratagems without raising the suspicions of Elbow and his kind.[49]

Where the limits of exemplary power are concerned, however, Barnardine is of course the most extreme instance. Like the Ralegh conspirators, he has been trundled out for execution only to be granted a last-minute reprieve—not once but in a seemingly endless procession of mock executions, all without effect except to inure him to the entire process. He is "a man that apprehends death no more dreadfully but as a drunken sleep; careless, reckless, and fearless of what's past, present, or to come" (IV. ii. 140–41), and so he remains at the close of the play, habituated to the poetics of exemplary power and punishment to the point that they have been drained of all effect. It might have been more productive to march him out to another kind of scaffold, to enforce his attendance at plays, where he might have been induced to regard, as he had never done with his own mock executions, the fictive as if it were real: to find, that is to say, his sense of apprehension expanded by a drama that developed in its audience a more pointed sense of what's past, present, and to come—a drama that fostered enhanced powers of observation and planning, and induced its audience to turn those powers upon their own circumstances and selves. But then, such a theater does not exist in the suburbs of Vienna, for all their affinities with the suburbs and Liberties of Shakespeare's London. It does not exist in the suburbs, but it does come to exist in the persons of Isabella and Angelo.

In her second conference with Angelo, Isabella acknowledges that women are frail, as frail "as the glasses wherein they view themselves, / Which are as easy broke as make forms" (II. iv. 124–25). The analogy itself breaks down at a crucial but significant juncture: where a virgin like Isabella is concerned, forming a new self in her glassy essence is inseparable from breaking it. What is true of procreation is also true of the deconstruction and reformation of the subject. "Best men," as Mariana observes, "are moulded out of faults" (V.i.437), and it is along the fault-lines of the self that the Duke works in his ghostly guise, not only by mediating between his penitents and their sins but also, in the case of Isabella, by fracturing and multiplying her sense of herself, her person, her *personae*. Well-schooled in the art of substitution, the Duke is an able tutor for his novice; having put Angelo in his own place, he persuades Isabella to do the same with Mariana, and thus initiates a process in which Isabella gradually relinquishes her sense of self as a fixed and essential entity and begins to view her role as a role, to regard herself as an interchangeable commodity and to apprehend that self with an enhanced sense of what's past, present, and to come:

> *Duke* We shall advise this wronged maid to stead up your appoint-
> ment, go in your place. If the encounter acknowledge itself

hereafter, it may compel him to her recompense; and hear,
by this is your brother saved, your honor untainted, the poor
Mariana advantaged, and the corrupt deputy scaled. The maid
I will frame, and make fit for his attempt. If you think well
to carry this as you may, the doubleness of the benefit defends
the deceit from reproof. What think you of it?

Isab. The image of it gives me content already, and I trust it will
grow to a most prosperous perfection.

(II.i.250–61)

The doubleness of the deceit is redoubled, however, when Isabella
is induced to project herself, both publicly and psychologically,
back into the situation of her surrogate. Having allowed Mariana
to take her part in Angelo's designs, Isabella then publicly adopts
the role she did not play in private, not only to accuse Angelo
of the crime he did not commit but also to shame herself twice
over, both by lying and by tarnishing her chaste image. The shame
is fictive, but playing the part nonetheless has a lasting effect.
When she next "takes [Mariana's] part," it is not to forward the
lie of her coerced seduction but to project this tarnished *persona*
back into the past, to incorporate Angelo's lust into her reformed
sense of herself:

> Look, if it please you, on this man condemn'd
> As if my brother liv'd. I partly think
> A due sincerity govern'd his deeds
> Till he did look on me.
>
> (V. i. 441–45)

Roy Battenhouse is unfortunately not alone in applauding what he
regards as Isabella's sense of equity here, in finding her plea admirable not for the mercy it shows but for the "truth" it acknowledges. Isabella *is* responsible for Angelo's lust, according to
Battenhouse, "since her *exhibiting* [my emphasis] herself . . . occasioned Angelo's propositioning."[50] What is being exhibited in Isabella's plea is not the guilt of the victim, however, but the power
of vicarious victimage. Isabella has not only taken Mariana's part;
she has come to view herself through Angelo's eyes, to incorporate
and turn upon herself the gaze of an Other for whom virtue is a
temptation to and a site for lustful desire.

Angelo is the Duke's surrogate, of course, and at the end of
Measure for Measure the master reclaims not only the position he
initially vacated but also the one that has been fashioned during
his "absence"—fashioned by the combination of Angelo's desire for

and Vincentio's manipulation of Isabella. The Duke proposes marriage rather than an unlawful liaison, but his proposition situates
Isabella all the more forcefully as an object of male desire; the
virgin novice, who had been preparing for a life as the bride of
Christ, is silent, the focus not merely of Vincentio's inquiring gaze
but of all eyes, onstage and off. That her silence is a shocked one
is undeniable; Shakespeare knew how to make a marriage comedy
unproblematic in its romantic couplings, even in plays—*The Merchant of Venice* is one—otherwise rife with significant and unan-
swered questions. Whether her silence can be taken as a sign of
resistance to the Duke's overture is questionable, however. Although well within the parameters of any given production, such
an interpretation must ignore the progressive displacement and
multiplication of selves Isabella has experienced under the Duke's
direction, the degree to which her participation in the Duke's scheme
of substitutions has already made her an object of exchange in an
economy of male desire, even to the point that she has come to
view and define herself through the eyes of such desire in its more
illicit manifestation. It is in a sense too late for resistance; even a
negative response would not restore the glass wherein she formerly
viewed a more integral and unfragmented self. Her shock at the
Duke's proposition is not because it is unimaginable but because,
as she realizes at this moment of retrospective clarification, it has
become inevitable. It is a shock and a retrospection that, from our
own vantage point, we can at best share.[51]

Angelo's glass is broken more dramatically, his self-regard more
clearly fractured and displaced when he is induced to view himself
and what's past, present, and to come through the eyes of an Other
who is at once entirely real and entirely imaginary:

> O my dread lord,
> I should be guiltier than my guiltiness
> To think I can be undiscernible,
> When I perceive your Grace, like power divine,
> Hath looked upon my passes. Then, good prince,
> No longer session hold upon my shame,
> But let my trial be mine own confession.
> Immediate sentence, then, and sequent death
> Is all the grace I beg.
>
> (V. i. 364–72)

Angelo has always been aware, even acutely so, that his passes have
been observed by power divine itself. He has been troubled, but
quite capable nonetheless of behaving as though his sins were those
of a third person. In the passage above, however, his sense of

excruciating and intolerable visibility stems not from this sense of divine surveillance nor even from his realization that the Duke has all too literally witnessed his abuses of office. Rather, it is the product of his own apprehension, of his full incorporation of the gaze of the Other turned upon his radically discernable self. This acute and apprehensive sense of being observed—of having been always and already observed—does not close the gap between the Duke and the Divinity, but rather issues from that gap; it is not a testament to the Christian allegory of the play but rather to the power that comes from dismantling, secularizing, and internalizing the structures of Christian anxiety, especially the psychological tyranny of pastoral inquiry, and from putting those structures into play on a new stage.

V

In 1634, Peter Studley published *The Looking-Glasse of Schisme,* a treatise that sought to establish the danger of radical Puritan sects by chronicling the "Execrable Murders, Done by Enoch ap Evans, a Downe-Right Separatist, on the Bodies of his Mother and Brother." Evans was apparently motivated by excessive "zeale to the word of God"; his matricide and fratricide stemmed from and, needless to say, concluded a family argument over what should be the "most convenient gesture in the act of receiving the sacred communion."[52] Both during and after his trial, Evans was as unrepentant and intransigent as Barnardine; unlike his fictive predecessor, however, he was marched out to the scaffold on the appointed day and hanged, in accord with his sentence, until dead.

The spectators at his execution were surprised and unsatisfied by Evans' behavior; even his fellow prisoners found it distasteful, and were especially outraged when Evans said he would like to break the hangman's pate. What is significant about the response of common citizen and fellow felon is, first of all, that it was shared, and second, that it was of relatively recent historical vintage. As J. A. Sharpe has recently detailed, such a response was a culturally determined one, and its genealogy extends back no further than the Reformation.[53] Beginning with those convicted of high treason in the sixteenth century and gradually extending even to provincial felons, civil and religious authorities combined in an extraordinary effort not merely to save the souls of the condemned by bringing them to a state of contrition but also, and more importantly, to enhance the didactic powers of exemplary punishment by staging a second, public confession from the scaffold—a "last dying speech" in which the condemned would anatomize their crimes, divorce themselves from their past misdeeds and beliefs, and embrace their fate as just, necessary, and an example to all. What is surprising in the period is how rare figures like Enoch ap Evans are, how often even committed traitors and rebels, at least in the extant published accounts, met their deaths not in defiance but with apparently sincere confessions, condemning themselves and praising the authorities that had brought them to the scaffold.[54]

The felon would narrate a history of his life, give it a shape and hence a meaning, define its errors and excesses; those gathered around the scaffold would listen, no longer mere spectators but an audience as well, and what they would witness would be not only an exemplary account of an errant life but also, and more crucially, an exemplary manifestation of the power of the state to foster an internalized obedience even among its most retrograde subjects. The narrative was meant to be incorporated, of course, the obedience internalized in the souls of those who watched and listened or read the widely circulated accounts that accompanied such confessions. There are important similarities between such a displacement and redeployment of confessional self-scrutiny and the contemporaneous phenomenon I have been tracing in terms of the popular stage, but important differences as well. Neither fortuitous events nor peculiar signs of an age more reverent than our own, scaffold confessions were culturally produced and determined manifestations of an effort to secularize and theatricalize confession, to enter it into the repertoire of available forms of ideological control, but only insofar as it could be fit into the existing structure of exemplary punishment. Although the situation of the scaffold audience might seem analogous to that of the audience at a play, the latter involves a vicarious engagement and energy that the former lacks. We are the rhetorically designated, directly addressed audience for the didactic and proselytizing message of a last dying speech; for it to be effective, we must not only believe it to be genuine but also have already inscribed within us, at least at some dormant or latent level, the ideological strictures and values being manifested before us. In contrast, we eavesdrop on a play; we are never the intended audience but always in the position of a conspirator and accomplice to an action and dramatic discourse that draws us into it precisely because we are not, in a certain sense, meant to see or hear it. Relying on an already inscribed structure of beliefs, the scaffold confession relies on belief in another sense as well: it must be perceived as real, a perception heightened, needless to say, by the subsequent execution. Theater relies not on belief but on a suspension of disbelief, an initial complicity and participation in the fiction before us that necessarily blurs or elides the boundary between the observing subject and the dramatic subject, the actual and the artificial person, the real and the imaginary.

It was a remarkable theater of complicity, a theater of apprehension in Heywood's sense of the term, that developed in the popular playhouses of Elizabethan and Jacobean England. *Measure for Measure* is not the purest example of such a theater but rather a critical reflection upon it—one that produces onstage, in the characters of Isabella and Angelo, an acute version of the apprehending subject that had, in the theatrical renovations of the previous decades, been produced in the audience itself. It is an ambivalent reflection on the power and cultural effects of Shakespearean dramaturgy, and for Shakespeare as well as for us its ambivalence is personified in the figure of Duke Vincentio. Mixing divinity with scurrility before our eyes, Shakespeare's Duke has long been, to say the least, a problematic figure. Edward Chalmers, who first noted his resemblance to James in 1799, regarded *Measure for Measure* as an unmistakable parody of the king; Albrecht saw the play as a royal homage, and until quite recently critics have operated within the confines of such contained antitheses.[55] And if James' countenance seems always to be peering out of the Duke's cowl, so does the image of the playwright himself. But however much James prided himself on spying into the secret recesses of his subjects' souls, the theater of apprehension staged in *Measure for Measure* was both unavailable to him and not fully within his own powers of containment or control. Nor were the apprehensive powers of Shakespeare's own playhouse orchestrated, as they are in the imaginary forum of this play, merely to augment the image of the dominant culture of his times or to supplement the system of exemplary power available to and endlessly manipulated by a monarch like James. The power of the stage was precisely the power of fiction, the power to induce an audience or an Angelo to view themselves as actors in their own lives, as artificial and artfully manipulated constructions, as indeed they were, whether they existed onstage or off, whether they were constituted by a playwright or by larger cultural forces of determination. Offstage, however, there was no Duke in a position to crystallize the enhanced and excruciating self-awareness that marks Angelo's crisis of full transparency or discernibility. To the degree that the stage served to reform its subjects, to make them more apprehending and apprehensive, it also exceeded the grasp of its period. If the apprehensive power of the stage produced what Norbert Elias would call an expanded domain of the superego, and hence an expanded avenue of access for forces of social and cultural control, it also produced an expanded cultural and self-awareness that the period in question was not fully equipped to manage or turn to its own advantage. However much the Duke's withdrawal and return adumbrates the transitional period in the English monarchy, his appropriation and theatricalization of pastoral apprehension traces a historical displacement that had not yet taken place on the scaffold of the state.

Imagining a forum for social control that is both outlawed, nostalgically appealing, and illicit in its imagined form—not a confessional forum but its theatrical displacement—*Measure for Measure* produces an image of its own historical situation, and at the same time it marks the distance between itself and the powers that be. The power the Duke wields is, as Leonard Tennenhouse has observed, a function of the marginal status and perspective he assumes along with his disguise. Far removed from power divine, the Duke nonetheless commands a kind of functional omniscience:

> Although the play takes care to make divinity a matter of seeming, Vincentio and the other disguised rulers function as if there were such a power at their service, a power that comes from peering into the secret recesses of their subjects' souls and seeing the criminal possibilities that reside there. Like God, the disguised figure can gaze on the state from a position outside of the social matrix.[56]

It is a perspective no actual monarch could command—that the state itself would only command after its full bureaucratization and its corresponding shift from an exemplary to a more acute and disciplinary form of power[57]—but it is also a marginal situation in which the period would have found another analogy, at once wholly secular and more immediate. If the Liberties of Vienna resemble the Liberties of Shakespeare's London in all respects but one, if the suburban houses being plucked down in *Measure for Measure* do not include the similarly threatened playhouses of Jacobean London, it is not because Shakespeare's stage is absent from his imaginary city. The play imagines, in a sense, the dismantling of that stage, but only by extending its marginal perspective and apprehensive powers throughout the community. The simile that develops between the Duke and the playwright is double-edged, as all similes are; similarity establishes difference as well as likeness, and the more Vincentio comes to be a figure for the playwright the greater the distance that is being marked between the apprehensive powers of the state and those of the stage.

Nor is the Duke the only figure of the playwright at the end of the play; there is also the ever intransigent Barnardine. As the case of Enoch ap Evans reminds us, such intransigence would not have saved Barnardine if he found himself on the stage of history rather than that of the theater, but this does not make Barnardine's fate a mere misrepresentation or mystification of history. In his global unconsciousness and radical inaccessibility, Barnardine represents the limits of even the Duke's power to control or contain, to induce and subvert the desires of his subjects. Like Prospero at the conclusion of *The Tempest*, the Duke pardons what exceeds his grasp: he licenses what he cannot control, in a magnanimous gesture meant to turn the manifest embodiment of his own limits into a display of his power to issue such a license, but the act can at best "flourish the deceit." The popular playhouses of Elizabethan and Jacobean England were granted a similar license, and in an equally equivocal gesture. In Marston's disguised-monarch plays, the unrepentant figures on stage at the end are disposed of in a different fashion. They are banished, exiled not from the country but to the suburbs of a city that thus purges itself of vice but only by making a place for it on the margins of community; in Shakespeare, no one is banished, but as a figure of uncontained license Barnardine is also a figure for the social and cultural terrain occupied by Elizabethan and Jacobean drama. As the Duke exits, Barnardine does not only stand *upon* the boards of Shakespeare's stage. He also stands *for* the place of that stage, and for the cultural and historical situation that formed the ground of its possibility.

5

Lying like Truth:
Riddle, Representation, and Treason

I

In 1600, violating ancient codes of hospitality and of fealty, the earl of Gowrie attempted to murder James VI of Scotland while the sovereign was staying at Gowrie's house in Perth. Gowrie and his accomplice were cut down in the attempt. But according to *Gowries Conspiracie,* printed in the same year *cum privilegio Regis,* the earl's corpse bore its wounds strangely. It refused to bleed until James, while searching the body for letters that might provide a clue to a deed inexplicable as that of a man acting under his own power and volition, discovered a "close parchment bag" in Gowrie's pocket and removed it. Immediately blood gushed from the corpse. Nature resumed its course, and with nature and James once more in control, the body of the traitor was once again free, and once again subject to natural and human laws. It was free, that is, to be transported to Edinburgh, presented to Parliament in a spectral session, duly found guilty of treason, and then hanged, drawn and quartered, and exhibited—on poles fixed at Edinburgh, Perth, Dundee, and Stirling. Gowrie's bag was found to be "full of magicall characters, and words of inchantment, wherein, it seemed, he put his confidence."[1]

Today we are uncertain which to be most incredulous about—the documented spectacle of execution, or the preternatural detail of this "devil's writ," as York describes the "oracles . . . hardly attained and hardly understood" that he snatches from Southwell's hand in *2 Henry VI* (I. iv. 69). Both are significant aspects of the representation of treason in the age, however. The traitor stands at an uncertain threshold of Renaissance society, athwart a line that sets off the human from the demonic, the natural from the unnatural, and the rational from the enigmatic and obscure realm of unreason. Treason is a twice-monstrous act: it is something awesome and terrifying in a way we find difficult to conceive—although period accounts, such as those describing the mood of London after the discovery of the Gunpowder Plot in 1605,[2] testify to its tumultuous repercussions even in failure—but it is monstrous, too, in that it is something made to show and reveal itself in both speech and spectacle. The fate of the Gunpowder conspirators provides but one example of a sequence that was typical, and could be described as the penal variety of a "King's Triumphs": first the confessions, then a procession through the city and an exhibition so that the populace could come to see the traitors "as the rarest sorts of monsters; fools to laugh at them, women and children to wonder, and all the common people to gaze."[3] In treason's procession as in the king's the city itself is the stage, and its streets form the scene for a mobile representation of power and authority. In the royal procession, however, the king himself appears and passes through a series of elaborate archways that provide, with their emblems and devices, a running commentary on his presence and his power. In chains as a sign and demonstration of that power, the traitor is himself a living gloss upon it and needs no further interpretation. But if his course is not graced in advance with the handiwork of the city's guilds, his wake is afterwards hung with treason's emblems. The final stage and ultimate performance of treason, often accompanied by a second, public confession, was of course on the scaffold, where the traitor was hanged and drawn and quartered for further display in death, according to a custom whose ritual was as much dramatic as it was juridical.[4]

There are suggestive analogies to be drawn between the one scaffold and the other—between the spectacle of the traitor on the platform of public execution and on the stage—but it would be wrong to equate the two. It is not that one is real, however, while the other is a mere show. Each belongs to the ritual and representation of treason in the Renaissance, but with a crucial difference. It is not treason that speaks from the place of execution, and in a sense it is no longer the body of the traitor that is painstakingly subjected to the law, and so shown to be human and natural once again. Confession and execution mark the return of the traitor to society and to himself, even in death. "Nothing in his life," as Malcolm says of the repentant Cawdor's execution, "Became him like the leaving of it" (I. iv. 7–8).[5] His death was fitting and becoming, in a sense, because it was only in leaving life that he again became *himself* and achieved again a certain decorum of self—as Gowrie did even in death when his bag of riddles was removed. Confession, execution, and dismemberment, unsettling as they may seem, were not so much punishment of the traitor as they were the demonstration that what had been a traitor was no longer, and that what had set him off from man and nature had been, like Gowrie's bag, lifted from him. When the body bleeds, treason has been effaced; execution is treason's epilogue, spoken by the law. In histories of the period, however, treason presents us with a more equivocal figure; on stage, it is something closer to treason itself that is enacted, and that speaks.

II

It is during the country troubles of Henry VIII that the language of treason begins, like masterless men, to come under renewed legislative scrutiny. Like so much else in the unsteady movement from a feudal to a nascent capitalist economy, it is within the antitheses of city and country, court and country that treason is defined. It is a country matter and a vagabond act in its own right—the act of one without a proper master, or one who denies his master as proper.[6] With the Treason Act of 1534, the explicit questioning of the king's authority becomes a matter of high treason, punishable by death. Making speech a capital offense provoked a long-lasting dispute with Parliament, one whose outlines can be traced through the years by the successive repeals and reenactments of the law. But whenever troubles arise, what you say again becomes an affair of life and death. The *Act for the punishment of diverse treasons* (1522) follows a time of pronounced civil strife, and again defines as guilty of high treason anyone who "by open preaching, express words, or sayings do expressly, directly and advisedly set forth and affirm that the King that here is is an heretic, schismatic, tyrant, infidel, or usurper of the crown."[7]

But the rebel is rarely so accommodatingly forthright. He "troubleth by biwaies," as Sir John Cheeke writes in *The Hurt of Sedicion* (1569): he wins others over to his cause not by outright, identifiable, and therefore governable lies, but by relying upon and taking advantage of the multiple senses of things, whether actions or words. The rebel or traitor is not a plain dealer, quite the opposite. "He cannot plainely withstand and useth subtilities of sophistrie," Cheeke continues, "mistaking the thing, but persuading men's minds, and abusing the plaine meaning of the honest to a wicked end of religious overthrow."[8] Cheeke confronts not treason's lie—so much is assumed—but the problem of its persuasiveness and the difficulty of identifying it in the making, before the damage is done and the rabble roused. Treason lies, but it lies like truth—as it must do. Underlying Cheeke's description of the traitor as one who makes verbal abuse a transitive act (whose primary object is always an indirect one—it abuses *to*) is the assumption that men could not be persuaded to rebellion by reason or by proper argument—that treason is explicable only as reason deluded or seduced, deceived by an abuser of words.

Yet if the traitor abuses words, he is also abused by them. Among the causes of the Yorkshire uprising of 1549, amid a discussion of the rebels' grievances and evil dispositions, Holinshed notes that "an other cause was, for trusting to a blind and fantasticall prophecie, where with they were seduced, thinking the same prophecie shuld come to passe, by the rebellions of Norffolke, of Devonshire, and other places."[9] The Yorkshire rebels were as much the victims of this "fantasticall prophecie" as they were its agents, and they were undone by the riddle that led them on with the hope of success. Here we encounter a recurrent topos in accounts of treason. As an explanation of cause the prophecy doesn't explain—it displaces the source of seduction from the rebels to an oracular utterance—but it does account for the actions of all, both the mob and its head. Something like Zeno's paradox operates in discussions of the cause of rebellion: an infinite regress of others who are to blame, the abusers or seducers, opens out into a series from which the figure of the Other ultimately crystallizes, and the note of the preternatural often begins to sound. But such riddles also highlight the fact that, for the Renaissance, treason is by definition a self-consuming act. "What commonwealth is it then," Cheeke asks the rebel, "to doo such abhominable enterprises after so vile a sort, that yee hinder that good yee would doo, and bring in that hurt yee would not, and so find that yee seek not, and follow that yee lose, and destroie yourselves by follie . . . . and so not onlie over-floweth us with the miserie, but also overwhelmeth you with the rage thereof?"[10] Given the enormity of his rebellion, the traitor too must have been somehow deceived. He is caught by a riddle or prophecy in an equivocal space between the truth and the lie, and he will prove his own ruination one way or the other—for the monstrosity and enigma of his act is that it threatens the foundations of order itself, and even in success could not survive the catastrophe it plots. The prophecy that gives a false and impossible hope of success to treason embodies its inevitable defeat, but it does not prescribe a limit to treason's catastrophe: facing a triumph that may well prove to be pyrrhic, authority is little consoled by treason's riddling delusion or the guarantee of its inevitable doom.

In these prophecies and riddles what we might dismiss as mere superstition constitutes in fact a rhetoric of rebellion. "When we speak or write doubtfully, that the sence may be taken in two ways,"

we are guilty, according to George Puttenham, of ambiguitas—or
in the Greek, of amphibology.[11] Puttenham ranks amphibology as
the worst abuse or vice in rhetoric, and his definitions and examples
are standard ones. What distinguishes *The Arte of English Poesie* from
its fellow handbooks of rhetoric is a twofold digression warning of
the social and political threat posed by the figure of amphibology.
If the traitor is an ambiguous figure for Holinshed, the vice or
trope of amphibology is for Puttenham the figure of treason itself.

Puttenham related amphibology not to sophistry, as Cheeke did,
but to a pre-Socratic past that is oracular as well as pagan.[12] "These
doubtfull speeches were used much in old times by their false
Prophets as appeareth by the Oracles of *Delphos* and of the *Sybilles*
prophecies devised by the religious persons of those days to abuse
the superstitious people, and to encomber their busie braynes with
vaine hope and vaine fear." Yet the punning prophecies of amphibology are also found closer to home, since "all our old British
and Saxon prophecies be of the same sort, that turne them on
which side ye will, the matter of them may be verified." Nor are
they simply relics of bygone days, for amphibologies return willfully
to trouble both the still developing national language and the security of the state itself:

> [They] carryeth generally such force in the heades of fonde people,
> that by the comfort of those blind prophecies many insurrections
> and rebellions have beene stirred up in this Realme, as that of Jacke
> Strawe, and Jacke Cade in Richard the secondes time, and in our
> own time, by a seditious fellow in Norffolke calling himself Captaine
> Ket, and others in other places of the Realme, lead altogether by
> certain propheticall rymes, which might be constred [sic] two or three
> wayes as well as that whereunto the rebelles applied it.

According to period accounts the rebellion led by Robert Kett in
1549 was guided from beginning to end by "fayned prophecies"
that seemed to promise success to the rebels' cause but were in fact
"as ambiguous as those uttered by older and more famous sooth-
sayers." Obscure or doubtful as the riddles were, they possessed a
persuasive force. "Still there was a charm, and mystery, a mighty
power to them."[13] Kett's rebellion was a massive one. Following a
minor enclosure riot at Attleborough in June of 1549, villagers
gathered at Wymondham on July 7 to celebrate an annual festival
and attend a play in honor of Thomas of Canterbury.[14] More fences
were torn down by the gathered crowd. A landlord himself, Kett
joined the mob after his own fences were lost, organized it and led
it as an army eventually numbering 16,000 men in a successful
seige of Norwich. Locally impressed and royal troops were de-

feated, a royal pardon offered and rejected. When Kett found himself under attack by 11,000 troops under the earl of Warwick it was an amphibological riddle that determined the course of what was intended to be a strategic retreat:

> The country gnoffes, Hob, Dick, and Hick
> With clubbes and clouted shoone
> Shall fill the vale
> Of Dussindale
> With slaughter'd bodies soon.[15]

Fill the vale they did: the oracle was fulfilled, although the bodies in the vale proved not to be, as the rebels had presumed they would, those of Warwick's men.

The riddle of treason lies, it seems, in the riddle itself. A riddle, a prophecy, a double meaning, an unsettling pun: "when a sentence may be turned both wayes," Abraham Fraunce says of amphibole, "so that a man shall be uncertayne what way to take."[16] The image is that of a crossroads where the only right route to take is both at once. Choose one route or reading and the crossroads will return to haunt you—as it did Oedipus, a regicide and riddle-ridden man, and as it often did the traitor, who found his final resting place there, at the crossroads.[17] A lie can be defined or outlawed, a veiled message unveiled. But these riddles, prophecies, or amphibologies involve something other than treason lying or disguising itself.[18] They exceed and usurp the intentions of the traitor himself, bifurcating choice and intentionality. Surprisingly, no source is suggested for the prophecy in cases such as Kett's, no agent demonic or otherwise is even obliquely mentioned. The traitor is seduced by a language without origin.

But if amphibology seduces the traitor, it also presents authority with a considerable dilemma, and with it we move into a linguistic sphere the law cannot control. There is a recognition of a certain power in language here, one which for all its aura of superstition and country lore is associated with decidedly real struggles and threats to the power of the throne. National tongues were not without their role in exercising and expanding that power. "Language," as the bishop of Avila remarked in 1492, "is the perfect instrument of empire."[19] Yet if we find in the Renaissance an increasing awareness and deployment of the power of language— power in a real sense, as a weapon for combat and control—we also find in it a charting of the boundaries of rule, beyond which authority can only watch and listen to treason's amphibolic spectacle.

III

In December of 1604 the Gowrie plot was briefly exhumed as
Gowrie, a lost play performed at least twice by the King's Players
and then banned with a minor rebuke to the company for having
thus brought the king to the scaffold.[20] While the direct representation of the king on stage might risk displeasure or imprisonment,
the staging of treason—preternatural and regicidal as it might be—
did not, and we can assume that Gowrie's "magicall characters, and
words of inchantment" made their appearance in the play. Some
two years after presumably performing in *Gowrie,* a year after the
Gunpowder Plot of 1605, one of the King's Players turned to Holinshed for the plot of a play rich in such elements, in which a
Scottish king is assaulted by a kinsman and a subject—while in
"double trust," as James was in 1600. *Macbeth* is perhaps the fullest
literary representation of treason's amphibology in its age. In 1606
it was performed for James at court: authority watched, and listened. Onstage is a Scotland rapidly succumbing to misrule, la-
mented and viewed from an English perspective by its former
countrymen—a description that fits the perspective of Malcolm and
his fellow refugees from Macbeth's bloody reign, but one that fits
the perspective of James as well, as he viewed the play. The Scotland
on the scaffold is one preliminary to the intersection of James' line
with Scottish royalty, but prophetic of it; it is also a Scotland inter-
fused with contemporary concerns of the English court. But the
fusion of times and places is not without its unsettling prospects
from the vantage point of the throne.

   Nearing the end of his fantastic career, Macbeth pauses and looks
back down the way he has come, recognizing behind him the doubtful crossroads and the way not taken in the riddles that once made
him resolute, bloody, and bold:

> I pull in resolution; and begin
> To doubt th' equivocation of the fiend,
> That lies like truth.
>
> (V. v. 41–43)

He has recognized the amphibology in the witches' riddles—the
duplicitous sense of "wood" in the one prophecy wherein he put
his confidence—and he will soon come to know that "none of woman
born" was not the impossible and inhuman reference he took it
for, but rather paltered with him in a double sense of "born." In
Macbeth's recognition the audience finds a peculiar one of its own.
For recognizing amphibology where one expected something more
univocal has been the experience of the audience since Macbeth's

drunken Porter made his entrance, so upsetting to Coleridge, and gave us his topical pronouncement. "Faith, here's an equivocator, that could swear in both scales against either scale; who committed treason enough for Gods sake, yet could not equivocate to heaven" (II. iii. 9ff.).

In 1606 the topical reference was a clear one, since Father Garnet's equivocation during his trial for complicity in the Gunpowder Plot was still an active and much publicized concern. While the reference was clear, however, the *relation* of Garnet's equivocation to the play was not. In its narrow historical context, "equivocation" has been of inestimable aid in dating *Macbeth* but of doubtful use as a key to the entanglements of truth, lie, and treason in the play.[21] What Shakespeare gives us is not treason's lie— something that the court might well have expected, something it could regulate, define, control, and perhaps anticipate—but treason's amphibology. Not Garnet's equivocation, but an equivocation that lies like truth.

According to James, Garnet lied. According to the Church he relied upon a theologically valid duplicity known as equivocation or mental reservation—qualifying his spoken utterances with unspoken emendations, forming a true if mixed response to the questions put to him. In the eyes (or ears) of God, he had not lied. During the sixteenth century the Church promulgated and defended such equivocation as a strategy for Catholics to employ when caught between conflicting demands for loyalty to Protestant rulers and to Rome, and it is equivocation as such—as mental reservation—that the audience of *Macbeth* had well in mind. The theological treatises on equivocation that begin with St. Raymond's *Summa* (1235) describe mental reservation, however, as a secondary, narrower form of equivocation.[22] The term used for its primary form is amphibology. The Church had better sense, however, than to recommend punning under oath as a pragmatic strategy for Catholics who had to skate between the truth and a lie. Although theologically sound, puns and amphibologies would be of dubious value if *control* of a situation was paramount. As our tales of treason suggest, amphibology resists control. Indeed, psychoanalytic theory draws an antithetical relationship between control and amphibology, since it is through parapraxes and puns that the unconscious breaches the defenses of the conscious mind.[23]

When Thomas James refers to Garnet in 1612, he echoes Fraunce's syntax and image of amphibole as a crossroads where choice is bifurcated, but it is an empty echo. "Al his Equivocations, wherein his tongue runs one way, and his meaning another, that you know not where to find him."[24] The intentions of the speaker *rule* here: mental reservation resides and resolves itself in the conscious intentions of the speaker. In *Macbeth*, from its foul-and-fair opening to the senseless slaughter of Macduff's family in an effort to crown, as Macbeth says, his "thoughts with acts," intention, act, and language are unruly, a matter of words unencompassed by definitions of truth and lie that "palter with us in a double sense" and that exceed Macbeth's intentions and his efforts to control, both compelling and undoing his resolution.

Shakespeare does not, then, merely project the concerns of the moment onto the screen of Scotland's past. When finally admitted by the Porter, Macduff questions him, and the doorkeeper responds in "multitudinous antitheses," glossing his previous reference to mental reservation with a demonstration of amphibology in comic guise, culminating in an (un)resolving pun on "lie":

Macd. What three things does drink especially provoke?

Por. Marry, sir, nose-painting, sleep, and urine. Lechery, sir, it provokes and unprovokes: it provokes the desire, but it takes away the performance. Therefore, much drink may be said an equivocator with lechery: it makes him, and it mars him; it sets him on, and it takes him off; it persuades him, and it disheartens him; makes him stand to, and not stand to: in conclusion, equivocates him in a sleep, and, giving him the lie, leaves him.

(II. iii. 26ff.)

It is when Macbeth returns to the heath and seeks out the three hags for a second set of prophecies that Shakespeare's design with equivocation and the interplay of times and places comes into its most dramatic focus. After hearing the riddles, Macbeth witnesses the "show of eight Kings" from Banquo's line. They form a procession that leads prophetically offstage to the royal audience they will culminate in, and the last of them holds a glass in his hand, presumably to catch the countenance of the king. Genealogy and prophecy are made manifest in a visible display, but there is another genealogy in the air as well, one heard rather than seen. Juxtaposed to the projection of James' line, the witches' riddles complicate its complimentary gesture with what amounts to a genealogy of treason and equivocation: the equivocation the audience knows, defined by James as treason's dissembling lie, has been contextualized or traced back to the less than reassuring figure of treason and rebellion we have been charting in this chapter.

Amphibology marks an aspect of language that neither treason nor authority can control. It is a power that cannot be trammeled up, mastered, or unequivocally defined, but it is a power: it compels and moves the speaker or auditor. From the perspective of authority, it does so illicitly—that is, in the place of authority and laws of state, reason, or sense. It is not when Macbeth lies but when the language he would use instead masters him that the power of amphibology strikes us, and its effects are not confined to the witches' riddles.

Language behaves strangely and impulsively in the play, as if with a will of its own. At times Macbeth seems to stride the blast of his own tongue, not so much speaking as he is spoken by his words and their insistent associations. A submerged current propels his speech even when Macbeth dissembles, and it surfaces during his description of the murdered Duncan in the form of a disassembled pun:

> . . . his gash'd stabs like a breach in nature
> For ruin's wasteful entrance: there, the murtherers
> Steeped in the color of their trade, their daggers
> Unmannerly breech'd with gore.
>
> (II. iii. 113–16)

The breach that is an opening in Duncan's flesh—allowing what is outside to intrude, spilling all that should remain within—returns to the mind's eye and ear when "breech'd" succeeds it so closely. The first suggests or prompts the second in something closer to free association than logical progression of thought.[25] Wound and unmannerly covering, the intrusion of the one homonym upon the other acts as a pun often does, making visualization of an image difficult. The breeches of gore are themselves breached: one image haunts the other, and we are uncertain which way to take.

With the amphibolic riddle, taking one course through it does not eliminate the other; in his own moving and self-persuading language, Macbeth relies and rides upon gliding significations of words, often with a powerful effect. Authority can either watch and listen to such motions, or it can engage them. In *Macbeth*, Shakespeare develops an unsettling affiliation between treason's spectacle and its audience. To engage treason's motions is to participate in them, threatening the otherwise clear antithesis that would seem to hold between rule and misrule and revealing the latter to be less the antithesis of rule than its alternating current, its overextension and in a sense its consequence. In England with Macduff, Malcolm dissembles. He lies about his own character and

tarnishes his reputation, confident that when the test of his com-
patriot has been made he can remove this mask of misrule as easily
as he donned it. But once on his face, it leaves a lasting impression.
For Macduff the experience is a discomposing one, for it reveals a
family resemblance between authority and its Other where no relation was expected. When Malcolm strips away the mask and swears,
"My first false speaking / Was this upon myself" (IV. iii. 130–31),
Macduff hesitates, uncertain whether it is Malcolm honest and pure
or Malcolm profligate who declares such an absolute division between his lies and his truths. The line he draws and the need to
draw it are equally difficult for Macduff to align with his notions
of a true ruler: "Such welcome and unwelcome things at once / 'Tis
hard to reconcile" (IV. iii. 138–39).

The words could have been spoken by Macbeth before Duncan's
murder, when still on the heath and wondering how to reconcile
the foul and fair tidings of the witches' greetings.[26] Both a metaphor
and a pun call for a simultaneous perception of likeness and difference; but unlike a metaphor, a pun cannot be reduced to a
simile—as Aristotle said any metaphor could be—in order to clarify
the lines of its similitude. Amphibology lies *like* truth: similitude
here is reason's dilemma, not its exegetical or legal solution. An
interplay of likeness and difference, amphibology is less readily
ruled than are the antitheses of authority.

IV

Amphibology belongs to treason's spectacle. What is effaced by the
time of treason's orderly procession and meticulous execution under the law is something more than a rhetorical figure or mere
wordplay, as we understand such terms today. When amphibology
surfaces in histories or on the stage it is accorded a power that is
generative rather than controlling or restraining. It is something
the traitor gives himself up to, and a part of what is generated out
of it is the traitor's arc of rebellion. In his study of the "uncomic
puns" in *Macbeth*—"breach" could be added to them—Kenneth Muir
suggests such puns possess a generative power since lost to dramatic
language, but he approaches them strictly within the history of
literary language and the stage. Characteristic of Shakespearean
drama, most pronounced in *Macbeth* yet absent from the stage after
the Restoration, the uncomic pun is a part of what separates Shakespeare's language from ours: "The Restoration dramatists were
admirably lucid, but their use of language was, in the last resort,
unimaginative. The banishing of the pun except for comic purposes

was the symbol of a radical defect: it was a turning away from the genius of the language."[27]

Muir's thesis is a striking one, but a part of what separates Shakespeare's language from ours is the (an)aesthetization that has taken place when amphibology thus resurfaces as a purely linguistic phenomenon whose significance is both entirely aesthetic and even limited to a single genre. For Puttenham the domain of amphibology and the threat posed by it are considerably broader, as they were for the later seventeenth century—which did more than "turn away" from its *genius linguae*. Indeed, the age subsequent to Shakespeare brought language under its full and controlled scrutiny, not as a spectacle but as something to chart, analyze, regulate, and even legislate into a clear and ordered discourse.[28] Modern grammars, prose style, and ideas of translation stem from the efforts of the Royal Society and others to master language, but the ordering and deployment of discourse is also a phenomenon inseparable from the creation of the modern state.[29] The consequences for the figure of the traitor, dramatic and rhetorical, are beyond the bounds of this study but relevant to it. What I have called amphibology, Puttenham also describes as ambiguity. I avoid the more familiar term because of its familiarity. Ambiguity, too, has enjoyed considerable popularity as an aesthetic phenomenon in this century. What the Latin fails to suggest—partly in its etymology, but more importantly in its modern usage—is the unruly but generative force associated with treason's figure. But the Greek term *becomes* unfamiliar. Its strangeness is a historical occurrence, and it seems more than a coincidence of history or philology that the seventeenth century is the period when the term begins to decline in usage and gives way to the familiar but relatively pallid "ambiguity."

Charting the course a more orderly commonwealth must take, Hobbes broadly attacks figurative language in *Leviathan*, often eliding metaphor with ambiguity as equivalent vices. While he employs the more familiar term, the figure of treason still informs his use, in 1651, of "ambiguity." "Metaphors, and senslesse and ambiguous words," he writes, "are like *ignes fatui;* and reasoning upon them, is wandering amongst innumerable absurdities; and their end [is] contention, and sedition."[30] Less clearly but still perceptibly, the association of treason and amphibology enters into Johnson's discussion of Shakespeare's wordplay. The quibble—a pun or a riddle—fascinates and seduces Shakespeare, acting upon him like an *ignis fatuus* or one of Atalanta's irresistible apples, but something more threatening also darkens its appeal:

A quibble is to Shakespeare, what luminous vapors are to the traveller; he follows it at all adventures, it is sure to lead him out of his way, and sure to engulf him in the mire. It has some malignant power over his mind, and its fascinations are irresistible. . . . A quibble is the golden apple for which he will always turn aside from his career, or stoop from his elevation. A quibble, poor and barren as it is, gave him such delight, that he was content to purchase it, by the sacrifice of reason, propriety, and truth. A quibble was to him the fatal Cleopatra for which he lost the world, and was content to lose it.[31]

A *malignant* power, seductive and alluring, charming us out of all propriety and even property. The description is a familiar one, even if the purely literary context is not. Johnson's words could easily have been penned by a Puttenham or a Holinshed or even a Hobbes. In the context of *Macbeth*—in the context made accessible to us by *Macbeth*—the reverberation of such a description is telling. The author of treason's spectacle has himself become a figure of the traitor, motivated and undone by treason's amphibolic tongue.

Like his author, Macbeth dies unrepentant. At the opening of the play, in the recounted deaths of Macdonwald and Cawdor, we encountered differing versions of treason's last act and final performance; at its close, the play returns to the question of treason's proper public representation, and from that question derives its penultimate dramatic impetus. Macbeth has run his bloody course and stands undone yet no longer deluded, facing Macduff but hesitant to engage with his doom. Macduff goads his rival into action with a reminder that treason has another stage available to it, if it refuses to go the way of a Macdonwald or a Cawdor:

> Then yield thee, coward
> And live to be the show and gaze o' th' time:
> We'll have thee, as our rarer monsters are,
> Painted upon a pole, and underwrit,
> "Here you may see the tyrant."
> (V. viii. 23–27)

Macduff threatens a life in captivity and a gallows procession which, staged in effigy, can be infinitely repeated—viewed and reviewed by Macbeth himself, among others. Macbeth is threatened, in a vertiginous sense, with a reduced, silent, purely spectacular version of *Macbeth* itself; he chooses instead to die in renewed rebellion. When he exits it is as a warrior and a traitor, in arms. Macduff returns, bearing Macbeth's head, and the traitor is no more.

Yet the entrance of Macbeth's head has a complex effect in a play that has so closely followed and adapted itself to treason's amphibolic course. For a brief time, the figure of the traitor has

merged with the figures of Shakespearean language and dramaturgy. For the duration of the play, we are taken beyond James'
reduced notion of equivocation as a mere lie and introduced to the
realm he was attempting to redefine: a realm less easily governed
by the reigning absolutes of Jacobean England, historically occupied by figures of sedition, here taken over by the dramatic and
rhetorical figures of Shakespearean dramaturgy. The impulsive
power of treason's tongue is a heightened and elaborated version
of Shakespeare's language. Macbeth speaks and is propelled by
words that lie like truth, and also like Shakespeare at the height of
his powers. But the incongruous kinship that develops between the
figures of the stage and those of treason is a restricted one. Macbeth's death marks the point where stage and treason must diverge,
and his disembodied head crystallizes their divergence. To the audience the visage is a familiar one, but it is also out of place, proper
to a different setting, customarily viewed on a different scaffold.
Macbeth's head in a sense doubles the stage it bloodies, such that
we end in a visual representation of the verbal pun: one scaffold
portrayed upon the boards of the other, in a closing reformation
of treason's spectacle.

V

Like *Macbeth,* Shakespeare's second tetralogy and *Measure for Measure* could be called "royal plays," chronicles of rule composed with
reigning ideologies well in mind. All were performed before royalty,
and from the viewpoint of their respective monarchs they readily
take the shape of dramatic compliments. In each case, however,
compliment is accompanied by a more complex design, radical in
its comprehensiveness. These are critical histories of the contemporaneous moment, anamorphic genealogies of power: they need
to be viewed from more than one perspective, and cannot be fully
comprehended from any single vantage point, no matter how privileged or dominant. Viewed from a marginal perspective—a perspective aligned with the cultural situation of the popular stage
itself, receptive to lines of affiliation drawn between that stage and
other eccentric or liminal phenomena—such plays take on the contours of amphibologies writ large. Shakespeare rehearses Tudor
and Jacobean ideologies with a fullness, a "two-eyedness" (in A. P.
Rossiter's phrase), that opens up a critical perspective on his own
day and age—on the cultural pretexts and practices that were shaping the larger dramaturgies of Elizabethan and Jacobean society.
The effect, to quote Louis Althusser once again, is to "make us

'perceive' . . . from the *inside,* by an *internal distance,* the very ideology" in which such plays and such a stage were held.

Held, but by no means fully contained. The relationship between literature and the culture that produces it is a complex and dynamic one, partly because culture itself is a complex and dynamic ensemble, a lived system of meanings, values, and practices. Culture in this sense is an ongoing composition, a process of definition, recreation, and modification, rather than merely the product of such activities. It is a *hegemony,* in the sense developed by Gramsci and recently expanded by Raymond Williams:

> It is a whole body of practices and expectations, over the whole of living: our senses and assignments of energy, our shaping perception of ourselves and our world. It is a lived system of meanings and values—constitutive and constituting. . . . a realized complex of experiences, relationships, and activities, with specific and changing pressures and limits. In practice, that is, hegemony can never be singular. Its internal structures are highly complex, . . . [and] it does not just passively exist as a form of dominance. It has to be continually renewed, recreated, defended, and modified. It is also continually resisted, limited, altered, challenged by pressures not at all its own.[32]

Hegemonic culture is, moreover, a historical dynamic, an ongoing, diachronic negotiation between the old and the new. The dominant culture in any given period cannot hope to include or even to account for all human aspirations and energies; present culture is continually limited, challenged, or modified by culture past and culture yet to come—or, for a less Dickensian formulation, by what Williams calls *residual* and *emergent* cultural phenomena.

The residual comprises elements of culture that were once fully articulated by former societies and situations: practices and institutions, meanings and values that have slipped into the past, but not far enough to be either monumentalized as tradition or to be fully removed from ongoing cultural processes. Residual cultures and cultural forces can be retrieved and revitalized; they are still available to the present, as alternatives and supplements to it. Emergent culture, by contrast, has yet to be fully articulated. The emergent is the leading edge of culture, a field of possibilities from which will emerge new classes and institutions, even new forms of the dominant culture, but which also includes alternatives never to be realized by or incorporated into the dominant order of things. Taken together, the residual and the emergent form the historical horizon of culture; marginal yet potent thresholds of the dominant social hierarchy, they represent "areas of human experience, aspiration, and achievement which the dominant culture neglects, opposes, represses, or even cannot recognize."³³

Lodged on the margins of culture at a time when those margins were especially rich and polyvalent, the Elizabethan popular stage enjoyed a unique and complex ideological perspective—or rather, a complex choice of perspectives. An emergent cultural formation, it also relied greatly upon those residual pastimes and practices that served as the conditions of its own emergence or possibility. Its place on the horizon or threshold of culture brought it into alignment with much that its own period found strange and un-familiar, and that alignment provided the stage with an anamorphic point of view: an ability not merely to see its own culture through the glass fashioned and provided by the dominant order, but also to view that order *through* its various cultural Others. The result is not so much a subversive drama as one rich in oblique commentary on its own times—on the relationships that prevailed between re-sidual, emergent, and dominant values, and on the processes and practices by which such relationships were created, maintained, redefined, or repressed.

We have been concerned with a select few Shakespearean plays, chosen because they reflect and put to use the ideological and cul-tural environment of the popular stage in a fashion that serves to articulate the broader dynamics of early modern culture. In Shake-speare's second tetralogy, for example, the taverns of Eastcheap, drawn from the playwright's own day and age, are not merely ele-ments of local color added to the dramatic enactment of the Tudor genealogy of power. In a sense, the contemporary scene displaces history, unmoors it from its comfortable anchorage in the past and conveys it into the present, translating Tudor myths of power into a vehicle for staging the cultural practices and tensions of Shake-speare's own moment in history. Hal's tavern companions and foils, as many critics have observed, are figures larger than themselves. In Shakespeare's representation, as we have seen, they become dra-matic surrogates of the marginal and popular cultures of Elizabe-than England, of all that was, under the transcategorical rubric of "the strange," granted license to occupy the horizon of possibility in early modern culture. Watching them upheld for a while, we are led to perceive such license in operation, to view it critically as a strategy of power. From such a perspective, the two parts of *Henry IV* reveal not a celebration of Tudor myths of power but rather a dramatic exploration of the ways in which that power was currently engaging residual, emergent, and otherwise strange cultures: bringing them

under the scrutiny of its gaze, even actively rehearsing and partic-
ipating in them, shaping its own rites of passage by passing *through*
its cultural Others—incorporating certain aspects of the strange,
making them familiar and absorbing them into the dominant culture, while radically rejecting or suppressing others.

The paradoxical end of such a process of cultural rehearsal
reminds us that reproducing the dynamics of a given culture,
whether an alien or a dominant one, does not necessarily reinforce
those dynamics; rehearsing the dynamics and practices of its own
culture at a second remove, Shakespeare's stage subjects the dominant culture of its time to the same dramaturgical process of es-
trangement through familiarity. The impact of the stage on the
period was not limited, however, to such critical speculations on
the reigning hierarchies of state. What I have called the rehearsal
of cultures in the period was itself part of a larger reformation of
manners, and one which would produce a fundamental reconfiguration of the subject, in both the political and the psychoanalytic
senses of the term.

In conduct books of the sixteenth and seventeenth centuries and
from the pulpit, the individual was being exhorted to view him or
herself in a new light, to interiorize a judgmental social perspective
and turn it upon the self, its actions, motives, weaknesses, and
desires, and thus to subject both the social and the psychological
self to a form of self-scrutiny that would eventually produce something like the modern subject—what has alternately been described
as the self-regulating bourgeois identity or the "sovereign individual" of modern capitalism.[34] The drama that emerged on the popular stage in the 1590s neither prescribed rules of behavior nor
proselytized its spectators to reform themselves; it did, however,
foster a complex theatrical transaction between that audience and
the artificial but affecting selves they were induced to view as both
others and as versions of themselves. Such a theater of (self) apprehension achieves its fullest embodiment in Shakespearean tragedy, but it is in *Measure for Measure* that Shakespeare most fully
reflects upon the role of his own dramatic practice in the larger
civilizing process of the period. The audience at a performance of
Hamlet was not, of course, subjected to the acute self-scrutiny and
internalized surveillance that is produced in Angelo and Isabella;
what we see in such figures is an imaginary intersection of the
affective powers of the stage and of the state, a theatricalization of
the subject which would make possible its internalized and psychologized self-regulation, but whose historical moment of possibility had yet to arrive.[35]

In *Macbeth,* it is the limits of authority—its capacity to redefine, incorporate, or reject what exceeds it—that are thrown into dramatic relief in a different sense. The contemporary scene engaged by the play is hardly restricted to James' lingering interest in demonology or even to the tumultuous aftermath of the Gunpowder Plot; at the heart of *Macbeth*'s dramaturgical concerns lies the developing absolutism of the Jacobean state. If sixteenth-century political cosmology precluded the possibility of a fully intentional treason—a traitor must in some sense be deluded to engage in a course of action which would, if successful, prove his own undoing—that same cosmology radically restricted the power of authority to control or contain treason's amphibology. Treason marked the threshold of political ideology, occupying a place that had traditionally and spectacularly been acknowledged by rituals of exclusion and execution staged on the threshold of society itself. James was endeavoring to extend that threshold, to redefine the boundaries of rule, and his claims for absolutism were invariably grounded in the figure of a king who could, from his quasi-divine perspective, spy into the mystery of things, including the indecipherable countenance and amphibolic tongue of treason.

"It is the glory of God," as Francis Bacon wrote in *The Great Instauration,* "to conceal a thing, but it is the glory of a King to find a thing out."[36] The discovery of the Gunpowder Plot presented James with an awesome opportunity to act out such a royal role on the public stage of history; in his speeches capitalizing on the prevention of the plot, in the controversy surrounding Father Garnet's equivocation, James repeatedly emphasized the mysterious powers of a king who could thus act as God's spy, successfully discriminating between loyalty and sedition, truth and lie. Such is not, however, the image or the situation of authority recreated in Shakespeare's play. References to equivocation and the spectacular genealogy of James that arises from the witches' cauldron of Act IV bring the history of Macbeth's treason into alignment with the contemporary scene, but that scene is itself critically distanced by the enactment not of treason's equivocation but of its full and uncontained amphibology. Watching such a play, James occupies the position of authority; what he views, however, is not a further aggrandizement of his absolute image but a dramatic articulation of the limits of proper rule and authority. The platform of Shakespeare's scaffold marks those limits, just as the scaffold of execution had traditionally marked them. James is a passive audience, "subjected" to a drama in which there is "no art / To find the mind's construction in the face" (I. iv. 12–13)—a drama more ambivalent, that is to say, than

Chapter Five

the one James had fashioned out of the seditious desires of Guy
Fawkes and his fellow conspirators. The king's position and perspective could be likened, in fact, to the situation of London itself
in the late sixteenth century, made into a passive audience and daily
subjected to the spectacle of its own limits and limitations that was
being staged in its Liberties. In the dramaturgical dynamics of royal
audience to amphibolic play, Shakespeare's scaffold relies upon and
recreates the cultural dynamics of its own marginal situation. Like
treason's amphibology, like the recreative and incontinent play of
residual and emergent cultures, Shakespeare's stage was lodged on
the threshold of authority, at the horizon of the period's powers
of containment or control.

The situation of the popular stage was a privileged one, marginal
yet ideologically complex and powerful; it was also a highly precarious one, threatened not only by the efforts of the city to suppress popular drama but also by the very popularity and success
of that drama. If the marginal situation of the popular stage was
a crucial element in the cultivation of Elizabethan and Jacobean
drama, we would expect that stage to suffer something of a sea
change as it came to occupy a new and apparently less ambivalent
place in the cultural landscape of the times. In Shakespeare's career,
to continue focusing on the playwright most intimately involved
with the popular playhouse, whose work spans the period of its
highest achievement and also extends into the early days of its
decline, such a change is indeed evident. Its customary name is
romance.

CHAPTER

6

"All That Monarchs Do": The Obscured Stages of Authority in Pericles

I

In 1605, the Queen's Revels Children performed *Eastward Ho!* at Blackfriars. The authors, Jonson, Chapman, and Marston, were soon apprehended and imprisoned, and for a time it was rumored that Jonson would suffer the loss of his nose and ears for satire directed against the king and his Scottish knights. A year later John Day's *The Isle of Gulls* resulted in similar charges, and again "sundry were committed to Bridewell."[1] When again at large, the company was reorganized as the Children of Blackfriars, but they ran into difficulty once more in 1608, this time managing to offend not only the king but the visiting French ambassador as well. A further round of imprisonments was one of the results; another was the dissolution of the company—one of the last of the boys' troupes—by order of James himself.

Another consequence, according to critical tradition, was the emergence of Shakespearean romance. When the Children of Blackfriars were forced to give up their lease, Richard Burbage, the owner of Blackfriars, redeemed the lease himself and retained it for his own company. For years, the private theaters of the city had been the exclusive province of boys' companies, but the age of strict division between private and public playhouse—the former located within the city walls and devoted largely to satirical comedy,[2] the latter situated on the outskirts of the city, where it pursued a more marginal and ideologically complex form of drama—was at an end. Popular drama had returned to the confines of the city. The future of the King's Men would include Blackfriars as its city residence, an intramural dramatic forum to supplement the stage they continued to occupy at the Globe. That future would also include, of course, the development of Shakespearean romance—a historical coincidence that can prove misleading, especially if taken as a sign that the romances were shaped to fit the tastes and expectations of a new, presumably more elite audience at Blackfriars.

In Alfred Harbage's view, such is the case: the romances bear the stamp of the coterie, as Harbage defined the playgoers who frequented theaters like Blackfriars and Paul's.[3] Harbage's coterie has proved, however, to be more of a critical fiction than an Elizabethan or Jacobean reality, an exaggeration not only of the differences between audiences attending plays within and without the city but also of their power to shape or determine a dramatic repertory.[4] Shakespeare's romances were, moreover, far from elite productions. They enjoyed a popularity as catholic as that of any of his earlier plays, and when they succeeded they did so in the Globe and at Court as well as at Blackfriars. Much to the bewilderment of modern critics, *Pericles* seems to have been one of the most popular romances, and it could hardly have been conditioned by either the audience or the stage facilities of the private theater. Written in 1607 or 1608, it may have preceded the acquisition of Blackfriars by as much as a year; even if the later date of composition is correct, the play could not have been staged before a "private" audience, elite or otherwise, at that time. When Burbage redeemed the lease on Blackfriars, the theater was in a state of disrepair, requiring extensive work before it could be reopened. The city was also in the throes of a new outbreak of plague, making it a propitious time for reconstruction: throughout 1608, performances at Blackfriars as at all theaters within the city were suppressed for the duration of the epidemic, which lasted well into the new year. Neither the King's Men nor any other company performed at Blackfriars during the initial years of *Pericles*' popularity, and the forum of the private theater cannot, as a consequence, explain the dramaturgical shift toward romance.

When popular drama moved out into the Liberties to appropriate their ambivalent terrain for its own purposes, it was able to do so only because the traditions that had shaped and maintained those Liberties were on the wane. A gap had opened in the social fabric, a temporary rift in the cultural landscape that provided the stage with a place on the ideological horizon, a marginal and anamorphic perspective on the cultural dynamics of its own times. Popular drama owed its birth, in other words, to an interim period in a larger historical transition, a period marked by the failure of the dominant culture to rearticulate itself in a fashion that would close off the gaps and seams opening on the margins of its domain. Such a historical interlude could not last long, however, and it was beginning to draw to a close in the first decade of the Jacobean period. One sign of the times came in the form of the Crown's increasing demands for the incorporation of the Liberties. London staunchly resisted the effort—however unhappy the city was over the incontinence of its margins, it was haunted by the specter of a rival urban body—and was successful in its opposition until 1637, when Charles brought the traditional liberty of the suburbs to a corporate conclusion.[5]

The king's harsh actions against the Children of Blackfriars also served as a warning that traditional forms of license would not necessarily prevail under the increasing absolutism of the Jacobean state. For marginal groups, former sources of power and ideological mobility were fast becoming insecure, sources of anxiety at best. One expression of that anxiety was Burbage's effort to broaden the financial and cultural base of his company, responding to a previously unfelt need by taking over Blackfriars himself. The advent of Shakespearean romance was another such expression. If the shift in theatrical setting and the shift in dramaturgy are at all related, they are apposite developments, independent yet homologous signs of a changing political and cultural climate. As a genre, Shakespearean romance reflects the shifting ground of popular drama in the city; it also reflects upon or articulates the broader tensions and contradictions of a culture poised on the verge of the modern world and the status of Shakespearean theater in such a world.

II

Upon deciphering Antiochus' riddle, Pericles first offers to conceal the *arcanum imperii* of the king's incest. "Who has a book of all that monarchs do, / He's more secure to keep it shut than shown" (I. i. 97–98). The offer to keep the king's secret safe only reveals, of course, that it is no longer either a secret or his own; the incestuous entanglements of legitimacy and authority have already been disclosed, and will continue to shape the main plot of the play. "We begin in incest," as C. L. Barber most succinctly put it, "and end in a sublime transformation of the motive."[6] In other respects, however, *Pericles* is something less than an open book. Where the actions of Pericles and his daughter are concerned, the play reveals a sense of taboo that is both far from universal and quite foreign to the familiar Greek romance upon which the play is based:[7] a sense of taboo that reveals significant cultural tensions and contradictions, and is produced by the intersection of genre, dramatic forum, and historical moment that we customarily call Shakespearean romance.

Consider, for example, Pericles' first act of any significance after fleeing Antioch. To the starving city of Tharsus, he presents a

shipment of grain, expecting nothing in return but "love / And har-
bourage for ourself, our ships and men" (I. iv. 99–100). It is a gift
without reserve, a demonstration of legitimate authority in action—
of a patriarchal power that does not feed upon its subjects or depen-
dents but rather nourishes and protects them. A true prince, as Pericles says, should be "no more but as the tops of trees / Which fence
the roots they grow by" (I. ii. 31–32), and it is in recognition of such
princely grace that the citizens erect a memorial to their benefactor,
in the form of a "statue to make him glorious" (II. Chorus. 14). In
and of itself, the scene is hardly problematic, the contrast with
Antiochus quite clear. Unspecified in Shakespeare's play, however,
is the setting for Pericles' princely performance; in Lawrence Twine's
The Patterne of Painful Adventures,[8] a relatively faithful Elizabethan
version of the Apollonius romance that was also one of Shakespeare's sources, the gift of grain takes place in the marketplace of
the city, where a safe harbor is not the only price attached to Apollonius' expression of princely bounty. The citizens of Tharsus must
also pay the going rate for wheat, namely "eight peeces of brasse
for every bushel" (262). When the bargain is completed, however,
Apollonius has second thoughts. "Doubting lest by this deede, he
should seem to put off the dignitie of a prince, and put on the
countenance of a merchant rather than a giver, when he had received the price of the wheate, he restored it back again to the use
and commoditie of the citie." Taken in payment and then returned,
the brass coin effaces the course of its circulation and restores
Apollonius' princely countenance; it even redoubles his generosity,
since it returns to the city in the form of a second gift—and so the
citizens treat it, not as money to be spent but as a gift to be in some
fashion reciprocated and returned to the giver. The citizens follow
Apollonius' example quite profoundly, in fact, for they translate
the brass coin returned to them into a monumental image of princely
generosity. "They erected in the marked [sic] place a monument
in the memoriall of him: his stature [sic] made of brasse standing
in a charret, holding corne in his right hand, and spurning it with
his left foot." Beginning as a monetary sign for the value of the
grain, the coin of the city—what Apollonius in fact spurned, although not with his foot—has been recast to represent the grain
according to the dictates of an alternate symbolic economy; the
money of the merchant has been translated into the image of the
prince, not by bearing his likeness, as in the case of a coin of the
realm, but by becoming that likeness in a manner more attuned to
princely decorum.

Apollonius' flurry of brass coins serves to remind us that a gift is never merely a gift. Gift-giving initiates a dialectical process of "prestation," according to the now-classic study of symbolic exchange by Marcel Mauss: a gift establishes a cycle of exchange, an obligation to accept the gift offered and to accept what it implies as well, that is, the obligation to give presents in return.[9] A gift marks the beginning of a coercive system of exchange, one that comes into play, as Pierre Bourdieu observes, in cultural situations where more overt systems of obligation or domination are unavailable:

> The gift, generosity, conspicuous distribution—the extreme case of which is potlatch—are operations of social alchemy which may be observed whenever the direct application of overt physical or economic violence is negatively sanctioned, and which tend to bring about the transmutation of economic capital into symbolic capital . . . an interested relationship is transmuted into a disinterested, gratuitous relationship, overt domination into misrecognized, "socially recognized" domination, in other words, legitimate authority.[10]

All gifts are to some degree "misrecognized," the obligations they embody cloaked in an aura of disinterested gratuity and gratitude. Through their acts of prestation, both Pericles and Apollonius achieve an indebted alliance with Tharsus that could easily bring the wrath of Antiochus down on the city. Pericles' alliance, however, is never quite represented as part of an exchange, except insofar as it is included in, or occluded by, the "love" he seeks. The mercantile traces of Apollonius' negotiations, the brass from which his statue is molded, are not allowed to mar the figure of Pericles raised by the city in Shakespeare's play; the "marked place" in *Pericles*, where the gift is given and the statue erected, is stripped of all distinguishing marks, including its designation as a marketplace. Nor is the initial scene at Tharsus the only instance in which the negotiations of authority are thus suppressed. When Pericles returns to Tharsus to deposit the infant Marina there, he sails off to resume his throne at Tyre—where he remains throughout the childhood and early adolescence of his daughter, despite the fact that she is "all his heart's delight." Apollonius, by contrast, is too grief-stricken over the loss of his wife to return to either her father's court or his own; he leaves his daughter behind in order to embark on a voyage around the Mediterranean, "meaning . . . to exercise the trade of merchandize," and until his return some fourteen years later is presumed lost at sea. Shakespeare's divergence here is an extreme one: what keeps father and daughter apart, and unknown

to one another until their climactic recognition scene, is left unex-
plained, resulting in a lapse of logical plot development that even
Gower, standing "i' th' gaps / To teach you the stages of our story"
(IV. Chorus. 8–9), cannot resolve.

According to Fredric Jameson, such lacunae mark significant
moments in the transmission and transformation of a genre, especially when that genre is romance. In *The Political Unconscious,*
Jameson defines romance as a genre of historical crisis—one that
surfaces most prominently at critical moments of transition in Western culture, and that seeks to provide imaginary solutions to real
but unprecedented social and cultural contradictions:

> As for romance, it would seem that its ultimate condition of figur-
> ation . . . is to be found in a transitional moment in which two dif-
> ferent modes of production, or moments of socioeconomic
> development, coexist. Their antagonism is not yet articulated in terms
> of the struggle of social classes, so that its resolution can be projected
> in the form of a nostalgic (or less often, a Utopian) harmony. Our
> principal experience of such transitional moments is evidently that
> of an organic social order in the process of penetration and subver-
> sion, reorganization and rationalization, by a nascent capitalism, yet
> still, for a long moment, coexisting with the latter. So Shakespearean
> romance . . . opposes the phantasmagoria of "imagination" to the
> bustling commercial activity at work all around it.[11]

Adopting Jameson's perspective for the moment, we would note
that the Apollonius romance was originally the product of the early
Middle Ages, and was shaped by the relatively comfortable cultural
contradictions of that world: it was the product, that is to say, of a
state of society in which trade and merchants were officially denounced by the Church but were also, for the most part, either
turned to its advantage or merely overlooked. "To fornicate is
always forbidden to anyone," as canon law aptly proclaimed, "but
to trade is sometimes allowed, and sometimes not."[12] With the development of a world economy in the sixteenth and seventeenth
centuries, however, cultural concern over the place and "trade of
merchandize" was significantly heightened; as Louis Dumont has
shown, the expanding commercial activities of the period were not
readily accommodated by existing ideologies but instead provoked
an escalating disparagement of trade and money in general, resulting in a state of severe cultural contradiction that would only
be resolved over the course of the next century and a half, as
economic theory evolved to the point that exchange and even profit
could be ideologically justified.[13] The countenance of a merchant
may be a source of anxiety for Apollonius, but that countenance

is fully repressed in Shakespeare's version of the story; what Jameson regards as the signature of Shakespearean romance, its efforts to dissociate itself from the "bustling commercial activity at work all around it," thus manifests itself in *Pericles,* and makes it a dramatic register and imaginary resolution of the cultural contradictions that *were* the early modern period.

Such a reading would conform to what Jameson regards as the ultimate horizon of literary interpretation, in which the occlusions and anxieties of a given genre are viewed as registers of the informing tensions and contradictions of distinct historical modes of production; the text is conditioned and determined by its place in Jameson's master narrative of History. Twine's *Painful Adventures,* however, occupies the same transitional moment in history, and in the three editions that were issued between 1576 and 1607 exhibits none of the mercantile anxieties produced when the same romance is brought on stage. Jameson would situate Shakespearean romance on the plane of historical modes of production, but in the case of *Pericles* such a strategy seems premature, producing a significant blindness to more immediate historical conditions of production. The popularity of Twine's version and the nature of Shakespeare's divergence from it suggest that not all the anxieties of the text are generic, that we are dealing with a critical moment in the life of a specific romance tradition—the Apollonius of Tyre story—at the point where that tradition intersects the more recent one of popular drama.

Nor is it adequate to refer, as Jameson does in his general comments on Shakespearean romance, to plays written for and quite successful upon the popular stage as being set apart from "the bustling commercial activity at work all around [them]." Drama was a thriving if unseemly business enterprise in early modern England, theaters sites of exchange, players regarded with the same ambivalence as merchants for their protean capacities to cross or violate the class boundaries and cultural hierarchies. Merchants and players were homologous figures in the moral imagination of the period, each representing a degree of social mobility that threatened to produce a state of social alchemy. According to William Harrison, merchants should be counted among the citizens or burghers of the commonwealth but were in fact increasingly difficult to fix within a strict social hierarchy, since "they often change estate with gentlemen, as gentlemen do with them, by a mutual conversion of one into the other."[14] And if merchants were confusing social categories and hierarchies, so were their fellow alchemists of the stage, according to the standard antitheatrical invectives:

> In Stage playes for a boy to put on the attyre, the gesture, the passions
> of a woman; for a meane person to take upon him the title of a
> Prince with counterfeit porte, and traine, is by outward signes to
> shewe themselves otherwise than they are, and so within the com-
> passe of a lye. . . . We are commanded by God to abide in the same
> calling wherein we were called, which is our ordinary vocation in a
> commonweale. . . . If privat men be suffered to forsake theire calling
> because they desire to walke gentlemen like in sattine & velvet, with
> a buckler at theire heeles, proportion is so broken, unitie dissolved,
> harmony confounded, that the whole must be dismembred and the
> prince or the heade cannot chuse but sicken.[15]

A player, according to a Jacobean character-book, was a jack-of-
all-trades, "a shifting companion" from the perspective of social
hierarchy:

> If his profession were single, hee would think himselfe a simple
> fellow, as hee doth all professions besides his owne: His owne there-
> fore is compounded of all Natures, all humours, all professions.[16]

If merchants changed place with gentlemen, the player's range was
more extensive, subjecting all social classes and categories, from
peasant to monarch, to a theatrical system of exchange and thereby
inculcating in the audience a potent sense of social mobility and of
the protean capacities of the self. Moreover, the player's profession
not only was compounded of all but also confounded cultural dis-
tinctions crucial to the reigning hierarchy of early modern London.
The player's work, his protean profession, was playing, and the
guilds of London viewed such a blurring of cultural realms as a
threat that was hardly limited to the narrow confines of the stage.

Merchants and players were twin figures for the period, ambivalent and discomfiting doubles; the popular stage itself was not
only a significant participant in the bustling commercial activity of
early modern London but was also located in the midst of various
licit and illicit trades, ranging from actual marketplaces to stalls of
foreign or unlicensed craftsmen to taverns and brothels, all of which
had enjoyed both liberty and license outside the city walls. Such a
situation was crucial to the emergence of popular drama, but it is
a situation that *Pericles* consistently seeks to distance itself from,
with a single exception. In the bawdyhouse at Mytilene, *Pericles* does
allow the marketplace and the trade of merchandise to be brought
on stage, and the exception is a significant one. In Shakespeare's
reworking of Marina's time in the brothel, we find ourselves on familiar but strange ground: familiar in terms of the popular stage
and its marginal situation and affiliations, strange in all the ways that
the brothel of *Pericles* sets itself apart from the taverns of Eastcheap

or the licentious suburbs of *Measure for Measure*. In the brothel, the countenance of a merchant comes into clearer focus as a source of anxiety, threatening to impinge not on the authority of a prince but on the authority and status of Shakespeare's dramatic enterprise itself.

III

Unlike her father, Marina enters a quite explicitly defined market-place, not as an agent of exchange but as the thing itself: a com-modity to be bought and sold, then sold again by a pander who hopes to shore up the "wenchless" fortunes of his brothel with her continually renewed use-value. She is, of course, a "piece of virtue," and so she remains. She preaches divinity in the whorehouse and converts its customers; she wins Lord Lysimachus not by anything she says but by the nobility and breeding evident in any word that passes her lips. In Twine, Apollonius' daughter Tharsia is no less determined to preserve her chastity than is her Shakespearean counterpart, but the two part company in the means they employ to convert their customers and, ultimately, their masters' trade. Where Marina preaches, Tharsia shows a shrewder sense both of business and of theater.

The lord of the city, Athanagoras—the counterpart to Lysima-chus—is her first customer; in the face of his desire she weeps, then offers to him neither her body nor a sermon nor even her speechless nobility, but rather the tale of her woeful adventures. She relates her part in the romance we have been reading, converting the desire of a man for a woman into the desire of an audience for a story, and with profitable results. In payment for the tale she tells, Athanagoras gives her twenty pieces of gold—twice the market value of her vir-ginity. In leaving he encounters her next customer; when asked how he found her, he wryly replies, "Never of any better," and then hides behind the door to watch and listen to the ensuing scene. Tharsia tells her new client of Athanagoras' generosity, and the man, Apor-tatus, offers her an even more inflated sum; she weeps, tells her story, and he too is satisfied. Upon leaving and discovering Athanagoras, Aportatus joins him outside the door—thus fulfilling the function for which he was named—to watch the scene played over, again and again. Tharsia and her story continue to appreciate in value, and the audience outside the room continues to grow.

What she converts the bawdyhouse into is a playhouse. Athana-goras fully understands what such a figure represents: he adopts Tharsia and removes her from the brothel to the "market place of the citie" where, with a broader audience and an expanded repertory, she will be able to "get store of money daily" (300). He becomes her sponsor, the equivalent of a patron or the owner of a theatrical company—or as Marx defined such a role, an entrepreneur who realizes the value of the songbird he has in his hands:

> A singer who sings like a bird is an unproductive worker. If she sells her song for money, she is to that extent a wage-laborer or merchant. But if the same singer is engaged by an entrepreneur who makes her sing to make money, then she becomes a productive worker, since she *produces* capital.[17]

It is difficult to imagine that Shakespeare, any less than Athanagoras, failed to realize what Tharsia represents. Not merely a figure born for the popular stage, she is a figure *of* the popular stage: she ruins her masters' trade not by driving them out of business but by converting a licensed yet illicit sexual transaction into the stage setting for a more theatrical form of exchange, creating a more profitable and inherently theatrical enterprise on the site of an incontinent but pervasive pastime.

Popular drama had been founded on an analogous translation of marginal pastimes into a new form and forum for theater. Popular playhouses like Shakespeare's had survived for years in the Liberties of London as profitable businesses, an enterprising form of theatricality dependent upon its close conjunction with other residual and emergent forms of cultural license. The particular conjunction that Tharsia achieves, that of a stage in the midst of a bawdyhouse, would in itself hardly have surprised Shakespeare's audience. According to contemporary accounts of spectators' activities in the popular theaters, performances took place in the midst of the theatrical equivalent to a bawdyhouse. The size of crowds in suburban theaters provided an anonymity which translated playgoing into an unrivaled opportunity for the less-than-aesthetic pursuits of sexual flirtation, seduction, assignation, and common prostitution. As Ann Jennalie Cook has recently argued, descriptions of "actes and bargaines of incontinencie" in the theaters are too pervasive to be entirely discounted.[18] Even if they could be discredited, claims that playhouses were "the very markets of bawdry" were made so frequently as to guarantee that brothel and playhouse would be indissolubly linked in the cultural imagination, making the two virtually synonymous. The promise of sexual assignation was also heightened by such accounts; whether fulfilled or not, such a prospect swelled the ranks of the paying playgoers considerably, underwriting the financial stability of popular drama and making bawds silent partners of any company of players. Like

Tharsia's customers, Shakespeare's audience was lured into the playhouse at least in part by the promise of illicit liaisons—an anticipation that, as Stephen Greenblatt has recently argued, the popular playhouse at once encouraged and transformed, displaced and incorporated into the erotic power and energy of the theater itself.[19]

Viewed in this light, the brothel scenes of *Pericles* bring the general anxiety over mercantile concerns into more specific focus; the play's unwillingness to represent the highly theatrical transaction between an actor and an audience, whether a prince before a populace or his daughter before prospective customers, marks an evasion of the economic and cultural roots of the popular stage itself. Elsewhere in *Pericles,* dramatic enactment is often preempted or supplanted by moral commentary posing as narrative; in the brothel scenes, the theatrical impetus that Tharsia turns to the profit of herself and her audience is suppressed in Marina's chaste performance. Theatricality itself—the capacity to submit oneself to another's desired fiction or compel another to submit to one's own, in a highly charged dissolution of the boundaries of identity—is displaced, divorced from the role Marina performs and relegated to the one she would have enacted, had she become the "creature of sale" that the bawd has in mind:

> Pray you, come hither awhile. You have fortunes coming upon you. Mark me: you must seem to do that forcefully which you commit willingly; despise profit where you have most gain. To weep that you live as you do makes pity in your lovers: seldom but that pity begets you a good opinion, and that opinion a mere profit.
>
> (IV. ii. 117ff.)

This is a speech to a fledgling player, replete with echoes from Shakespeare's corpus: Hamlet addressing the players, Polonius counselling Laertes, even a touch of Bottom worked in for good measure. Here, however, theatricality is reduced to mere role-playing in pursuit of profit. Playing and the bawdy "trade of merchandize," closely associated in early modern culture and in Shakespearean representation of the past, have attained an equivalence that is no longer a source of theatrical energy but rather of an anxiety that marks a fundamental contradiction between Shakespearean romance, at least in this manifestation of it, and the cultural grounds of possibility for popular drama.

If the anxieties of the play over exchange and transactions of the marketplace and the theater are in any way relevant to the larger social and economic contradictions of the period, it is in the context of this narrowing-down of the theatrical. Theatricality was, of course, the mark of the player's profession, his business or enterprise; traditionally, it had also been what distinguished a player from his fellow social alchemist, the merchant. "By a mutual conversion of one into the other," as Harrison complained, merchants and gentlemen actually changed places in the social hierarchy; players, by contrast, performed a deceptive imitation of such mobility, an apparent permutation of social categories that was at once ideologically powerful and a theatrical illusion. The theatricality that had formerly distinguished the player, however, was shifting ground in the period, undergoing what amounted to a cultural transvaluation.

In the broadened and "placeless market" of an expanding world economy, "impersonality and impersonation . . . suddenly thrust themselves forward as vexing issues."[20] At the time when theatricality was being banished from the stage of *Pericles*, it was in the process of being appropriated by the marketplace. "Man in business," as John Hall wrote, "is but a Theatricall person, and in a manner but personates himselfe . . . in his retired and hid actions, he pulls off his disguise and acts openly."[21] Displaced by history from the province of the stage to that of the marketplace, theatricality here suffers a radical reduction, becoming a mere impersonation that serves at once to enable and to mystify the pursuit of profit. Although the moral connotations of disguising oneself or one's motives have since continued to fluctuate, the theatrical has yet to escape from the narrow stage it came to occupy in the course of the seventeenth century—a narrow stage that has already become the confines of the theatrical in *Pericles*.

Hall's distinction between what a man does in business and what he does when retired or hid from public view also carries the seeds of a full and in many ways unprecedented dichotomy between the public and the private—a dichotomy around which the Enlightenment would articulate itself, within which Shakespeare's heterogeneous world could only occupy the no-man's-land of an excluded middle. As the theatrical and the mercantile were mutually displaced to fit the configurations of such a dichotomy, a new concept of the self or the person would arise. Hobbes' famous definition of the self as a *persona* stems from a discussion of social and other contracts, of man in the marketplace, and is elucidated by the necessary identification with the actor. "So that a *person*, is the same as an *actor* is, both on the stage and in common conversation; and to personate, is to act, or *represent* himself, or another."[22] Behind Hobbes' effort to delineate the confused social and personal boundaries of a new age lies a rigid distinction between natural and artificial persons or personations, representations of oneself and another, which again could only exclude the middle ground formerly occupied by phenomena like the popular stage—by a theatricality that was at once less easily contained, more mobile, and more vertiginous.

It had been a certain capacity for a different form of the theatrical, for an intense submission to and exploration of alternative values and desires, that had made the popular stage remarkably receptive to the residual and emergent cultural phenomena which shared its place on the ideological horizon of Elizabethan and Jacobean London. To the extent that such a capacity is reduced or repressed in *Pericles,* the play represents not so much a turning point in Shakespeare's career as a concerted turning away from the cultural contexts and associations that had shaped his dramaturgy in the past. Speaking from the perspective of literary tradition, Howard Felperin suggests that *Pericles* "reveals Shakespeare reassessing the premises on which his art had always been based";[23] from the standpoint of the present study Felperin's phrase is a felicitous one, especially if taken more literally than its author intended. The premises or grounds being reassessed include the place of the stage itself; in what it obscures or suppresses, *Pericles* reveals Shakespeare's systematic effort to dissociate his art from the marginal contexts and affiliations that had formerly served as the grounds of its possibility. As such, it is less a transitional work than an experiment never repeated, unsatisfying in its gaps and seams yet illuminating because of them, serving to demonstrate—for Shakespeare as for us—the crucial role played by the marginality of the popular stage and the critical resources it found available to it on the ideological threshold of its age.

IV

An experiment never repeated: unlike *The Winter's Tale* or *The Tempest, Pericles* represents a radical effort to dissociate the popular stage from its cultural contexts and theatrical grounds of possibility—an effort to imagine, in fact, that popular drama could be a purely aesthetic phenomenon, free from history and from historical determination. In later Shakespearean romance, the utopian impulse of the genre turns to the problematics and imaginary resolution of social and class divisions or to searching explorations of colonial ideology and the limits of patriarchal power and authority; here, utopian desire attempts to imagine a purely aesthetic realm governed by a purely aesthetic and not yet available figure, that of the author.

Gower introduces *Pericles* as a tale of universal significance, ancient but unaging, forever timely and uncontaminated by historical or cultural contexts:

> From ashes ancient Gower is come,
> Assuming man's infirmities,
> To glad your ear, and please your eyes.
> It hath been sung at festivals,
> On ember-eves and holy-ales;
> And lords and ladies in their lives
> Have read it for restoratives:
> The purchase is to make men glorious,
> Et bonum quo antiquius eo melius.
> If you, born in these latter times,
> When wit's more ripe, accept my rimes,
> And that to hear an old man sing
> May to your wishes pleasure bring
> I life would wish, and that I might
> Waste it for you like taper-light.
>
> (I. Chorus. 2–16)

Although choral prologues and interludes are not alien to Shakespearean dramaturgy, Gower is a unique figure. His is not the voice of history such as we encounter in *Henry V* but of history's occlusion or antithesis; not the voice of time, as in *The Winter's Tale*, but of a timeless authority. Gower also represents, of course, one of Shakespeare's sources: reincarnated on stage, he occupies the place of both author and authority and seeks to legitimize the play in the way a father or a monarch legitimizes a genealogy, by authorizing it in a rather full sense of the term.

Shakespeare had never before felt compelled to bring his authors or authorities on stage; that he does so here, in a romance structured around the genealogical entanglements and contaminations of authority, should at least give us pause. Although Gower claims to stand at the limits of theatrical representation—to stand "i' th' gaps to teach you / The stages of our story"—his role is far from an illuminating one. "The effect," as Muriel Bradbrook writes, "is to offer a point of view which is not authoritative . . . but is to be scanned from a Jacobean perspective."[24] Scanned from such a perspective, Gower in fact conceals as much as he reveals, especially where the genealogical entanglements of Shakespeare's sources are concerned. His presence as an authorial figure obscures the discomfiting significance of Twine's *Painfull Adventures;* presenting himself as an authoritative supplement to theatrical representation, he serves in fact as an antitheatrical agent, an embodiment of the

play's effort to divorce itself from the cultural grounds of theatricality in Jacobean London. As such he is a proleptic figure, an
anticipation not of later configurations of Shakespearean romance
but of an emerging figure of the author that would eventually
eclipse the popular stage and Shakespearean dramaturgy.

It would have seemed fatal, as Stephen Greenblatt has reflected,
to be imitated by Shakespeare: "He possessed a limitless talent for
entering into the consciousness of another, perceiving its deepest
structures as a manipulable fiction, reinscribing it into his own
narrative form."[25] This is not to mystify Shakespeare as an author
but rather to recognize that his corpus is grounded not in a univocal
perspective but in a multiplicity and heterogeneity of voices, an
incorporation and appropriation of a wide range of alternative and
marginal perspectives. Shakespeare stands at the threshold or horizon of professional authorship and the modern construction of the
author, but that horizon was already coming into view. Although Ben
Jonson was one of Shakespeare's contemporaries not taken in by
Gower's claims to an ageless authority, finding *Pericles* as "stale / as
the shrieve's crusts," Jonson is nonetheless one of Gower's de-
scendants, at least in his efforts to carve out a literary and properly
aesthetic realm for his plays. As Peter Stallybrass and Allon White
have recently noted, the figure of the author promulgated in Jonson's publication of his plays is a figure who seeks, like Gower in
Pericles, to displace drama from its marginal and theatrical conditions of production:

> The "authorship" of [Jonson's] plays, indeed, was an act performed
> *on* and *against* the theatrical script, so as to efface its real conditions
> of production. The *Workes* which Jonson published in 1616 were the
> result of a labour whereby his plays appeared as literary texts, mi-
> raculously freed from the contagion of the marketplace.[26]

It was an effort that would succeed fully only in retrospect, when
the figure of the Jonsonian author would be appropriated by the
Restoration stage to authorize and legitimize a more proper, and
properly aesthetic, form of theater.

It is to Jonson, however, that we owe a final glimpse of the
marginal situation of the popular stage, the "licentious liberties" it
occupied and appropriated to its own heterogeneous ends. Some
things come into clearest view as they are about to disappear from
the stage of history, and it is such a view of the popular stage that
Jonson provides in *Bartholomew Fair.* Performed on the popular
stage, the action of the play is also set on the grounds of that stage,
in the Liberties outside the city walls and the marketplace and

fairgrounds of Smithfield. The place of the stage is brought on
stage, in what is presented as an ironic reification of a passing phase
of history. The Stage-Keeper of the Induction is an anachronism,
a figure of the theatrical past who has performed his duties since
the days of Tarlton but is soon supplanted by a Scrivener who
announces a new social contract for theater, and a new theatrical
era. What we are about to see will not be a mere successor to the
theatrical past, however; it will also be a demystification of that past,
particularly of the marginal contexts of Shakespearean romance.
The author of *Bartholomew Fair,* according to the Scrivener, can only
present things as they are:

> If there be never a servant-monster i' the Fair, who can help it? he
> says; nor a nest of antics? He is loth to make Nature afraid in his
> plays, like those that beget *Tales, Tempests,* and such like drolleries, to
> mix his head with other men's heels.
>
> ("The Induction on the Stage," 128–32)[27]

Dryden praised Jonson for making "an excellent lazar of the fair";[28]
as a figure for the popular stage, Jonson's fair also has a larger
historical resonance. Reducing the ideological range and license of
popular drama to its sheerly material marginality, Jonson recalls
something of the history of that marginality; he collapses popular
drama into its prehistory, making a lazar not only of the fair but
of the popular stage as well.

Jonson does not seem to have agreed with Dryden concerning
his success: he did not include *Bartholomew Fair* in his *Workes* of
1616, nor was it published with Jonson's corpus until after his death.
Even as an ironic and parodic review of the place of the popular
stage, the play gives sufficient range and license to the enormities
of the Liberties that the imprimatur of the author could not fully
purge the taint of the stage. The vitality of *Bartholomew Fair* makes
it a less radical effort to divorce popular drama from its cultural
grounds than Shakespeare's effort in *Pericles,* but taken together
the two serve to register the shift that was taking place in the cultural
landscape of the period, and to clarify the role that the rise of the
author would play in the impending eclipse of Jacobean popular
drama. And if *Pericles* was an experiment never repeated by Shakespeare, it was also an experiment written for and performed on
the popular stage, and its literary fortunes consequently testify to
the limits of any work that seeks to obscure or escape its historical
conditions of possibility. Gower's claims to universal significance
were belied not only by Jonson but also by subsequent literary
history; his perspective nonetheless anticipates predominant views

in this century of the motives and nature of Shakespearean romance. *Pericles* stands as an unwitting but necessary qualification to such idealizing tendencies, a reminder that a work of art achieves such an aura of ahistorical significance not because it has successfully transcended or risen above the cultural conditions of its production and reception, but rather because it has remained inextricably bound to them and has engaged them fully: contained and to an extent determined by its specific cultural context, and only to that extent able to clarify, question, or transform the bonds and boundaries of the culture that produced it.

Notes

PREFACE

1. See Michel Foucault, *Madness and Civilization*, trans. Richard Howard (New York: Random House, 1971). Also relevant are Foucault's comments on the politics of space in an interview with the editors of *Hérodote;* see "Questions on Geography," in *Power/Knowledge: Selected Interviews and Other Writings, 1972–1977*, ed. Colin Gordon (New York: Pantheon, 1980), pp. 63–77.

2. See Clifford Geertz, "Thick Description: Toward an Interpretive Theory of Culture," in *The Interpretation of Cultures* (New York: Basic Books, 1973), pp. 3–32.

3. For a collection that brings together examples of both, and attempts at greater length to articulate differences and similarities, see *Political Shakespeare: New Essays in Cultural Materialism*, ed. Jonathan Dollimore and Alan Sinfield (Ithaca: Cornell University Press, 1985).

4. See Raymond Williams, *Marxism and Literature* (Oxford: Oxford University Press, 1978), p. 112.

5. My own formulation of a semiotics or poetics of cultural production is indebted to Stephen Greenblatt's description of "cultural poetics" in *Renaissance Self-Fashioning: From More to Shakespeare* (Chicago: University of Chicago Press, 1980). For more recent discussions of New Historicism and cultural materialism, see Louis Montrose, "Renaissance Literary Studies and the Subject of History," *English Literary Renaissance* 16 (1986): 5–12, and in the same volume, Jean Howard, "The New Historicism in Renaissance Studies," 13–43.

6. Clifford Geertz, "Blurred Genres: The Refiguration of Social Thought," *The American Scholar* 49 (1980): 167; for the origin of the phrase "cultural performance," see Milton Singer, "The Cultural Pattern of Indian Civilization: A Preliminary Report of a Methodological Field Study," *Far Eastern Quarterly* 15 (1953): 27.

7. Frank Lentricchia, *Criticism and Social Change* (Chicago: University of Chicago Press, 1983), p. 70.

CHAPTER 1

1. Fernand Braudel characterizes the walled town as "aloof" in *Capitalism and Material Life*, trans. M. Kochan (New York: Harper and Row, 1973),

p. 382. For Wyngaerde's Panorama, see G. E. Mitton, *Maps of Old London* (London: A. & C. Black, 1908).

2. Muriel C. Bradbrook, *English Dramatic Form* (London: Chatto & Windus, 1965), p. 41.

3. On theater in France, see Elie Konigson, "Religious Drama and Urban Society in France at the End of the Middle Ages," in *Drama and Society*, ed. James Redmond (Cambridge: Cambridge University Press, 1979), pp. 23–36.

4. Victor Ehrenberg, *Sophocles and Pericles* (Oxford: Basil Blackwell, 1954), p. 6. On the place of Athenian drama in fifth-century society, see Harold C. Baldry, "Theatre and Society in Greek and Roman Antiquity," in Redmond, *Drama and Society*, pp. 1–21.

5. Richard Schechner, *Essays on Performance Theory, 1970–1976* (New York: Drama Book Specialists, 1977), p. 115.

6. The phrase is Phillip Stubbes', in *The Anatomie of Abuses* . . . (1583), in the *New Shakespeare Society*, ed. F. J. Furnivall (London, 1877–82), series 6, pt. 1, 141.

7. For an admirable study of antitheatricalism in Western culture, see Jonas Barish, *The Anti-Theatrical Prejudice* (Berkeley: University of California Press, 1981).

8. See Sydney Anglo, *Spectacle, Pageantry, and Early Tudor Policy* (Oxford: Oxford University Press, 1969); Natalie Z. Davis, "The Social and the Body Sacred in Sixteenth-Century Lyon," *Past and Present* 90 (1981): 40–71; Richard C. Trexler, *Public Life in Renaissance Florence* (New York: Academic Press, 1980); André Leroi-Gourhan, *Le geste et la parole* (Paris: Editions Albin Michel, 1965), 2:138–205; Henri Lefebvre, *Le droit et la ville* (Paris: Presses universitaires de France, 1978).

The two sources closest to my own approach, and immensely fruitful, are Charles Phythian-Adams, "Ceremony and the Citizen: The Communal Year at Coventry, 1450–1550," in *The Early Modern Town*, ed. Peter Clark (London: Longman, 1976), pp. 106–28; and Joseph Rykwert, *The Idea of a Town: The Anthropology of Urban Form in Rome, Italy, and the Ancient World* (Princeton: Princeton University Press, 1976). Also of considerable value are two more recent studies: Denis Cosgrove, *Social Formation and Symbolic Landscape* (Totowa, N.J.: Barnes and Noble, 1985), and Peter Stallybrass and Allon White, *The Politics and Poetics of Transgression* (Ithaca: Cornell University Press, 1986).

9. Johan Huizinga, *The Waning of the Middle Ages* (New York: Doubleday, 1954), p. 9.

10. Lefebvre, *Le droit et la ville*, p. 53.

11. For the phrase and for an admirable discussion of culture as a symbolic action, see Clifford Geertz, "Thick Description," pp. 30–32.

12. The account of the procession (usually attributed to Mulcaster) is most easily accessible in Arthur F. Kinney, *Elizabethan Backgrounds: Historical Documents of the Age of Elizabeth I* (Hamden, Conn.: Archon, 1975), pp. 7–40; my page references are to this edition. The procession was also described by the Venetian ambassador, Il Schifanoya; see the *Calendar of State Papers (Venetian), 1558–1580*, 7:12–16. Also see David Bergeron,

English Civic Pageantry, 1558–1642 (London: Edward Arnold, 1972), pp. 12–29.

13. Clifford Geertz, "Centers, Kings, and Charisma: Reflections on the Symbolics of Power," in *Culture and Its Creators,* ed. Joseph Ben-David and Jerry N. Clark (Chicago: University of Chicago Press, 1977), p. 160. For a fuller but complementary view of Elizabeth's adroit negotiations of power, see Louis Adrian Montrose, " 'Eliza, Queene of shepheardes,' and the Pastoral of Power," *English Literary Renaissance* 10 (1980): 153–82, and Jonathan Goldberg, *James I and the Politics of Literature* (Baltimore: Johns Hopkins University Press, 1983).

14. Donald Lupton, *London and the Country Carbonadoed and Quartered into Severall Characters* (London, 1632), p. 3.

15. Charles Phythian-Adams, *The Desolation of a City: Coventry and the Urban Crisis of the Late Middle Ages* (Cambridge: Cambridge University Press, 1979), p. 178.

16. For efforts to read the early modern town as a ritual inscription, see Davis, "The Social and the Body Sacred," and Phythian-Adams, "Ceremony and the Citizen," for their studies of Lyon and Coventry.

17. The quotation is from an essay put together by Stephen Orgel from Gordon's notes and rough drafts, "Roles and Mysteries," in *The Renaissance Imagination: Essays and Lectures by D. J. Gordon,* ed. Stephen Orgel (Berkeley: University of California Press, 1980), p. 18.

18. All quotations from Stow are from the two-volume *Survay* edited by C. L. Kingsford (Oxford: Clarendon Press, 1909); volume and page numbers will hereafter be cited in the text.

19. Stephen Orgel, *The Illusion of Power* (Berkeley: University of California Press, 1975), p. 24.

20. For the details of that growth, see W. K. Jordan, *The Charities of London 1480–1660* (London: G. Allen & Unwin, 1960); Norman G. Brett-James, *The Growth of Stuart London* (London: G. Allen & Unwin, 1935), esp. pp. 67–126; Harold Priestley, *London: The Years of Change* (London: Frederick Muller, 1966); and F. J. Fisher, "London as an 'Engine of Economic Growth,' " in *The Early Modern Town,* ed. Peter Clark (London: Longman, 1971), pp. 205–15.

21. On rhetorical topoi and the cultivation of ambivalence, see Joel B. Altman, *The Tudor Play of Mind* (Berkeley: University of California Press, 1979).

22. See the *Rhetorica ad Herennium* (11.2.17) and Aristotle's *Topics* (163b, 24–30). For a full discussion of memory places and their relation to actual places, see Frances Yates, *The Art of Memory* (Chicago: University of Chicago Press, 1966), pp. 1–49; and Terry Comito, *The Idea of the Garden in the Renaissance* (New Brunswick, N.J.: Rutgers University Press, 1978), pp. 51–88.

23. Max Weber, *General Economic History,* trans. F. H. Knight (New York: Greenberg, 1927), p. 265.

24. Ernst Cassirer, *The Individual and the Cosmos in Renaissance Philosophy,* trans. M. Domandi (Philadelphia: University of Pennsylvania Press, 1979), p. 135.

25. Ibid.

26. Comito, *The Idea of the Garden*, p. 53. For Cicero, see *De Oratore* 2.34.146; 2.39.162.

27. See Robert J. Thornton, *Space, Time, and Culture among the Iraqw of Tanzania* (New York: Academic Press, 1980), esp. pp. 9–20.

28. Walter Benjamin, *Illuminations*, trans. H. Zohn (New York: Schocken Books, 1976), pp. 257–58.

29. *The Complete Works of John Lyly*, ed. R. W. Bond (Oxford: Oxford University Press, 1902), 3:115. On London's development in the sixteenth century, see Fisher, "London as an 'Engine of Economic Growth,' " pp. 205–15.

30. *27 Henry 8*, c. 19.

31. Braudel, *Capitalism and Material Life*, p. 398.

32. Virginia Gildersleeve, *Government Regulations of the Elizabethan Drama* (New York: Burt Franklin, 1961), p. 140.

33. Ibid., p. 137.

34. Michel Foucault, *Discipline and Punish: The Birth of the Prison*, trans. A. Sheridan (New York: Pantheon, 1977), p. 187.

35. In order of appearance, see Louis Adrian Montrose, " 'Eliza, Queene of Shepherdes' "; Emmanuel Le Roy Ladurie, *Carnival in Romans*, trans. M. Feeney (New York: Braziller, 1979); Carlo Ginzburg, *The Cheese and the Worms: The Cosmos of a Sixteenth-Century Miller*, trans. A. and J. Tedeschi (Baltimore: The Johns Hopkins University Press, 1980); Stephen J. Greenblatt, "Invisible Bullets: Renaissance Authority and Its Subversion, *Henry IV* and *Henry V*," in *Political Shakespeare: New Essays in Cultural Materialism*, ed. Jonathan Dollimore and Alan Sinfield (Ithaca: Cornell University Press, 1985), pp. 18–47; Alan MacFarlane, *The Justice and the Mare's Ale: Law and Disorder in Seventeenth-Century England* (New York: Cambridge University Press, 1981).

36. Geertz, "Blurred Genres," p. 167.

37. Wallace T. MacCaffrey, "Place and Patronage in Elizabethan Politics," in *Elizabethan Government and Society*, ed. S. T. Bindoff et al. (London: Athlone Press, 1961), p. 97.

38. For the concept of "privileged visibility" as well as Elizabeth's pronouncement, see Greenblatt, "Invisible Bullets," p. 44.

Chapter 2

1. Erich Auerbach, "Philology and *Weltliteratur*," trans. M. and E. Said, *Centennial Review* 13 (1969): 14. For London's last lepers and an essential survey of the city's lazar-houses, see Marjorie B. Honeybourne, "The Leper Hospitals of the London Area," *London and Middlesex Archaeological Society Transactions* 21 (1963): 3–61.

2. John Stockwood, *A Sermon Preached at Paules Crosse . . .* (London, 1578), p. 134.

3. The most useful single study of the playhouses is Glynne Wickham, *Early English Stages, 1300–1600*, 3 vols. (London: Routledge & Kegan Paul,

1963); see also Walter C. Hodges, *The Globe Restored* (London: Oxford University Press, 1968), and *A New Companion to Shakespeare Studies*, ed. K. Muir and S. Schoenbaum (Cambridge: Cambridge University Press, 1971).

4. O. L. Brownstein, "A Record of London Inn-Playhouses from 1565 to 1590," *Shakespeare Quarterly* 22 (1971): 23.

5. On London's lazar-houses, see Honeybourne, "Leper Hospitals"; Charles A. Mercier, *Leper Houses and Medieval Hospitals* (London: Lewis, 1915); Rotha Mary Clay, *The Medieval Hospitals of England* (London: Methuen, 1909).

6. Foucault, *Madness and Civilization*, p. 4.

7. *Patrologiae cursus completus, series graeca*, ed. J. P. Migne (Paris, 1841–64), 36: 579.

8. Honeybourne, "Leper Hospitals," p. 5.

9. Foucault, *Madness and Civilization*, p. 6.

10. For the interpretive conflation, and a well-informed inquiry into the cultural significance of leprosy, see Peter Richards, *The Medieval Leper and His Northern Heirs* (Totowa, N.J.: Rowman & Littlefield, 1971), pp. 5–56.

11. Ibid., p. 51.

12. Ibid., p. 53.

13. Braudel, *Capitalism and Material Life*, pp. 397–98.

14. Along with marginal spectacle, the Liberties were also the site of marketplaces. For a study of the suburbs as places where "the contradictions between commerce and celebration" in early modern London were topographically expressed, see Susan Wells, "Jacobean City Comedy and the Ideology of the City," *ELH* 48 (1981): 37–60. A more general but inspired account of the marketplace as a liminal phenomenon can be found in Jean-Christophe Agnew, "The Threshold of Exchange: Speculations on the Market," *Radical History Review* 21 (1979): 99–118.

15. Reprinted in Clay, *Medieval Hospitals*, pp. 273–76.

16. For Turner's definition of liminality, see *Dramas, Fields, and Metaphors: Symbolic Action in Human Society* (Ithaca: Cornell University Press, 1974), pp. 231–71, and *The Ritual Process: Structure and Anti-Structure* (Ithaca: Cornell University Press, 1977), pp. 94–131. Essays by Turner and others are collected in *Secular Ritual*, ed. S. F. Moore and B. G. Myeroff (Amsterdam: Van Gorcum, 1977).

17. Van Gennep, *The Rites of Passage*, trans. M. B. Vizidom and G. L. Caffee (Chicago: University of Chicago Press, 1960), pp. 15–26.

18. On the public exposure of criminals in ancient Greece, see Louis Gernet, *Anthropologie de la Grèce antique* (Paris: Maspero, 1968), pp. 289–90.

19. Mary Douglas, *Purity and Danger: An Analysis of Concepts of Pollution and Taboo* (Middlesex: Pelican Books, 1970), pp. 114–53.

20. Guy Debord, *Society of the Spectacle* (Detroit: Black and Red, 1977), chap. 1. 23.

21. Sir Henry's obsequies in 1586 cost over 1,500 pounds, leaving the family bankrupt and unable to pay for Sir Philip's funeral a few months

later; Elizabeth subsidized the latter's funeral procession and burial. See Lawrence Stone, "The Anatomy of the Elizabethan Aristocracy," *The Economic History Review* 28 (1948): 12–13.

22. I quote from the second English edition (London, 1635), p. 32; Botero's treatise was originally published in 1588.

23. Cited by Derrick Sherwin Bailey, *Sexual Relation in Christian Thought* (New York: Harper and Row, 1959), p. 162.

24. See "La pharmacie de Platon," in *La Dissémination* (Paris: Editions de Seuil, 1972), pp. 71–197, esp. 108–53.

25. For Freud's brief but influential essay, see "The Antithetical Sense of Primal Words," in *Character and Culture*, ed. P. Rieff (New York: Collier, 1963), pp. 44–50.

26. Tony Tanner, "Licence and Licencing: To the Presse or to the Spunge," *The Journal of the History of Ideas* 38 (1977): 5. The quotation from Chesterfield is cited by Tanner, p. 5.

27. On the economic threat of the Liberties to the City, see Peter Clark, "Town Occupations and Town Economies," in *Crisis and Order in English Towns 1500–1700,* ed. P. Clark and P. Slack (London: Routledge & Kegan Paul, 1972), pp. 156–61.

28. Christopher Hill, *The World Turned Upside Down* (Middlesex: Penguin, 1975), p. 40.

29. For Burke's use of the term, see his *Permanence and Change* (Los Altos: Hermes, 1954), pp. 71ff.

30. From a sermon delivered in 1577, cited by E. K. Chambers, *The Elizabethan Stage* (Oxford: Clarendon Press, 1923), 4:197.

31. Orgel, *The Illusion of Power,* p. 2.

32. Muriel Bradbrook, *The Rise of the Common Player* (Cambridge: Harvard University Press, 1962), p. 74.

33. E. K. Chambers, *The Medieval Stage* (Oxford: Clarendon Press, 1903), 2:7–9.

34. Altman, *Tudor Play,* p. 269.

35. Sir Thomas Elyot, *The image of governance* (London, 1540–41), p. 69.

36. For a full discussion and bibliography on the recent debate about the place and potential of ritualized misrule, see Natalie Z. Davis, *Society and Culture in Early Modern France* (Stanford: Stanford University Press, 1975), pp. 97–123.

37. "The Remembrancia," in *Dramatic Records of the City of London,* ed. E. K. Chambers (London: The Malone Society, 1907), 1:1, 48. The *OED* fails to note Woodrofe's usage; the earliest example it gives of "incontinence" without reference to sexual appetite is from 1641.

38. See J. Dover Wilson, "The Puritan Attack upon the Stage," in *The Cambridge History of English Literature,* ed. A. W. Ward and A. R. Waller (Cambridge: Cambridge University Press, 1966), 6:381.

39. Thomas Nashe, *The Wonderfulle yeare* (London, 1603), D1r.

40. "The Remembrancia," p. 68.

41. Ibid., p. 77.

42. For the Protean player, as well as an excellent study of the reciprocal relationship between Elizabethan drama and culture, see Louis Adrian Montrose, "The Purpose of Playing: Reflections on a Shakespearean Anthropology," *Helios*, n.s. 7 (1980): 51–74.

43. Stephen Gosson, *Plays Confuted in Five Actions* (London, 1582), G7v.

44. See *The Elizabethan World Picture* (London: Chatto & Windus, 1967), esp. pp. 9–17. For a succinct critique of Tillyard's view, see Montrose, "The Purpose of Playing," pp. 54–57.

45. Montrose, "The Purpose of Playing," p. 54.

46. Muriel Bradbrook, *The Common Monument* (Cambridge: Cambridge University Press, 1976), p. 51.

47. See Alfred Harbage, *Shakespeare and the Rival Traditions* (Bloomington: Indiana University Press, 1970), p. 85.

48. S. L. Bethell, *Shakespeare and the Popular Dramatic Tradition* (London: Staples Press, 1948); A. P. Rossiter, *Angel with Horns* (London: Longman, 1961).

49. Robert Weimann, *Shakespeare and the Popular Tradition in the Theater*, ed. R. Schwartz (Baltimore: The Johns Hopkins University Press, 1978), p. 177.

50. Maurice Godelier, *Perspectives in Marxist Anthropology* (Cambridge: Cambridge University Press, 1977), p. 5.

51. Hayden White, "Literature and Social Action: Reflections on the Reflection Theory of Art," *New Literary History* 11 (1980): 364.

52. Terry Eagleton, *Criticism and Ideology* (London: New Left Books, 1976), p. 72.

53. Louis Althusser, *Lenin and Philosophy* (London: New Left Books, 1971), pp. 222–23.

CHAPTER 3

1. See Jean Céard, *La nature et les prodiges: l'insolite au 16e siècle, en France* (Geneva: Droz, 1977), p. 460. For a related study of the shifting cultural significance of "monsters," see Katharine Park and Lorraine J. Daston, "Unnatural Conceptions: The Study of Monsters in Sixteenth- and Seventeenth-Century France and England," *Past and Present* 92 (1981): 20–54.

2. *Thomas Platter's Travels in England, 1599*, trans. Clare Williams (London: Jonathan Cape, 1937), pp. 171–73. I have modified Williams' translation slightly. For the original, see *Thomas Platters des Jungeren Englandfahrt im Jahre 1599*, ed. Hans Hecht (Halle: N. Niemeyer, 1929).

3. The most thorough study is still Julius von Schlosser, *Die Kunst und Wunderkammer der Spätrenaissance* (Leipzig, 1908). See also Alma Stephanie Wittlin's useful work, *The Museum: Its History and Its Tasks in Education* (London: Routledge & Kegan Paul, 1949); the sections on the early collection at Dresden in *The Splendors of Dresden: Five Centuries of Art Collecting in Dresden* (New York: George Braziller, 1978), pp. 19–25, 75–77; Niels von Holst, *Creators, Collectors, and Connoisseurs: The Anatomy of Public Taste*

from Antiquity to the Present Day (New York: G. P. Putnam's Sons, 1967), pp. 103–7, 144. E. H. Gombrich makes brief comments of interest in "The Museum: Past, Present and Future," *Critical Inquiry* 3 (1977): 449.

4. Francis Bacon, *Works*, ed. James Spedding et al. (London, 1859), 3:330–31.

5. Cited by Margaret Hodgen in her useful and thorough *Early Anthropology in the Sixteenth and Seventeenth Centuries* (Philadelphia: University of Pennsylvania Press, 1964), p. 302.

6. The phrase is Jonson's, referring to the anti-masque of *The Masque of Queens;* see *Ben Jonson: Selected Masques,* ed. Stephen Orgel (New Haven, 1975), p. 81.

7. Jean de Léry, *Voyage fait en la Terre du Brésil* (1578); cited by J. H. Elliott, *The Old World and the New* (London: Cambridge University Press, 1970), p. 22.

8. A contemporary account of the voyage, written by George Best, appears under the title *The Three Voyages of Martin Frobisher,* ed. Richard Collinson (London: The Hakluyt Society, 1863). For the fate of the family, see Sidney Lee, *Elizabethan and Other Essays,* ed. Frederick S. Boas (Clarendon: Oxford University Press, 1929), p. 275; also J. R. Hale, "Geographical and Mental Horizons," in *The Age of the Renaissance,* ed. Denys Hays (London, 1967), p. 335.

9. Henri II's entry was chronicled in two prose accounts and one verse. The fullest, from which I have quoted, is *C'est la Deduction du sumpteux ordre plaisantz spectacles et magnifiques theatre dresses, et exhibes par les citoiens de Rouen ville Metropolitane du payes de Normandie, A la sacre Maieste due Tres Christian Roy de France, Henry second, leur soverain Seigneur, Et a Tres illustre dame, ma Dame Katharine de Medicis* (Rouen, 1551); reprinted as *Entree a rouen du Roi Henri II et de la Reine Catherine de Medicis* (Rouen, 1885), Kiiiv. An excellent and full-length study of the entry has been made by Margaret M. McGowan, "Form and Themes in Henri II's Entry into Rouen," *Renaissance Drama,* n.s. 1 (1968): 199–252.

Hodgen erroneously reports the villages outside of Bordeaux in 1565, in *Early Anthropology,* p. 112. Gilbert Chinard mentions the Bordeaux festivities parenthetically while discussing the Rouen Entry, and may be the source of confusion of two quite different ceremonies; see Chinard, *L'exotisme americain dans la littérature Française au 16e siècle* (Paris, 1911), pp. 105–6.

10. For the history of the use of a sciamachy in royal entries, see Sidney Anglo, "The Evolution of the Early Tudor Disguising, Pageant, and Mask," *Renaissance Drama,* n.s. 1 (1968): 13–18.

11. *Calendar of State Papers (Spanish), 1550–1552,* 10:182.

12. See Erwin Panofsky, *Studies in Iconology: Humanistic Themes in the Art of the Renaissance* (New York: Harper & Row, 1962), 13–18. I am indebted for this reference and a clarifying discussion on the point to Professor Terry Comito.

13. The French ship is shown in an illuminated edition of the *Entrée;* see the reproduction in Roy Strong, *Splendor at Court: Renaissance Spectacle and the Theater of Power* (Boston: Houghton Mifflin 1973), pp. 88–89.

14. *Calendar of State Papers (Spanish)*, 182.

15. The one exception was the exclusion of the previous day's triumphal references to the acquisition of Boulogne—suppressed, as Simon Renard reports, in order not to offend the English spectators present. See McGowan, "Forms and Themes," p. 80.

16. On conspicuous expenditure and its devastating effects on the English aristocracy, see Stone, "The Anatomy of the Elizabethan Aristocracy," 3–13. Charles Pythian-Adams provides an excellent analysis of the rhetoric of civil ceremony in "Ceremony and the Citizen," pp. 106–28.

17. For efforts to "justify" Renaissance interest in other cultures as a precursor of Enlightenment ethnography, see Hodgen, *Early Anthropology*, and to a lesser degree, John Howland Rowe, "The Renaissance Foundations of Anthropology," *American Anthropologist* 67 (1965): 1–14. For an illuminating counterargument, see James A. Boon, "Comparative De-enlightenment: Paradox and Limits in the History of Ethnology," *Daedalus* 109 (1980): 73–91.

18. Thomas Heywood, *An Apology for Actors* (1612); in *Shakespeare Society Papers* (London, 1843), 15:40.

19. *Autobiographical Tracts of Dr. John Dee*, ed. James Crossley (London: The Chetham Society, 1851).

20. In *Statutes of the Realm*, 1:47.

21. J. R. Hale, "Sixteenth-Century Explanations of War and Violence," *Past and Present* 51 (1971): 6.

22. Cited by Christopher Hill, *Change and Continuity in Seventeenth-Century England* (London: Weidenfeld and Nicolson, 1974), p. 20.

23. Foucault, *Madness and Civilization*, pp. 36–37.

24. Bradbrook, *The Living Monument*, p. 43.

25. Reprinted in the *New Shakespeare Society*, ed. Frederick V. Furnival (London, 1877–82), series 6, pts. 4–6, 149.

26. C. L. Barber, *Shakespeare's Festive Comedy* (New York: The World Publishing Co., 1968), p. 149.

27. Cited by Natalie Z. Davis, "Proverbial Wisdom and Popular Errors," in her *Society and Culture in Early Modern France* (Stanford: Stanford University Press, 1975), p. 249.

28. Sir Thomas Browne, *Selected Writings*, ed. Geoffrey Keynes (Chicago: University of Chicago Press, 1968), p. 227.

29. See Davis, *Society and Culture*, pp. 245–64.

30. *Platter's Travels*, p. 170. See also Chambers, *The Elizabethan Stage*, 2:365–66.

31. All quotations from *Henry IV* and *Henry V* are from the Arden Shakespeare, ed. A. C. Humphreys.

32. Jonas A. Barish, "The Turning Away of Prince Hal," *Shakespeare Studies* 1 (1965): 13.

33. See *The Statutes of Wales*, ed. Ivor Bowen (London: T. Fisher Unwin, 1908), p. 75.

34. *An Epitome of the Psalmes, or briefe meditations upon the same*, trans. Richard Taverner (1539); cited by Richard Foster Jones, *The Triumph of the English Language* (Stanford: Stanford University Press, 1966), p. 29.

35. See Jones, *Triumph.* Also useful is J. L. Moore, *Tudor-Stuart Views on the Growth, Status, and Destiny of the English Language,* in *Studien zur Englischen Philologie* 41 (1910).

36. Richard Mulcaster, *The First Part of the Elementarie* (1582; rpt. Menston: Scolar Press, 1970), p. 158.

37. Robert Weimann, "Shakespeare and the Study of Metaphor," *New Literary History* 6 (1974): 166.

38. From the prefatory epistle to *The Shepheardes Calendar,* by "E. K."; in *The Poetical Works of Edmund Spenser,* ed. J. C. Smith and E. de Selincourt (London: Oxford University Press, 1961), p. 417.

39. Bakhtin, *Rabelais and His World,* trans. H. Iswolsky (Cambridge: MIT Press, 1968), pp. 470–71.

40. "Of Repenting," in Montaigne's *Essayes,* trans. John Florio (New York: Modern Library, 1933), p. 731.

41. Roger Ascham, *The Scholemaster* (1570); cited in Jones, *Triumph,* p. 15.

42. "The Excellencie of the English Tongue" (1596?), in *The Survey of Cornwall,* ed. F. E. Halliday (London, 1953), p. 305. Carew's "towardness" is an example of what Stephen Greenblatt defines as "improvisation" in *Renaissance Self-Fashioning,* pp. 222–24.

43. William Empson, "Falstaff and Mr. Dover Wilson," *Kenyon Review* 15 (1953): 247. Shakespeare does not employ the legend directly, but its popular acceptation was at the heart of Henry's Elizabethan image as the first truly *English* king of the realm. It was the original "King's English" that Henry learned; his influence appears to have been significant in shaping Chancery English into what would become, by Shakespeare's day, the standard of the nation. See Malcolm Richardson, "Henry V, the English Chancery, and Chancery English," *Speculum* 55 (1980): 726–50.

44. On the cultural heterogeneity of *Henry IV* and Hal's appetites, see Erich Auerbach, *Mimesis,* trans. W. R. Trask (Princeton: Princeton University Press, 1974), pp. 312–33.

45. For an insightful reading of Hal's rehearsal of Francis—focused on the prince's efforts to awaken, even momentarily, the apprentice's discontent—see Stephen Greenblatt, "Invisible Bullets: Renaissance Authority and Its Subversion," *Glyph* 8 (1981): 40–60.

46. See Richard Helgerson, *The Elizabethan Prodigals* (Berkeley: University of California Press, 1977).

47. Glendower's Welsh certainly was. Unlike Cornish and other Celtic tongues, Welsh resisted the pressures of assimilation and suppression quite ably, despite juridical efforts to control or outlaw it; Welsh remained a strange tongue, a discomfiting reminder that Wales continued to be a foreign and hostile colony, ruled and to an extent subjected but never quite controlled by Tudor power. See R. R. Davies, "Colonial Wales," *Past and Present* 65 (1974): 3–23, and "Race Relations in Post-Conquest Wales: Confrontation and Compromise," in *Transactions of the Honourable Society of Cymmrodorion* (1974), pp. 32–56.

In a period devoted to the collection of alien customs, persons, and languages, understanding and use were not necessarily interdependent. In November of 1608, Captain Peter Wynne encountered a previously unknown tribe of Indians while on an exploratory expedition from James-town. Their dialect was unfamiliar, but the civilian authorities on the expedition solved the linguistic dilemma without apparent difficulty. Noting that the natives' tongue sounded as strange as Wynne's Welsh, perhaps even similar to it, they assigned him the task of translation. "The people of Monacan speak a far differing language from the subjects of Powhatan," as Wynne himself reported to Sir John Egerton on November 21, "their pronunciation being very like Welsh, so that gentlemen in our company desired me to be their interpreter."

48. See the Arden edition, p. 63 n. 19.

49. Empson, "Falstaff and Mr. Dover Wilson," 221.

50. Barber, *Shakespeare's Festive Comedy*, pp. 217ff.

51. Barish, "The Turning Away of Prince Hal," p. 10.

52. Davis, *Society and Culture*, p. 256.

53. George Puttenham, *The Arte of English Poesie* (1589; rpt. Westminster: Constable & Co., 1895), p. 96.

54. See Chambers, *The Elizabethan Stage*, 4:221–22, for the letter from the mayor to the Privy Council. Glynne Wickham called the order "a watershed in English theatrical history.... Its advent spelt the end of a predominately amateur and casual theatre and the start of the strictly professional and commercial theatre that we know"; see "The Privy Council Order of 1597 for the Destruction of all London's Theatres," in *The Elizabethan Theatre*, ed. D. Galloway (Toronto: Macmillan, 1969), 1:21.

55. See Max Weber, *General Economic History*, trans. F. H. Knight (New York: Greenberg, 1927), p. 265.

56. From the *Anarchia Anglicana* (1649); the passage is cited in full by Alan Simpson, *Puritanism in Old and New England* (Chicago: University of Chicago Press, 1955), pp. 54–55.

57. John Dryden, "The Defence of the Epilogue," in *Critical and Miscellaneous Prose Works*, ed. E. Malone (London, 1800), p. 232. For the history of such "surveillance," understood in Dryden's sense of observing Error, see Foucault, *Discipline and Punish*.

58. See M. L. Radoff, "Influence of French Farce in *Henry V* and *The Merry Wives*," *Modern Language Notes* 48 (1933): 427–35.

CHAPTER 4

1. Niccolò Machiavelli, *The Prince*, trans. and ed. Robert M. Adams (New York: Norton, 1977), p. 22. I have amended the translation slightly.

2. Gentillet's treatise, written in 1576, was published in English translation in 1602. See Innocent Gentillet, *A discourse upon the meanes of wel governing and maintaining in good peace, a kingdome, or other principalitie. Divided into three parts, namely, The Counsell, The Religion, and the Policie, which*

a Prince ought to hold and follow, Against Nicholas Machiavelli the Florentine (London, 1602).

3. Norman N. Holland, *"Measure for Measure:* The Duke and the Prince," *Comparative Literature* 11 (1959): 16.

4. Stephen Greenblatt, "Shakespeare and the Exorcists," in *Shakespeare and the Question of Theory,* ed. Patricia Parker and Geoffrey Hartman (Methuen: New York and London, 1985), pp. 176–77.

5. Leo Salingar, *Shakespeare and the Traditions of Comedy* (Cambridge: Cambridge University Press, 1974), p. 322.

6. John Aubrey, *Miscellanies Upon Various Subjects* (London, 1890), pp. 218–19.

Europae Speculum was first published in an unauthorized version in 1605. An edition with the author's corrections was published after Sandys' death; see Sir Edwin Sandys, *Europae Speculum* (Hague, 1629).

7. Cited by Stephen Greenblatt, *Renaissance Self-Fashioning,* p. 88.

8. From a letter to Adam Newton, 1 January 1608; for the full text, see *Two Biographies of William Bedell,* ed. E. S. Shuckburgh (Cambridge: Cambridge University Press, 1902), p. 229.

9. The edition used can be found in *The Selected Writings of Fulke Greville,* ed. Joan Rees (London: Athlone Press, 1973).

10. On the imaginary construct of Catholicism in the period, see Carol Z. Weiner, "The Beleaguered Isle: A Study of Elizabethan and Jacobean Anti-Catholicism," *Past and Present* 51 (1971): 27–62.

11. *A Mirrour for Magistrates of Cyties* (London, 1584), Aiiiiv.

12. Edward Coke, *The Third Part of the Institutes of the Laws of England,* epilogue; cited by Harold Skulsky, "Pain, Law, and Conscience in *Measure for Measure," The Journal of the History of Ideas* 75 (1964): 157.

13. Quoted in Stephen Greenblatt, "Invisible Bullets," p. 44.

14. For documents relevant to the execution, see Kinney, ed., *Elizabethan Backgrounds,* pp. 213–36.

15. Ibid., p. 226.

16. *The Basilicon Doron of James VI,* ed. James Craigie (Edinburgh and London: Blackwood and Sons, 1944), p. 162.

17. Stephen Orgel, "Making Greatness Familiar," *Genre* 15 (1982): 47.

18. Heywood, *Apology,* pp. 52, 54.

19. *A Refutation of the Apology for Actors* (London, 1615; rpt. New York: Garland, 1973), H3v.

20. Ibid., H2v.

21. For the phrase, see William Tyndale, *The Obedience of a Christian Man,* in *Doctrinal Treatises . . . by William Tyndale,* ed. H. Walter (Cambridge, 1848), p. 265; on the *psychotyrrani* of confession, see Stephen Ozment, *The Reformation in the Cities* (New Haven: Yale University Press, 1975).

22. For example, see Anthony Munday's echoes of Tyndale on auricular confession: "For that is not a good meanes to correct sinne. For that it be secret, it ought not to be revealed openlie, but by such meanes to be reformed as Christ himselfe alloweth in his Gospel"; cited in Chambers, *The Elizabethan Stage,* 4:212.

23. On the history of confession, see Henry Charles Lea, *A History of Auricular Confession and Indulgences in the Latin Church*, 3 vols. (Philadelphia and London, 1896). Borromeo's technological obsessions are reported in a valuable study of confessional practices by John Bossy, "The Social History of Confession in the Age of the Reformation," *Transactions of the Royal Historical Society*, 5th series, 25 (1975): 21–38.

24. Bossy, "Confession," p. 24.

25. For accounts of behavior in church, see Carl Bridenbaugh, *Vexed and Troubled Englishmen, 1590–1642* (Oxford: Oxford University Press, 1976), p. 191.

26. Michel Foucault, *The History of Sexuality*, trans. Robert Hurley (New York: Pantheon, 1978), pp. 61–62.

27. For Luther's anxieties over confession, see Ozment, *Reformation*, p. 51.

28. William Tyndale, *Obedience*, p. 337.

29. Cited in Charles Wordsworth, *Evangelical Repentance* (London, 1841), p. 80.

30. See Andrew Gurr, *The Shakespearean Stage, 1574–1642* (Cambridge: Cambridge University Press, 1970), pp. 73–74.

31. Heywood, *Apology*, p. 21.

32. See Robert Weimann, "Society and the Individual in Shakespeare's Conception of Character," *Shakespeare Survey* 34 (1981): 23–31.

33. Lea, *A History of Auricular Confession*, 1:253.

34. Norbert Elias, *Power and Civility*, trans. Edward Jephcott (New York: Pantheon, 1982), pp. 292–93.

35. William Bavande, cited in Chambers, *The Elizabethan Stage*, 4:100.

36. Stephen Greenblatt, "The Cultivation of Anxiety: King Lear and His Heirs," *Raritan* 2 (1982): 103.

37. Montrose, "The Purpose of Playing," p. 68.

38. For a related argument, see Weimann, "Society and the Individual," pp. 23–31.

39. Quotations are from the Arden edition, edited by J. W. Lever (London: Methuen, 1979).

40. Leonard Tennenhouse, "Representing Power: *Measure for Measure* in Its Time," *Genre* 15 (1982): 139–58.

41. Goldberg, *James I*, p. 239.

42. Other characters in other plays don false friar's robes and hear illicit confessions, but they are either villains like the assassins in Webster's *The White Devil* or figures of clear and unproblematic religious satire, parodying the mummery and subterfuge practiced by the genuine but, from a Protestant perspective, no less illegitimate article. However ambivalent we may find Shakespeare's Duke, he stands out among such company and in such a country as Reformation England. On the Duke's disguise in the context of Elizabethan and Jacobean dramatic practice, see Rosalind Miles, *The Problem of "Measure for Measure"* (New York: Barnes and Noble, 1976), pp. 167–96.

43. *Basilicon Doron*, p. 45.

44. Sir John Harrington, *Nugae Antiquae* (London, 1804), 1:180.

45. On the cultural dynamics of Elizabeth's reign, see Montrose, " 'Eliza, Queene of Shepheardes,' " pp. 153–82; and "Gifts and Reasons: The Contexts of Peele's *Arraygnement of Paris,*" *ELH* 47 (1980): 433–61.

46. *The True Narration of the Entertainment of his Royall Majestie* (London, 1603), D3v.

47. Cited by Lucy Aiken, *Memoirs of the Court of King James the First* (London, 1823), 1:174.

48. Ibid.

49. On thieves' cant, see the introduction to Gamini Salgado, ed., *Cony Catchers and Bawdy Baskets* (Harmondsworth: Penguin, 1972); Peter Burke, "Languages and Anti-languages in Early Modern Italy," *History Workshop Journal* 11 (1981): 24–32; M. A. K. Halliday, "Anti-languages," *American Anthropologist* 78 (1976): 570–84.

50. Roy Battenhouse, "*Measure for Measure* and King James," *Clio* 7 (1978): 200.

51. Carolyn Asp has given a reading of Isabella's situation which, in its Lacanian interpretation of the male gaze, complements my own but concludes with an effort to assert Isabella's independence, albeit a subtly nuanced one. "[Isabella's] silence to his proposal must not be taken as assent, but perhaps as just the opposite, a move of power and independence, a stepping out of the circuit of desire. Finally, on stage, Isabella is an icon who does not speak but who focuses the gaze. We, the spectators, gaze upon her and translate her as our desire interprets; she remains unvanquished, virgin." Asp's interpretation was presented at a session on "Gender and Sexuality in Shakespeare" at the Modern Language Association, Washington, D.C., December 30, 1984; I quote from a synopsis of that talk published as "Desire, the Gaze and the Woman in *Measure for Measure,*" *The Shakespeare Newsletter* (Winter, 1984): 40. For a reading of Shakespearean silence as a voice of power that would support Asp's view, see Jonathan Goldberg, "Shakespearean Inscriptions: The Voicing of Power," in *Shakespeare and the Question of Theory,* ed. Patricia Parker and Geoffrey Hartman (London: Methuen, 1985), pp. 116–37.

I would regard Asp's reading as a projection of feminist desire, but not necessarily irrelevant to the designs of the play. The conclusion in a sense produces the need for such a projection, not because it provides us with an exemplary figure of feminist resistance or independence but because it makes us feel the loss, see the progressive foreclosure, of such a figure. At the end, Isabella is not an emblem of an alternative construction of the Woman; her silence is, however, a site that alternative construction can and must occupy.

52. Peter Studley, *The Looking-Glasse of Schisme: Wherein by a Briefe and True Narration of the Execrable Murders, Done by Enoch ap Evans, a Downe-Right Separatist, on the Bodies of his Mother and Brother, with the Cause Mooving him Thereunto, the Disobedience of that Sect, against Royall Majesty, and the Lawes of our Church is Plainly Set Forth* (London, 1634), p. 35.

53. J. A. Sharpe, " 'Last Dying Speeches': Religion, Ideology and Public Execution in Seventeenth-Century England," *Past and Present* 107 (1986): 165. Sharpe also records the case of Evans (p. 155) and I am indebted to him throughout these paragraphs.

54. For an examination of this phenomenon in cases of high treason, see Lacey B. Smith, "English Treason Trials and Confessions in the Sixteenth Century," *Journal of the History of Ideas* 15 (1954): 471–98.

55. See Lever's introduction to the Arden edition, p. xlviii.

56. Tennenhouse, "Representing Power," 143–44.

57. For the emergence of a disciplinary power grounded in an internalized sense of surveillance, see Foucault, *Discipline and Punish*. For an argument that revises and complements Foucault, and also contains a powerful analysis of the early novel and its contribution to the formation of the modern subject, see John Bender, *Imagining the Penitentiary: Fiction and the Architecture of Mind in Eighteenth-Century England* (Chicago: University of Chicago Press, 1987).

CHAPTER 5

1. *Gowries Conspiracie* (1600); printed in *The Harleian Miscellany* (London, 1808), 2:345.

2. John Nichols, *The Progresses . . . of James the First* (London, 1828), 2:38–43.

3. *The King's Booke* (1605); cited in Henry N. Paul, *The Royal Play of Macbeth* (New York: Macmillan, 1950), p. 230.

4. On the frequency of apparently spontaneous public confessions, see Smith, "English Treason Trials," pp. 471–98. On the cultural poetics of public execution, see Samuel Y. Edgerton, Jr., "*Manniera* and *Manneia:* Decorum and Decapitation in the Sixteenth Century," in *The Meaning of Mannerism*, ed. F. W. Robinson and S. G. Nichols (Hanover, N.H.: University Press of New England, 1972), pp. 67–103.

5. All quotations are from the Arden *Macbeth*, ed. Kenneth Muir (London: Methuen, 1951).

6. See Chambers, *The Elizabethan Stage*, 1:276–79, for the extension of the Vagabond Act to players in 1572.

7. *English Historical Documents*, 5:480.

8. In Holinshed, *Chronicles of England, Scotland, and Ireland* (1580?; rpt. London: J. Johnson, 1807–8), 3:1009. Cheeke is included in full by Holinshed, pp. 987–1011.

9. Ibid., p. 985.

10. Ibid., pp. 1004–5.

11. George Puttenham, *The Arte of English Poesie*, p. 267.

12. On oracular possession and rhetoric, see Plato's *Phaedrus* (244a–e). Aristotle discusses the relation between amphibology and oracles, citing a duplicitous prophecy from Herodotus (*Rhetoric*, 1407a–b); see also Quintilian, *Institutio Oratoria* (7.9) and Cicero, *De divinatione* (2.56).

13. Frederic W. Russell, *Kett's Rebellion in Norfolk* (London, 1859), p. 142. Russell is a useful compilation of period accounts, chiefly Southerton and Nevylle. Holinshed also describes the prophetic elements of the uprising. For a modern study, see Julian Cornwall, *Revolt of the Peasantry, 1549* (London: Routledge & Kegan Paul, 1977).

14. The uprising provides a context for the frequent charges made in the later century, that playhouses served as sites for the hatching of treasonous plots. Playhouses "give opportunity to the refuze sort of evill disposed & ungodly people . . . the said Stage Plaies beeinge the very places of theire Randevous appoynted by them to meete with such other as wear to ioigne with them in theire designes & mutinous attemptes, beeinge allso the ordinarye places for maisterles men to come together and recreate themselves." The Lord Mayor and Alderman to the Privy Council, July 28, 1597; in Chambers, *The Elizabethan Stage*, 4:321.

15. Russell, *Kett's Rebellion*, p. 142.

16. *The Lawyers Logicke* (1588; rpt. Menston: Scolar Press, 1969), p. 27.

17. According to Jean-Pierre Vernant, amphibology is the wellspring of Greek tragedy, most prominent in *Oedipus Rex;* see *Mythe et tragédie en Grèce ancienne* (Paris: F. Maspero, 1972), pp. 21–40, 101–31.

18. When the country matter of treason tunnels under the foundations of the state itself in the Gunpowder Plot, we may have an example of the conspirators invoking and attempting to use this "country confidence" to their advantage. In his letter to the Tower with instructions for the interrogation of Guy Fawkes, James inquired about the circulation of a "crewallie villanouse pasquil . . . which spake something of harvest and prophesied my destruction." Cited in B. N. de Luna, *Jonson's Romish Plot* (Oxford: Clarendon Press, 1967), p. 223 n. 1.

19. Cited by Stephen J. Greenblatt, "Learning to Curse: Aspects of Linguistic Colonialism in the Sixteenth Century," in *First Images of America*, ed. F. Chiapelli (Berkeley: University of California Press, 1976), 2:562.

20. The play and its problems at court are known only from a letter of 8 December 1604, cited in Chambers, 1:328.

21. See Paul, *The Royal Play*, pp. 226–48.

22. For a full chronology, see the entry under "Mental Reservation" in *The Catholic Encyclopaedia* (New York: Robert Appleton, 1911), 10:195–96.

23. Relevant would be Freud's *The Psychopathology of Everyday Life* (New York: Norton, 1965), and *Jokes and Their Relation to the Unconscious* (New York: Norton, 1960). For Jacques Lacan, see *Ecrits*, trans. Alan Sheridan (New York: Norton, 1977), pp. 146–79.

24. *The Jesuits Downefall;* cited in Frank L. Huntley, "Macbeth and the Background of Jesuitical Equivocation," *PMLA* 79 (1964): 400 n. 45.

25. On this passage, see Cleanth Brooks, *The Well-Wrought Urn* (New York: Harcourt, Brace & World, 1947), pp. 37ff.

26. On the opening scenes of *Macbeth*, and the role of the witches in the play, see two essays by Harry Berger, Jr.: "The Early Scenes of *Macbeth:* Preface to a New Interpretation," *ELH* 47 (1980): 1–31, and "Text Against

Performance in Shakespeare: The Example of *Macbeth*," *Genre* 14 (1981): 49–80. For a reading of James I's efforts to incorporate equivocation into the rhetoric and dramaturgy of rule, see Goldberg, *James I*, pp. 113–63.

27. Muir, "The Uncomic Pun," *Cambridge Journal* 3 (1950): 484. Comic or not, paronomasia lacks the force associated with amphibology, even in its etymology. Fraunce's "amphibole" is actually the most correct form, in that the word's root, *bole*, is not swallowed up by the *logos* suffix. Meaning both to strike on all sides and to be struck on all sides, "amphibole" is itself an amphibole.

On the relation of *comic* puns and figures of sedition, see Weimann, *Shakespeare and the Popular Tradition*, pp. 135–48.

28. See R. F. Jones, "Science and English Prose Style in the Third Quarter of the Seventeenth Century," in *Seventeenth-Century Prose*, ed. S. E. Fish (New York: Oxford University Press, 1971), pp. 53–90, for an account of Joseph Glanvill's day before the bar of the Royal Society. Originally an imitator of Browne, Glanvill revised all his works, expunging metaphors and figures, then came before a full session of the society for their approval, openly confessing the error of his ways and vowing not to stray from the path of a clear style again.

29. See Michel Foucault, *The Order of Things* (New York: Vintage Books, 1971), esp. pp. 78–208.

30. *Leviathan*, ed. C. B. Macpherson (Harmondsworth: Penguin, 1972), pp. 116–17.

31. "Preface to Shakespeare," in *The Complete Works of Samuel Johnson*, ed. A. Sherbo (New Haven: Yale University Press, 1968), 7:74.

32. Williams, *Marxism and Literature*, pp. 110, 112.

33. Ibid., pp. 123–24.

34. For the "self-regulating" bourgeois identity, see Stallybrass and White, *Transgression*, p. 88; for the notion of the sovereign individual, see Nicholas Abercrombie, Stephen Hill, and Bryan S. Turner, *Sovereign Individuals of Capitalism* (London: Allen and Unwin, 1986).

35. For a complementary genealogy of the modern, psychologized notion of the self and its historical construction, see Stephen Greenblatt, "Psychoanalysis and Renaissance Culture," in *Literary Theory/Renaissance Texts*, ed. Patricia Parker and David Quint (Baltimore: The Johns Hopkins University Press, 1986), pp. 210–24.

36. Cited by Orgel, *The Illusion of Power*, p. 55.

Chapter 6

1. Cited by Marchette Chute, *Shakespeare of London* (New York: Dutton, 1949), p. 289.

2. Of the plays presented in theaters within the city through 1613, 85 percent were comedies and 15 percent tragedies; in the public playhouses, 49 percent were comedies, 30 percent tragedies, and 21 percent histories. Of the comedies that survive from the boys' companies, the overwhelming

majority are satiric. For the figures and further discussion, see Alfred Harbage, *Shakespeare and the Rival Traditions* (Bloomington: Indiana University Press, 1970), pp. 85ff.

3. Ibid., esp. pp. 3–119.

4. The extreme distinction between a popular and an elite audience has frequently and persuasively been challenged, most recently by Ann Jennalie Cook, *The Privileged Playgoers of Shakespeare's London* (Princeton: Princeton University Press, 1981).

The use of "private" to describe theaters like Blackfriars is in itself misleading insofar as it suggests a socially uniform audience with preestablished tastes and expectations. Stephen Orgel argues that the only theater "private" in this sense was the one found at Court. "The public playhouse [within or without the city] is built by producers and theatrical entrepreneurs, the directors of theatrical companies, and its audience is their creation. The public theater will be successful only to the extent that individual citizens, potential spectators, are willing to compose themselves into that audience the producers have imagined. But private theaters [such as at Court] are the creation of their audiences, and are often designed not only for a particular group but for a particular production or occasion" (*The Illusion of Power*, p. 6).

5. Harold Priestley, *London: The Years of Change* (London: Frederick Muller, 1966), pp. 48ff.

6. C. L. Barber, " 'Thou That Beget'st Him That Did Thee Beget': Transformation in *Pericles* and *The Winter's Tale*," *Shakespeare Survey* 22 (1969): 64.

7. Presumed to originate in a lost Greek version written no later than the third century A.D., the Apollonius of Tyre story belongs to a subgenre sometimes characterized as Greek or Mediterranean romance. For a discussion, see Samuel L. Wolff, *The Greek Romances in Elizabethan Prose Fiction* (New York: Columbia University Press, 1912), and Arthur Heiserman, *The Novel before the Novel* (Chicago: University of Chicago Press, 1977); on Shakespeare's romances and their critical fortunes, see F. David Hoeniger, "Shakespeare's Romances Since 1958: A Retrospect," *Shakespeare Survey* 29 (1976): 1–10.

8. The edition of Twine used, and all page references, are from W. C. Hazlitt, *Shakespeare's Library* (London, 1875).

9. See Marcel Mauss, *The Gift*, trans. I. Cunningham (New York: Norton, 1967).

10. Bourdieu, *Outline of a Theory of Practice*, trans. R. Nice (Cambridge: Cambridge University Press, 1977), p. 192.

11. Fredric Jameson, *The Political Unconscious: Narrative as a Socially Symbolic Act* (Ithaca: Cornell University Press, 1981), p. 148.

12. Cited by Raymond de Roover, "The Scholastic Attitude toward Trade and Entrepreneurship," in *Capitalism and the Reformation*, ed. M. J. Kitch (London: Longman, 1969), p. 95.

13. Louis Dumont, *From Mandeville to Marx: The Genesis and Triumph of Economic Ideology* (Chicago: University of Chicago Press, 1977).

14. William Harrison, *The Description of England*, ed. G. Edelen (Ithaca: Cornell University Press, 1968), p. 115.

15. Stephen Gosson, *Plays Confuted in Five Actions* (London, 1582), G7v.

16. Cited by Montrose, "The Purpose of Playing," p. 51.

17. Karl Marx, *Capital*, trans. B. Fowkes (New York: Vintage, 1977), 1:1044.

18. Ann Jennalie Cook, " 'Bargaines of Incontinencie': Bawdy Behavior in the Playhouses," *Shakespeare Studies* 10 (1977): 271–90.

19. See Stephen Greenblatt, "Fiction and Friction," in *Reconstructing Individualism: Autonomy, Individuality, and the Self in Western Thought*, ed. Thomas C. Heller, Morton Sosna, and David Wellbery (Stanford: Stanford University Press, 1986), pp. 30–52.

20. Agnew, "The Theshold of Exchange," p. 112.

21. John Hall, *The Advancement of Learning*, ed. A. K. Croston (Liverpool: University Press, 1953), p. 37.

22. Thomas Hobbes, *Leviathan*, ed. C. B. MacPherson (Middlesex: Penguin Books, 1972), p. 217.

23. Howard Felperin, *Shakespearean Romance* (Princeton: Princeton University Press, 1972), p. 173.

24. Bradbrook, *The Common Monument*, p. 186.

25. Greenblatt, *Renaissance Self-Fashioning*, p. 252.

26. Stallybrass and White, *Transgression*, p. 75.

27. *Bartholomew Fair*, ed. E. A. Horsman (London: Methuen, 1960).

28. Cited by Stallybrass and White, *Transgression*, p. 72.

Index

Pericles (continued)
37; antitheatricality of, 143–45;
anxieties over exchange, 138,
140–41; anxieties over
Liberties, 141, 144–47, 150–51;
and figure of the author, 147–
51; occlusions in, 137–48;
popularity of, 136; and Twine's
Painful Adventures, 138–44
Phythian-Adams, Charles, 13,
154 n. 8, 155 n. 15, 155 n. 16
Plague, 21, 49–50, 136
Platter, Thomas, 60, 62, 63, 73,
75, 76, 159 n. 2, 161 n. 30
Plays Confuted in Five Actions, 51
Popular drama: cultural distance
of, 52, 54; incontinent forms of,
49–51, 53, 55; and internal
distantiation, 57, 129; interstitial
forms of, 48–49; and license of
Liberties, vii, ix–x, 8–9, 22–23,
25, 27–31, 47–59
Priestley, Harold, 155 n. 20, 170 n. 5
Prince, The, 88–92
Pseudodoxia Epidemica, 74
Public executions, 39–40, 116–18,
88–91, 104–6, 111–12
Puritans, 34, 44, 45, 51, 72, 111
Puttenham, George, 84, 120, 127,
128, 163 n. 53, 167 n. 11

Quene's Majestie's Passage, The, 11–
12
Quintilian, 167 n. 12

Radoff, M. L., 163 n. 58
Ralegh, Sir Walter, 106, 107
Rankins, William, 34
Raymond, Saint, 123
Reformation, 86, 88, 91–100, 102,
108, 111, 129, 132
Rehearsal of cultures, 60–87
passim; Catholic ritual, 85–

defined, 69; and development
of vernacular, 74–75, 76–79,
82, 86; European subcultures,
70–75; New World, 64–69; and
popular drama, 69–70, 84–85;
popular rituals, 72–73
Richards, Peter, 35, 157 n. 10–12
Richardson, Malcolm, 162 n. 43
Ritual, vs. theatricality, 91, 112–
13. *See also* Marginal ritual and
spectacle
Romance: and Elizabethan power,
105, 107; Shakespearean, 134–
38, 140–41, 143, 145, 147–51,
170 n. 7
Roover, Raymond de, 170 n. 12
Rossiter, A. P., 54, 129, 159 n. 48
Rowe, John Howland, 161 n. 17
Russell, Frederic W., 168 n. 13
Rykwert, Joseph, 154 n. 8

Salingar, Leo, 91, 92, 164 n. 5
Sandys, Sir Edwin, 92, 164 n. 6
Schechner, Richard, 7, 8, 154 n. 5
Shakespeare, vii, xi, 8, 19, 59, 90–
92, 127, 148–49, 162 n. 43;
bricolage in, 72; career of, x, 55,
84–85; critical distance upon
culture, 30, 54, 59, 129–31;
cultural license of theater, 75,
84, 86, 134; and Machiavelli,
90–91; and rehearsal of
cultures, 69–86, 129. Works: *As
You Like It*, 23; *Hamlet*, 132, 145;
Henry V, 80–82, 86–87, 148; *2
Henry VI*, 34, 116; *Merchant of
Venice*, 110; *The Merry Wives of
Windsor*, 87; *Julius Caesar*, 75;
The Tempest, 64, 115, 147; *The
Winter's Tale*, 147. See also *Henry
IV*; *Macbeth*; *Measure for Measure*;
Pericles
Sharpe, J. A., 111, 167 n. 53

Printed and bound by CPI Group (UK) Ltd, Croydon, CR0 4YY